Homeopathy pocket

**Foundations
Guidelines**

**Homeopathic
Remedies
A–Z**

GW00771541

Glossary
Author
Bibliography
Index

www.media4u.com

Author: Almut Brandl M.D.
Cover Illustration: Lucie Mikyna, Franka Krueger
Photographs: Deutsche Homöopathie-Union (DHU),
Sertürner Bildarchiv, Sertürner Arzneimittel GmbH
English Translation: Sabine Kaempfe
Copy Editing: Adrienne Penfield, Mary V. Burke
Printer: Koesel GmbH, 87435 Kempten, Germany, www.koeselbuch.de
Publisher: Börm Bruckmeier Publishing LLC, www.media4u.com

Printed in Germany
ISBN 1-59103-250-4

Introduction and Acknowledgements

Homeopathy pocket is aimed at medical doctors, students of medicine and practitioners who have identified homeopathy as being their method for treating and curing patients. On the other hand this paperback is intended to inform the medically untrained person who has an interest in being treated homeopathically. To be accessible to the general reader almost every medical term is explained in a glossary. You find these terms in the text in *italics*. Furthermore a comprehensive list of diseases has been added which can be used even by the lay person when choosing a remedy.

Do not be misled into thinking that this little book can entirely explain homeopathy. On the contrary, homeopathy requires a thorough study of its own. May the **Homeopathy pocket** reveal to the reader the virtues of this fascinating healing method.

May the **Homeopathy pocket** act as memory aid to all those involved in daily service to their patients and may it be helpful to all the other readers looking for a solution to their health problems.

I want to express my gratitude to my teachers, especially Ulrich Fischer, Bruno Jakobs and George Vithoulkas as well as Dr. Liffler who gave me the opportunity to practice classical homeopathy at the German clinic of Hof Bellevue.

All photographs in this book were kindly made available by the Deutsche Homöopathie-Union. Without the initiative of my publisher Dr. Phillipp Boerm this book would never have materialized.

Special thanks go to my parents and to Barbara Falkenroth, Ute Buttgereit, Andreas Lindenthal, Elisabeth Mueller and Ute Heppelmann for corrections and creative advice. Finally I want to thank all my patients for their openess in letting me join them on their way to homeopathic healing.

Almut Brandl, M.D.   June 2003

To P. T.

Additional titles in this series:
Differential Diagnosis pocket
Drug pocket 2003
Drug Therapy pocket
ECG pocket
Medical Abbreviations pocket
Medical Spanish Dictionary pocket
Medical Spanish pocket
Medical Spanish pocket plus
Normal Values pocket
Surgery pocket

Börm Bruckmeier Publishing LLC on the Internet:
www.media4u.com

Contents

Homeopathic Remedies 29

List of Equivalent Terms	29
Abrotanum	47
Aconitum napellus	50
Aethusa cynapium	53
Agaricus muscarius	55
Allium cepa	58
Aloe	60
Alumina	62
Ambra grisea	65
Anacardium orientale	67
Antimonium crudum	69
Antimonium sulphuratum aurantiacum	71
Antimonium tartarium	72
Apis mellifica	74
Argentum nitricum	77
Arnica montana	80
Arsenicum album	83
Aurum metallicum	86
Baryta carbonica	90
Belladonna	93
Bromium	96
Bryonia	99

Foundations of Homeopathy 9

Generalities	9
The Concept of Health and Disease	9
The Law of Similars	10
Provings and Symptom Pictures	11
Potencies	12

Guidelines for the Practitioner 16

The Practitioner's Duty	16
Homeopathic Case-taking	16
Searching for a Remedy	19
Doctrine of Miasms	22
Choice of Potency and Dosage	22
Homeopathy and the Single Remedy	24
Reactions to a Remedy and Healing Process	25

6 Contents

Calcarea carbonica	102	Gelsemium	1
Calcarea phosphorica	105	Glonoinum	16
Calcarea sulphurica	108	Graphites	17
Camphora	110	Helleborus niger	17
Cannabis indica	112	Hepar sulphuris	17
Cantharis	114	Hyoscyamus niger	18
Capsicum	116	Hypericum	18
Carbo vegetabilis	119	Ignatia	18
Causticum	122	Iodium	18
Chamomilla	126	Ipecacuanha	19
Chelidonium	128	Kali bichromicum	19:
China officinalis	130	Kali carbonicum	194
Cimicifuga	133	Kali phosphoricum	197
Cina	135	Kali sulphuricum	199
Cocculus	137	Lac caninum	202
Coffea	139	Lachesis	204
Colocynthis	142	Ledum	208
Conium maculatum	144	Lilium tigrinum	210
Crotalus horridus	148	Lycopodium	213
Cuprum metallicum	151	Magnesia carbonica	216
Dulcamara	153	Magnesia muriatica	218
Eupatorium perfoliatum	156	Magnesia phosphorica	220
Ferrum metallicum	158	Medorrhinum	222
Ferrum phosphoricum	161	Mercurius solubilis	225
Fluoricum acidum	163	Natrum carbonicum	228

Natrum muriaticum	230	Syphilinum	295
Natrum sulphuricum	233	Tarentula hispanica	298
Nitricum acidum	235	Thuja	301
Nux moschata	238	Tuberculinum	305
Nux vomica	240	Veratrum album	308
Opium	243	Zincum metallicum	311
Petroleum	245		
Phosphoricum acidum	247		
Phosphorus	250	Diseases	315
Phytolacca	253		
Picrinicum acidum	255		
Platinum	257	Glossary	367
Plumbum	260		
Podophyllum	262		
Psorinum	264	About the Author	379
Pulsatilla	267		
Rhus toxicodendron	270		
Sepia	273	Bibliography	380
Silicea	276		
Spongia	279		
Stannum	281	Index	393
Staphisagria	283		
Stramonium	287		
Sulphur	290		
Sulphuricum acidum	293		

Foundations of Homeopathy

▪ Generalities

Dr. Samuel Hahnemann who is known as the founder of homeopathy, was born on April 10, 1755 in Meissen on the river Elbe and died in Paris on July 2, 1843. Hahnemann is the author of the *Organon of the Medical Art*, which is still the essential text on homeopathy.

Homeopathy takes a holistic approach, which means that body, soul and mind are regarded as one entity. Well ahead of his time, Hahnemann was a physician who thought holistically. He considered the entire lifestyle of his patients to be important.

In order to be able to find the right way of healing an individual from a holistic perspective, it is of the

Birthplace   Photo: DHU

utmost importance to perceive the person in the totality of his or her environment. Homeopathic treatment is a regulatory therapy. A well chosen remedy provides a stimulus from within the patient, triggering the inner healing power of the body. If the homeopathic method is used in an optimal way, it becomes a medical art.

▪ The Concept of Health and Disease

Hahnemann describes a healthy person as follows: "In the healthy human state, the spirit-like life force (autocracy) that enlivens the material organism as dynamis, governs without restriction and keeps all parts of the organism in admirable, harmonious, vital operation, as regards both feelings and functions, so that our indwelling, rational spirit can freely avail itself of this living, healthy instrument for the higher purposes of our existence." (§ 9)

According to Hahnemann, a disturbance in this life principle lies at the basis of every disease.

George Vithoulkas, whose goal in life was the propagation of classical homeopathy throughout the world and who in 1996 was awarded the Alternative Nobel Prize for this reason, founded the Athens Clinic for Homeopathy in 1970. Since 1995, he has been teaching at the International Academy for Classical Homeopathy, on the Greek island of Alonissos. For Vithoulkas, health means freedom – freedom from pain in the physical body, freedom from passion on the emotional level, and freedom from selfishness in the mental sphere. In this respect, the parameter for measuring the health of an individual is his creativity. In order to be able to judge the seriousness of a disease in a patient, Vithoulkas developed a system with a hierarchical structure, whereby mental disturbances are more central and therefore more serious than emotional disorders, and the latter more serious than physical complaints. Within one level (mental, emotional, and/or physical), the degree of threat to the patient's life is the measure by which to judge the gravity of the disease.

Despite this systematic approach, the overall guiding principle of the homeopath is that the person is a whole, complete living being and this entity exists in a moving equilibrium.

■ The Law of Similars

"**Similia similibus curentur**" is the general principle of homeopathy that Hahnemann discovered: "Let like be cured with like". The meaning of the Law of Similars is that a substance that provokes symptoms in a healthy person is able to cure similar symptoms in a sick person. Therefore, one must find the remedy that produces the most similar symptoms in a healthy person to cure the sick person. Let us take as an example Allium cepa, the onion. As we know, the onion produces in a healthy person some discharge of fluid in the mucous membranes of the eyes, the nose, and the mouth. Following the Law of Similars, Allium cepa is prescribed for a runny nose.

■ Provings and Symptom Pictures

To assess the effect on the healthy person, so-called 'provings' are carried out, during which a certain substance is given to a person. Thereafter, every single event is recorded, in terms of not only physical but also emotional and mental symptoms. Further knowledge about the effects of a remedy is gained from toxicology, the science of toxic effects on the body. Finally, reports on cured cases confirm the symptom picture of a homeopathically chosen remedy.

The collected findings about the effect of a remedy constitute the symptom picture or remedy picture, as it is called. To date, substances from plants (e.g. Belladonna, the deadly nightshade), animals (e.g. Apis mellifica, the honeybee), minerals (e.g. Natrum muriaticum, sodium chloride), and synthetic substances, as well as nosodes, have been tested in a homeopathic proving. Nosodes are taken from secretions from the body of a sick person. Medorrhinum, which is made from gonorrheal pus, could be mentioned here as an example.

The symptom pictures of all the proven substances are collected in the **Materia Medica**. Each Materia Medica has its own structure, depending on the author. For each remedy, all symptoms that appear in a healthy person are listed. Some indication on the origins of the substance, toxicology, pharmacology, and general and guiding symptoms is followed by symptoms of the mind and the psyche and the physical symptoms (starting at the head, going down to the feet, and ending with skin and sleep symptoms). Hereafter, the modalities are listed (i.e. circumstances affecting the complaints in such a way that they get worse or better), followed by some indications on the relationship between remedies and a description of so-called similar remedies (i.e. producing a similar symptom picture).

Hahnemann writes: "Let all that is supposition, merely asserted or even fabricated, be entirely excluded from such a Materia Medica. Let everything be the pure language of nature, carefully and sincerely interrogated." (§ 144)

■ Potencies

Through his method of diluting, using succussion or trituration at each stage, Hahnemann discovered that the effects of poisoning from the drugs diminished, while increasing the healing powers, according to the Law of Similars.

This kind of strengthening of the curative effect of a medicinal substance is also called potentization or dynamization. The action of substances diluted in this way, and in which no molecules of the original substance can be detected any longer, can be regarded as information from the original substance being transferred onto the carrier substance through the process of potentization. This is comparable with a recording on an audiotape. The material has not changed chemically but the information has been saved. Through the right information, stored in the

Hahnemann   Photo: DHU

well chosen homeopathic remedy, the patient receives the stimulus to heal him-, herself.

Potentization follows strict rules. Of crucial importance are the number of the different potentization steps (always dilution and succussion or trituration; marked with a number) and the ratio of dilution (marked with a letter): for example, 12x, 30c, Q XVIII. For the decimal-potencies (x potencies), the dilution is carried out at a ratio of 1:10; for the centesimal potencies (c potencies), the ratio is 1:100. The single steps of dilution with intermittent succussion are carried out several times. In the case of a 5x potency, this means that a 1:10 dilution has taken place 5 times in a row, with succussion at each step. In the same way, a 10c potency has undergone dilution 10 times at a ratio of 1:100, with the corresponding succussion steps.

The so-called LM, or more correctly Q-potency, comes from the Latin Quinquagiesmillesima = 50,000. The LM is produced by diluting a 3c potency at a ratio of 1:50,000. Potencies are increased in the usual way with the same ratio.

Korsakoff potencies (named after the Russian lay-homeopath, von Korsakoff, 1789–1853) are made using the same vial each time. Dilution is performed with the remainder after emptying the glass and refilling it.

Highly poisonous remedies like Aconite, Mercurius or Lachesis are still toxic at a lower potency (for example 2x). But from 6x onwards, they too may also be used homeopathically without concern. In chemical terms, one could say that from a 24x or a 12c it is no longer possible to find a single molecule of the original substance.

The succussion strokes necessary for dilution should be carried out on the ball of the thumb or on a leather-bound book. The exact guidelines for making homeopathic remedies are laid down in the relevant pharmacopeia (HPUS).

The following forms for administration are manufactured: alcohol solutions (= dilutio/dil.), lactose tablets (tbl.), triturations of lactose (= trituratio/trit.), saccharose globules (= globuli/glob.), and injections (ampoule).

There are certainly many diseases which can be combated homeopathically without the help of a therapist. These are simple acute diseases which can possibly be treated by oneself. However, in general the diagnosis should be made by a homeopathic practitioner and the progress of the therapy monitored by this doctor. Common complaints that seem irrelevant may be the precursor of a life-threatening disease.

The list of diseases included below may be of help when looking for a remedy. Common diseases are listed, together with a short explanation and mention of the most important homeopathic remedies to be used in such a case. The index at the end of the book may be of further use in this respect.

For the selection of the appropriate remedy, it is crucial to compare the symptoms of the disease with the symptom picture; both should correspond with each other as far as possible. In classical homeopathy, only one remedy is given at a time and this remedy should be as similar as possible to the overall disease picture. In self-medication, medium potencies (like 12x, 8c) should be used. Potencies higher than 30c should not be used without authorization. If no improvement takes place in due course, then any further treatment should be referred to a professional therapist.

All chronic diseases should be treated constitutionally by an experienced homeopath. Chronic conditions are associated with a tendency to contract certain acute diseases – such as, for example, recurrent throat infections. In such cases, neither the lay person nor a trained professional are advised to self-medicate, since it is well known that it is easier to see the mote in one's neighbor's eye than the beam in one's own, which is the one to be treated. Constitutional therapy will be explained in the following chapters. Those who are already receiving a constitutional homeopathic treatment should always contact their therapist in the event of an acute complaint and before taking any remedy, as the wrong remedy may thwart the success of a long-term therapy.

Those who have understood the Law of Similars will know that the widespread understanding that homeopathy can not harm a person, can not possibly be true. An incorrectly given homeopathic remedy will produce symptoms of a proving in the sick person after repeated doses, just as in a healthy individual. For this reason, it is necessary to warn readers, in the strongest possible terms, not to use homeopathic medicines without careful consideration. Not every minor complaint or mild indisposition needs a homeopathic remedy.

If you are still interested and want to know more, you may of course also read the following introduction, written for the therapist. This may help you to get a better understanding of homeopathy and improve your chances of success in the search for a homeopathic remedy. The patient will learn why cooperation, open-mindedness, and self-observation are crucially important for successful treatment.

Guidelines for the Practitioner

■ The Practitioner's Duty

Hahnemann starts out his essential text, the *Organon of the Medical Art*: "The physician's highest and only calling is to make the sick healthy, to cure, as it is called." (§ 1)

Organon   Photo: DHU

Before you are able to heal, it is important to ascertain exactly what the patient is suffering from. The disease and its causation have to be found and the diagnosis has to be made. This applies also to the use of homeopathy. Although homeopathy is a relatively old form of therapy, we should not disregard modern diagnostic techniques.

Once the diagnosis has been made, you have to find the optimal therapy for each patient. In this respect, homeopathy is one of many other forms of therapy. Combining conventional and homeopathic therapy is perfectly feasible and often best benefits the patient.

■ Homeopathic Case-taking

To understand the patient fully and perceive him or her wholly, and thus be able to select the appropriate remedy, the practitioner has to be focussed, unprejudiced, and alert from the first moment of the encounter with the patient. Further conditions for good case-taking are an excellent and open relationship, full of trust, between practitioner and patient, as well as a quiet atmosphere, time, and patience.

It was Hahnemann who stated that taking a case "demands nothing of the medical-art practitioner except freedom from bias and healthy senses, attention while observing and fidelity in recording the image of the disease" (§ 83).

The first impression of the patient – his or her appearance and body language – is important. The case history begins with a report from the patient, in his or her own words. In addition, during the subsequent directed interview, leading questions should be avoided as far as possible.

You should attempt to record **all symptoms**, i.e. you should take down all complaints where the following elements are known:

- Causation
- Localization
- Sensations (e.g. characteristics of the pain – stinging/cutting/ burning/throbbing)
- Modalities (circumstances under which complaints get better or worse)
- Concomitant symptoms

During the entire interview, the practitioner should observe the patient carefully and mark in his/her notes the intensity of the reported symptoms by underlining them.

To aid your memory, a questionnaire, containing extensive blank spaces, has proven to be helpful. In some homeopathic clinics, patients are asked to complete a questionnaire prior to their consultation. While this may be helpful, the essence of the case-taking occurs within the relationship between patient and practitioner, in meeting face to face. A case-history given by a third person may be useful. This is imperative when dealing with children, persons who are mentally ill, and unconscious patients.

It goes without saying that after the case-history has been taken, a physical examination follows.

The following text displays an example of the structure of a well-taken case-history:

1. Main complaint, which instigated the patient request for treatment
2. Other complaints
3. Further symptoms: at this stage, every organ from head to foot – in this order – needs to be examined
4. Gynecological case-history in female patients: menstruation, pregnancy
5. Medical history: operations, accidents, childhood diseases, vaccinations, previous treatment, medication...
6. Family history: diseases of family members, causes of death, hereditary diseases...
7. General symptoms
   a) Diet: appetite, thirst, cravings for and aversions to certain foods or drinks, intolerances to certain substances, if applicable
   b) Symptoms relating to temperature (chilliness, feverishness)
   c) Perspiration
   d) Influence of climate: At the seaside, in the mountains, open air
   e) Sleep: position, insomnia, grinding teeth, talking in sleep, dreams
   f) Lunar phases
   g) Time of day of occurrence
   h) Seasons
8. Mental and emotional symptoms
   a) Intellect, memory, concentration
   b) Fears
   c) Self-confidence
   d) Introversion, extroversion, shyness, desires or dislike of company
   e) Mood, suicidal thoughts, aggressiveness

f) Reaction to grief and consolation
g) Other personal characteristics: domineering/yielding,
ambitious, jealous, talkative, hasty, restless, impatient,
dissatisfied, stubborn, indecisive, pedantic, orderly, avaricious,
miserly, distrustful, self-accusatory, compassionate
h) Relationships
i) Sexual sphere
9. Biographical and social case-history (profession, hobbies, religion)
10. Physical examination

It is a skill to take a good case-history in homeopathy. The case-history
is crucial for finding the remedy. Treatment will be successful if the
homoeopath succeeds in fully understanding the patient in his/her
uniqueness as a human being.

■ Searching for a Remedy

During the search for a remedy, you have to look for the essential
element, enabling you to acquire a correct overview of the situation.
You should step back and try to get the whole picture of the case,
identify the main problem of the patient, the characteristics of the case.
There are many ways to take a case and to search for a remedy, in order
to achieve your goal.

Grading of Symptoms: If no remedy picture becomes apparent,
provided that the practitioner has a thorough knowledge of the Materia
Medica, then the complaints should be graded. This means that the
most important complaints are identified and classified as follows:
All symptoms of great intensity, which are described spontaneously and
firmly by the patient (as underlined in the notes), are of particular
importance. Also, complaints that have been present for a long time
and have gradually become worse are taken into special consideration,
as well as the so-called complete symptoms. Generally speaking, the
causation, i.e. the event that triggered the complaint, is of crucial
importance. Examples include headache following a head injury, asthma

after receiving a shock, or depression since the death of a spouse. In this hierarchical system, mental and emotional symptoms have more weight than general symptoms. Both of these involve the whole person. General symptoms, on the other hand, are graded higher than local symptoms. Striking individual symptomss are more important than pathognomonic ones which are characteristic of a known disease. For example, if bronchial asthma improves when the patient lies on his/her *abdomen*, this would be considered unusual and thus a striking symptom.

In the *Organon*, in **paragraph 153**, Hahnemann says: "In the search for a homeopathically specific remedy, that is, in the comparison of the complex of the natural disease's signs with the symptom sets of the available medicines (in order to find among them an artificial disease potence that corresponds in similarity to the malady to be cured) **the more striking, exceptional, unusual, and odd (characteristic) signs and symptoms of the disease case are to be especially and almost solely kept in view**. These, above all, must correspond to very similar ones in the symptom set of the medicinesought if it is to be the most fitting one for cure. The more common and indeterminate symptoms (lack of appetite, headache, lassitude, restless sleep, discomfort, etc.) are to be seen with almost every disease and medicine and thus deserve little attention unless they are more closely characterized."

The symptoms chosen are listed in hierarchical order:

1. Causation
2. Mental and emotional symptoms
3. General symptoms
    - sensations and modalities affecting the entire person
    - sexuality, menstruation
    - appetite/thirst; desires and aversions to food
    - characteristics of excretions, secretions, and discharges
    - sleep and dreams
4. Local symptoms with their modalities and concomitant symptoms

Repertorization: As it is almost unfeasible to know in-depth the numerous drug pictures and in particular to remember which symptoms were produced by a certain remedy, homeopaths have created symptom indices designated as repertories.

In these repertories, symptoms are listed in logical and alphabetical order. Beside each symptom is found the remedies that produced it during a homeopathic proving. In order to save space, abbreviations are used, e.g. Nat. m for Natrum muriaticum.

Two distinguished editors of repertories were Dr. Clemens von Bönninghausen (1785–1864), who was the first to publish a repertory in 1846, and James Tyler Kent (1849–1916), who in 1877 published the most comprehensive repertory in English, the *Repertory of the Homoeopathic Materia Medica and a Word Index.*

Kent structured his repertory in chapters (mental and emotional symptoms, all parts of the body from the head to foot, sleep symptoms, sensation of temperature, perspiration, skin, generalities, i.e. complaints which affect the whole body). Within each chapter, symptoms are listed in the following order: indication of side of the body (where the symptom appears); time of occurrence; modalities (circumstances under which a symptom gets better or worse); indication of where the symptom is extending to. Within each sub-section, symptoms are listed alphabetically. Even modern repertories are structured in this way.

In the repertories, remedies in a given sub-section are usually presented in various grades. Kent attributed the grades in the following way: if the symptom is produced many times and can be confirmed by cured cases, the remedy for this symptom receives the second grade. If the symptom occurs only once or a few times, the remedy for this symptom is listed in the first grade.

Because of the vast amount of data, computer programs have been developed for homeopathy, which make the search for a remedy a lot easier. You may find software for repertorization programs as well as Materia Medica programs with search functions. A computer can certainly be an invaluable tool in the hands of an experienced homeopath, but it will never take his/her place.

During repertorization, the homeopath looks up every single symptom from the graded list, and tries to find the remedy, either working with a written repertorization sheet or by computer, looking for all those remedies which appear in every sub-section, or in most of them. Obviously, the symptom grades have to be taken into account. With the help of the Materia Medica, the resulting remedies are then compared with the overall state of the sick patient.

Key symptoms or the main symptoms of a drug picture should not contradict the complaints of the patient; however, there are no 'negative' symptoms. This is to say, if a certain symptom from a drug picture is missing in a patient this does not exclude this remedy from being prescribed.

Repertorization and comparing with the Materia Medica aim at finding the 'simillimum', the remedy indicated for an individual person.

■ Doctrine of Miasms

In classical Greek, the word 'miasma' means something like a 'defect' or 'pollution'. Hahnemann used this term to express the idea that mankind carries the marks of their ancestors and their environment. The chronic miasm of mankind can be dormant, which means that it is not necessarily manifested in a disease that becomes apparent.

Hahnemann introduced the theory of miasms especially for the treatment of patients with chronic disorders. Since then, his concept has been developed further in many different directions but will be discussed no further in the context of this book.

■ Choice of Potency and Dosage

Potency as well as dosage of the carefully chosen remedy must correspond with the individual case. However, the choice of the right remedy is by far more important than potency and dosage.

The potency should be selected with regard to the overall state of the immune system and the vital force of the patient. Strong individuals with robust constitutions can cope with very high potencies, e.g. a 50,000c. If you were to give such a high potency, the remedy picture should match the case of the patient very well, the result being a truly remarkable cure.

Weak patients should not receive high potencies. Their vital force cannot cope with such a strong stimulus. In these cases, it is preferable to prescribe lower potencies, like 6x, 3c or Q-potencies.

For the treatment of patients with chronic diseases, Q-potencies are recommended. They can provide a milder cure and have the capacity to adapt to individual susceptibility. **Q-potencies** should be prescribed in diluted form. This allows one to increase the potency slightly by striking the vial against one hand before giving the next dose, thus giving the organism a new stimulus. Q-potencies can be adapted to individual susceptibility more easily. You may vary the amount of drops; dilute more than once in water; or repeat the dose more often, after longer intervals, or in much shorter intervals in an acute case. For patients who are extremely sensitive, smelling the remedy in the vile may be sufficient. Q-potencies may be repeated frequently without interfering with the effect of the previous dose.

In general, low potencies (e.g. 6x) relate to organic disorders, medium potencies (e.g. 12x, 10c) to functional disorders, and higher potencies (from 24x and 12c onwards) to psychological symptoms.

Medicinal substances which have almost no drug effect develop their potential only around the 8x potency. Strong poisons will only be able to provoke a profound healing process in the organism above a 12x potency.

The decision on which **dosage** to use in homeopathy is based on a completely different approach to that in allopathic medicine. In homeopathy, it is the organism that receives a signal, a piece of information to stimulate the ability to heal itself. One globule, or one drop or tablet, is sufficient at any one time. Several globules contain the same information as a single one.

If you treat with c- or x- potencies, you always have to wait for the end of the reaction after administering the dose, irrespective of whether the remedy is potentized by the Korsakoff method or with multiple vials. A homeopathic remedy should not be repeated prior to running its course. The rule is: **no further dose of a remedy should be given as long as there is an improvement!** If the same drug picture presents itself after the remedy has run its course, then the same potency should be repeated until its effect is exhausted, which means it produces no effect at all or only for a brief period of time. After this, a higher potency should be prescribed, e.g. 30c, 200c, 1000c.

In an acute disease, you may, after administration of the first dose, dilute the remedy in a glass of water and 'pluss' it (stir vigorously) before giving a new dose (one sip or one spoonful of the medicated water).

In general, lower x-potencies require more frequent repetition, e.g. several times a day; higher c-potencies may last for weeks or even months. Only when the original symptoms, on which the prescription was based, reappear can the remedy may be given again. Remember, as long as the patient is feeling better in general, nothing must be given. Dr. G.H.G.Jahr (German homeopath,1800–1875) writes: "The teaching must insist on the fact that, in all cases, only **one single** remedy is given, which fits the case as closely as possible. It should not be interrupted by a different remedy in its course until it can clearly be seen that no further curative effect is to be expected if you were to use it again or wait any longer".

- **Homeopathy and the Single Remedy**

In classical homeopathy, you work only with one single remedy and not with a combination of different remedies. The patient receives the remedy which offers a symptom picture that matches the picture of the disease of the patient as closely as possible. This remedy will then trigger a response leading to self-healing.

The homeopathic remedy is often compared with the news on the radio. Just try to imagine how difficult it would be to have to listen simultaneously to different news coming from different radios, possibly even in different languages. That is how the organism must feel when receiving more than one remedy at a time or a mixture of different remedies. After such a treatment with a multitude of remedies, it becomes difficult to treat the patient homeopathically because the whole case has been confused by the multitude of proving symptoms.

Reactions to a Remedy and Healing Process

Vithoulkas gives the following description of the reaction to a similar remedy. He writes that the symptomatology of a given disease is the result of the immune system trying to keep the organism in equilibrium, despite the many unfavorable circumstances. Vithoulkas assumes an inner knowledge within the organism that chooses the optimum symptoms for healing. However, the organism is not strong enough to push the symptoms as far as cure. By giving a **similar remedy**, the symptoms get stronger and a homeopathic provocation takes place, which starts the healing process. Often, aggressive acute diseases have almost reached the climax of the disease process, so that the homeopathic provocation can hardly be noticed, or even not noticed at all; the patient just gets better directly. In chronic disease, there should be a homeopathic reaction after the remedy has been given; with the more gently acting Q-potencies, the provocation is sometimes only very mild.

The moment at which a reaction sets in is different in every remedy. Sometimes the effect comes immediately, sometimes only after a week or two.

In general, remedies that go together well with sudden, aggressive acute conditions should act quickly, i.e. the curative effect should set in within a few minutes or hours at the most. Remedies for curing chronic diseases with an insidious and slow progression are also slow in their mode of action.

The closer the remedy matches the disease, the faster it will act in an efficacious and permanent way. The greater the resonance between symptom picture and disease manifestation, the greater the success in healing. Once the healing process starts, it must not be interrupted. The most important criteria for judging the correct course of cure were formulated by Dr. Constantin Hering (1800–1880), and are known as **Hering's Law:**

"Cure must proceed from centre to circumference...from the top downwards, from within outwards, from more important to less important organs, from the head to the hands and feet. Symptoms which disappear in the reverse order of their coming are removed permanently."

Particularly in chronic diseases, the organism is not able to restore health immediately. Thus, cure is a process which unfolds before your eyes.

According to Hering's Law: if complaints move from inward to outward (that is, away from more central and vital organs to more peripheral ones), from mental to emotional conditions, and finally to physical disorders, you may consider the patient about to be cured. Likewise, the process towards good health is progressing as long as the symptoms move from above downwards, that is from head to foot. Also, a reappearance of former diseases in a chronologically reversed order is a sign of recovery. For example, in the case of a patient with a psychiatric condition who has previously suffered from bronchial asthma and has a history of neurodermatitis during childhood, you will witness the reappearance of the bronchial asthma and later of the eczema during the healing process before the cure is completed.

Only when you are certain that the prescribed remedy is ineffective, or complaints move in the wrong direction, should you look at the case again and search for a remedy that fits the case. Obviously, there may be other obstacles to cure, e.g. drug abuse, unhealthy lifestyle of the patient, or the use of strong aromatic substances like coffee and camphor.

Also, in cases where proving symptoms appear, i.e. symptoms which were not originally part of the disease but which may have been caused by the remedy, and at the same time the patient does not feel any relief, the remedy has not been correctly selected. You should then wait for the proving symptoms to disappear and look at the case again.

If, on the other hand, the general condition of the patient is improving and symptoms from the symptom picture, previously unseen, appear alongside the others, this merely confirms the correct choice of the remedy.

The practitioner must wait patiently and observe. As long as symptoms and signs follow the right direction and the right order according to Hering's Law, and the patient feels better in general, then you must not intervene.

If after an initial provocation and a long-lasting improvement the original disease manifests again, then the simillimum may be repeated. If, however, a permanent but new symptom combination manifests, a different remedy, the so-called **follow-up remedy**, should be selected. In choosing a follow-up remedy, the well known relationships between remedies may be helpful as a guideline (e.g. complementary remedies). However, it will always be the individual symptoms that lead to the selection of a homeopathic remedy.

On this subject, Hahnemann writes in the *Organon of the Medical Art*: "During treatment, every noticeably progressing and conspicuously increasing improvement is a state which, as long as it persists, generally excludes any repetition of the medicine being used, because all the good being produced by the medicine is still hastening towards completion." (§ 246)

Please note:
In the next chapter, which contains the various remedies, main symptoms are normally separated from the modalities belonging to them by a semicolon or a comma.

Medical terms in *italic* are explained in the glossary (p. 367).

Key-symptoms are usually written in **bold**.

Homeopathic Remedies

This text is an introduction to a selection of remedies. It is in some way a concise **materia medica.** Please note that the presentation of a given remedy lists neither all known symptoms nor all potential indications.

List of Equivalent Terms

A given remedy is often referred to by different names in the literature and in colloquial use; for this reason, we have inserted a List of Equivalent Terms at the beginning of the text. It lists the term that is used throughout this book in **bold**, and gives the page number where a detailed explanation of the homeopathic remedy can be found.

Term	Latin	English	Page
A			
Abrotanum	Artemisia Abrotanum	Southernwood	47
Acidum hydrofluoricum	**Fluoricum acidum**	Hydrofluoric acid	163
Aconitum napellus		Wolfsbane, Monkshood	50
Actaea racemosa	**Cimicifuga,** Cimicifuga serpentaria	Black Cohosh, Black Snakeroot	133
Aethusa cynapium		Fool's Parsley	53
Agaricus muscarius	Amanita muscaria	Bug Agaric, Fly Agaric	55
AgNO3	**Argentum nitricum,** Lapis infernalis	Nitrate of Silver, Lunar Caustic, AgNO3	77
Al_2O_3	**Alumina,** Argila pura,	Oxide of Aluminium, Pure Clay	62
Allium cepa		Red onion	58
Aloe	Aloe socotrina	Socotrine Aloes	60
Aloe socotrina	**Aloe**	Socotrine Aloes	60

Term	Latin	English	Page
Alumina	Argila pura, Aluminium	Oxide of Aluminium, Pure Clay, Al_2O_3	62
Aluminium	**Alumina**, Argila pura,	Oxide of Aluminium, Pure Clay, Al_2O_3	62
Amanita muscaria	**Agaricus muscarius**	Bug Agaric, Fly Agaric	55
Amara dulcis	**Dulcamara**, Dulcis amara, Solanum dulcamara	Bittersweet	153
Ambergris	**Ambra grisea**		65
Ambra grisea		Ambergris	65
Ambra grisea		Ambergris	65
Anacardium orientale		Marking Nut	67
Anamirta cocculus	**Cocculus**, Menispermum cocculus	Indian Cockle	137
Antimonium crudum		Black Sulphide of Antimony, Sb_2S_3	69
Antimonium sulphuratum aurantiacum		Golden Sulphuret of Antimony, Sb_2S_5	71
Antimonium tartaricum	Tartarus stibiatus, Tartarus emeticus	Tartar Emetic, $(C_4H_4O_6 (SbO) K)_2 + H_2O$	72
Antimony, Golden Sulphuret of	**Antimonium sulphuratum aurantiacum**	Sb_2S_5	71
Apis mellifica		Honeybee-poison	74
Apple, bitter	**Colocynthis** Citrullus colocynthis, Cucumis	Bitter Cucumber	142
Arbor Vitae	Thuja occidentalis	**Thuja**	301
Argentum nitricum	Lapis infernalis	Nitrate of Silver, Lunar Caustic, $AgNO3$	77
Argila pura	**Alumina**, Aluminium	Oxide of Aluminium, Pure Clay, Al_2O_3	62
Arnica montana		Leopard's Bane, Fall Herb	80
Arsenic Trioxide	**Arsenicum album**	As_2O_3, White Arsenic	83

Term	Latin	English	Page
Arsenicum album		As$_2$O$_3$, Arsenic Trioxide, White Arsenic	83
Artemisia Abrotanum	**Abrotanum**	Southernwood	47
Artemisia Cina	**Cina**	Wormseed	135
As$_2$O$_3$	**Arsenicum album**	Arsenic Trioxide, White Arsenic	83
Atropa belladonna	**Belladonna**	Deadly Nightshade	93
Aurum foliatum	**Aurum metallicum**	Gold	86
Aurum metallicum	Aurum foliatum	Gold	86
B			
BaCO	**Baryta carbonica**	Carbonate of Barium	90
Barium, Carbonate of	**Baryta carbonica**	BaCO	90
Baryta carbonica		Carbonate of Barium, BaCO	90
Belladonna	Atropa belladonna	Deadly Nightshade	93
Bichromate of Potassium	**Kali bichromicum**	Potash, K$_2$((CrO$_3$)(CrO$_4$))	192
Bitter Apple	**Colocynthis,** Citrullus colocynthis, Cucumis	Bitter Cucumber	142
Bitter Cucumber	**Colocynthis**, Citrullus colocynthis, Cucumis	Bitter Apple	142
Bittersweet	**Dulcamara**, Amara dulcis, Dulcis amara, Solanum dulcamara		153
Black Cohosh	**Cimicifuga,** Actaea racemosa, Cimicifuga serpentaria	Black Snakeroot	133
Black hellebore	**Helleborus niger**	Christmas Rose	174
Black Snakeroot	**Cimicifuga,** Actaea racemosa, Cimicifuga serpentaria	Black Cohosh	133
Black Sulphide of Antimony	**Antimonium crudum**	Sb$_2$S$_3$	69

Term	Latin	English	Page
Blacklead	**Graphites,** Plumbago		171
Boneset	**Eupatorium perfoliatum**	Thoroughwort	156
Brazilian Rattlesnake	**Crotalus horridus**	Rattlesnake	148
Brimstone	**Sulphur**	Sulphur	290
Bromine	**Bromium**		96
Bromium		Bromine	96
Bryonia	Bryonia alba, Vitis alba, Vitis diaboli	Wild Hops, White Bryony	99
Bryonia alba	**Bryonia,** Vitis alba, Vitis diaboli	Wild Hops, White Bryony	99
Bug Agaric	Amanita muscaria	Fly Agaric	55
Bushmaster	**Lachesis,** Lachesis muta, Surucucu		204

C

Term	Latin	English	Page
$(C_4H_4O_6 (SbO) K)_2 + H_2O$	**Antimonium tartaricum,** Tartarus stibiatus, Tartarus emeticus	Tartar Emetic	72
$C_6H_2(NO_2)_3(OH)$	**Picrinicum Acidum,** Trinitrophenol	Picric Acid	255
Calcarea carbonica (Hahnemanni)	**Calcarea carbonica (Hahnemanni)**	Lime of Oystershells, Carbonate of Lime	102
Calcarea phosphorica		Phosphate of Lime	105
Calcarea sulphuratum Hahnemanni	Hepar sulphuris calcareum	**Hepar sulphuris**	177
Calcarea sulphurica		Sulphate of Lime, Plaster of Paris, Gypsum, $CaSO4$	108
Camphor Tree	**Camphora.** Laurus Camphora	Camphor	110
Camphora	Laurus Camphora	Camphor Tree, Camphor	110
Cannabis indica		Hashish, Indian Hemp, Marijuana	112

Term	Latin	English	Page
Cantharis	Cantharis officinalis, Lytta vesicatoria	Spanish Fly	114
Cantharis officinalis	**Cantharis**, Lytta vesicatoria	Spanish Fly	114
Capsicum	Capsicum annuum	Cayenne-Pepper, Spanish Pepper	116
Capsicum annuum	**Capsicum**	Cayenne-Pepper, Spanish Pepper	116
Carbo vegetabilis		Vegetable Charcoal	119
Carbonate of Barium	**Baryta carbonica**	BaCO	90
Carbonate of Lime	**Calcarea carbonica (Hahnemanni)**	Lime of Oystershells	102
Carbonate of Magnesia	**Magnesia carbonica**		216
Carbonate of Potassium	**Kali carbonicum**	Potash, K_2CO_3	194
Carbonate of Sodium	**Natrum carbonicum**	Soda, $NaCO_3$	228
CaSO4	**Calcarea sulphurica**	Sulphate of Lime, Plaster of Paris, Gypsum	108
Causticum	Tinctura acris sine Kalio	Hahnemann's Tinctura acris sine Kalio	122
Cayenne-Pepper	**Capsicum**, Capsicum annuum	Spanish Pepper	116
Celandine, Greater	**Chelidonium**, Chelidonium majus	Greater Celandine	128
Chamomilla	Matricaria chamomilla	Common Chamomile	126
Charcoal	**Carbo vegetabilis**	Vegetable Charcoal	119
Chelidonium	**Chelidonium**, Chelidonium majus	Greater Celandine	128
Chelidonium majus	**Chelidonium**	Greater Celandine	128
China officinalis	Cinchona succirubra, Cortex peruviana		130
Chloride of Magnesia	**Magnesia muriatica**, Magnesium chloratum		218

Term	Latin	English	Page
Chloride of Sodium	**Natrum muriaticum,** Natrum chloratum	Common Salt, Sea Salt, NaCl	230
Christmas Rose	**Helleborus niger**	Black hellebore	174
Cimicifuga	Actaea racemosa Cimicifuga serpentaria	Black Cohosh, Black Snakeroot	133
Cimicifuga serpentaria	**Cimicifuga,** Actaea racemosa	Black Cohosh, Black Snakeroot	133
Cina	Artemisia Cina	Wormseed	135
Cinchona succirubra	**China officinalis,** Cortex peruviana		130
Citrullus colocynthis	**Colocynthis,** Cucumis	Bitter Apple, Bitter Cucumber	142
Clay, pure	**Alumina,** Argila pura,	Oxide of Aluminium, Al_2O_3	62
Club Moss (spores)	**Lycopodium,** Lycopodium clavatum		213
Cocculus	Anamirta cocculus, Menispermum cocculus	Indian Cockle	137
Coffea	Coffea arabica, Coffea cruda	Coffee, Coffee Tree	139
Coffea arabica	**Coffea,** Coffea cruda	Coffee, Coffee Tree	139
Coffea cruda	**Coffea,** Coffea arabica	Coffee, Coffee Tree	139
Coffee	**Coffea,** Coffea arabica, Coffea cruda	Coffee Tree	139
Colocynthis	Citrullus colocynthis, Cucumis	Bitter Apple, Bitter Cucumber	142
Common Chamomile	**Chamomilla,** Matricaria chamomilla		126
Common Salt	**Natrum muriaticum,** Natrum chloratum	Sea Salt, NaCl, Chloride of Sodium	230
Conium maculatum		Poison Hemlock	144
Copper	**Cuprum metallicum**		151

Term	Latin	English	Page
Cortex peruviana	**China officinalis,** Cinchona succirubra		130
Crotalus horridus		Rattlesnake, Brazilian Rattlesnake	148
Crude Rock-oil	**Petroleum,** Oleum petrae album	Mineral oil	245
Cucumber, bitter	**Colocynthis** Citrullus colocynthis, Cucumis	Bitter Apple	142
Cucumis	**Colocynthis** Citrullus colocynthis	Bitter Apple, Bitter Cucumber	142
Cuprum metallicum		Copper	151
Cuttlefish	**Sepia,** Sepia officinalis		273

D

Term	Latin	English	Page
Datura stramonium	**Stramonium**	Thornapple	287
Deadly Nightshade	**Belladonna,** Atropa belladonna		93
Delphinium staphisagria	**Staphisagria**	Stavesacre, Louse Wort	283
Dog's Milk	**Lac caninum**		202
Dulcamara	Amara dulcis, Dulcis amara, Solanum dulcamara	Bittersweet	153
Dulcis amara	**Dulcamara,** Amara dulcis, Solanum dulcamara	Bittersweet	153

E

Term	Latin	English	Page
Eupatorium perfoliatum		Boneset, Thoroughwort	156
Euspongia officinalis	**Spongia,** Spongia marina tosta	Roasted Sponge	279

F

Term	Latin	English	Page
Fall Herb	**Arnica montana**	Leopard's Bane	80
$FePO_4$	**Ferrum phosphoricum**	Phosphate of Iron	161

Term	Latin	English	Page
Ferrum metallicum		Iron	158
Ferrum phosphoricum		Phosphate of Iron, FePO$_4$	161
Flint, Pure	**Silicea**	H$_2$SiO$_3$, Silica	276
Fluoricum acidum	Acidum hydrofluoricum	Hydrofluoric acid	163
Fly Agaric	Amanita muscaria	Bug Agaric	55
Fool's Parsley	**Aethusa cynapium**		53

G

Garden-poppy	**Opium,** Papaver somniferum	Poppy	243
Gelsemium	Gelsemium Sempervirens	Yellow Jasmine	166
Gelsemium Sempervirens	**Gelsemium**	Yellow Jasmine	166
Glauber's Salt	**Natrum sulphuricum**	Sodium Sulfate, Sulfate of Soda, Na$_2$SO$_4$	233
Glonoinum		Nitroglycerine, Glycerol trinitrate	169
Glycerol trinitrate	**Glonoinum**	Nitroglycerine	169
Gold	**Aurum metallicum,** Aurum foliatum		86
Golden Sulphuret of Antimony	**Antimonium sulphuratum aurantiacum**	Sb$_2$S$_5$	71
Graphites	Plumbago	Blacklead	171
Greater Celandine	**Chelidonium,** Chelidonium majus		128
Gypsum	**Calcarea sulphurica**	Sulphate of Lime, Plaster of Paris, CaSO4	108

H

H$_2$SiO$_3$	**Silicea**	Silica, Pure Flint	276
Hahnemann's Tinctura acris sine Kalio	**Causticum,** Tinctura acris sine Kalio		122
Hashish	**Cannabis indica**	Indian Hemp, Marijuana	112
Helleborus albus	**Veratrum album**	White Hellebore	308

Term	Latin	English	Page
Helleborus niger		Christmas Rose, Black hellebore	174
Hemlock, Poison	**Conium maculatum**	Poison Hemlock	144
Hemp, Indian	**Cannabis indica**	Hashish, Marijuana	112
Henbane	**Hyoscyamus niger**		180
Hepar sulphuris	Calcarea sulphuratum Hahnemanni, Hepar sulphuris calcareum		177
Hepar sulphuris calcareum	Calcarea sulphuratum Hahnemanni	**Hepar sulphuris**	177
Honeybee-poison	**Apis mellifica**		74
Hops, Wild	**Bryonia**, Bryonia alba, Vitis alba, Vitis diaboli	White Bryony	99
Hydrargyrum	**Mercurius solubilis**	Quicksilver, Mercury	225
Hydrofluoric acid	**Fluoricum acidum,** Acidum hydrofluoricum		163
Hyoscyamus niger		Henbane	180
Hypericum	Hypericum perforatum	St. John's Wort	183
Hypericum perforatum	**Hypericum**	St. John's Wort	183
I			
Ignatia	Ignatia Amara, Strychnos Ignatii	St. Ignatius Bean	185
Ignatia Amara	**Ignatia,** Strychnos Ignatii	St. Ignatius Bean	185
Indian Cockle	**Cocculus**, Menispermum cocculus	Anamirta cocculus	137
Indian Hemp	**Cannabis indica**	Hashish, Marijuana	112
Iodine	**Iodum**		188
Iodum		Iodine	188
Ipecacuanha	Uragoga ipecacuanha	Ipecacuanha Root	190
Ipecacuanha Root	**Ipecacuanha**, Uragoga ipecacuanha		190

Term	Latin	English	Page
Iron	**Ferrum metallicum**		158
J			
Jasmine, Yellow	**Gelsemium**, Gelsemium Sempervirens		166
K			
$K_2((CrO_3)(CrO_4))$	**Kali bichromicum**	Bichromate of Potassium	192
K_2CO_3	**Kali carbonicum**	Carbonate of Potassium, Potash, K_2CO_3	194
K_2SO_4	**Kali sulphuricum**	Sulphate of Potassium	199
Kali bichromicum		Bichromate of Potassium, $K_2((CrO_3)(CrO_4))$	192
Kali carbonicum		Carbonate of Potassium, Potash, K_2CO_3	194
Kali phosphoricum		Phosphate of Potassium, KH_2PO_4	197
Kali sulphuricum		Sulphate of Potassium, K_2SO_4	199
KH_2PO_4	**Kali phosphoricum**	Phosphate of Potassium	197
L			
Labrador Tea	**Ledum**, Ledum palustre	Marsh Tea	208
Lac caninum		Dog's Milk	202
Lachesis	Lachesis muta, Surucucu	Bushmaster	204
Lachesis muta	**Lachesis**, Surucucu	Bushmaster	204
Lapis infernalis	**Argentum nitricum**	Nitrate of Silver, Lunar Caustic, AgNO3	77
Laurus Camphora	**Camphora**	Camphor Tree, Camphor	110
Lead	**Plumbum**		
Ledum	Ledum palustre	Marsh Tea, Labrador Tea	208
Ledum palustre	**Ledum**	Marsh Tea, Labrador Tea	208
Leopard's Bane	**Arnica montana**	Fall Herb	80
Lilium tigrinum		Tiger Lily	210

Term	Latin	English	Page
Lime of Oystershells	**Calcarea carbonica (Hahnemanni)**	Carbonate of Lime	102
Lime, Sulphate of	**Calcarea sulphurica**	Sulphate of Lime, Plaster of Paris, Gypsum, CaSO4	108
Louse Wort	**Staphisagria**, Delphinium staphisagria	Stavesacre	283
Luesinum	**Syphilinum**	Nosode from luetic ulceration	295
Lunar Caustic	**Argentum nitricum**, Lapis infernalis	Nitrate of Silver, AgNO3	77
Lycopodium	Lycopodium clavatum	Club Moss (spores)	213
Lycopodium clavatum	**Lycopodium**	Club Moss (spores)	213
Lycosa hispanica	**Tarentula hispanica**, Tarantula fasciiventris	Spanish Spider, Spanish Tarentula	298
Lytta vesicatoria	**Cantharis**, Cantharis officinalis	Spanish Fly	114

M

Term	Latin	English	Page
Magnesia carbonica		Carbonate of Magnesia	216
Magnesia muriatica	Magnesium chloratum	Chloride of Magnesia	218
Magnesia phosphorica		Phosphate of Magnesia	220
Magnesia, Phosphate of	**Magnesia phosphorica**		220
Magnesium chloratum	**Magnesia muriatica**	Chloride of Magnesia	218
Marijuana	**Cannabis indica**	Hashish, Indian Hemp	112
Marking Nut	**Anacardium orientale**		67
Marsh Tea	**Ledum**, Ledum palustre	Labrador Tea	208
Matricaria chamomilla	**Chamomilla**	Common Chamomile	126
May Apple	**Podophyllum**, Podophyllum peltatum		262
Medorrhinum		Nosode from gonorrheal pus	222
Menispermum cocculus	**Cocculus**, Anamirta cocculus	Indian Cockle	137

Term	Latin	English	Page
Mercurius solubilis	Hydrargyrum	Quicksilver, Mercury	225
Mercury	**Mercurius solubilis,** Hydrargyrum	Quicksilver	225
Mineral oil	**Petroleum,** Oleum petrae album	Crude Rock-oil	245
Monkshood	**Aconitum napellus**	Wolfsbane	50
Myristica fragrans	**Nux moschata**	Nutmeg	238
N			
Na₂SO₄	**Natrum sulphuricum**	Sodium Sulfate, Sulfate of Soda, Glauber's Salt	233
NaCl	**Natrum muriaticum,** Natrum chloratum	Common Salt, Sea Salt, Chloride of Sodium	230
NaCO₃	**Natrum carbonicum**	Carbonate of Sodium, Soda	228
Natrum carbonicum		Carbonate of Sodium, Soda, NaCO₃	228
Natrum chloratum	**Natrum muriaticum**	Common Salt, Sea Salt, NaCl, Chloride of Sodium	230
Natrum muriaticum	Natrum chloratum	Common Salt, Sea Salt, NaCl, Chloride of Sodium	230
Natrum sulphuricum		Sodium Sulfate, Sulfate of Soda, Glauber's Salt, Na₂SO₄	233
Nitrate of Silver	**Argentum nitricum,** Lapis infernalis	Lunar Caustic, AgNO3	77
Nitric acid	**Nitricum acidum,** Spiritus nitri acidus		235
Nitricum acidum	Spiritus nitri acidus	Nitric acid	235
Nitroglycerine	**Glonoinum**	Glycerol trinitrate	169
Nutmeg	**Nux moschata,** Myristica fragrans		238
Nux moschata	Myristica fragrans	Nutmeg	238
Nux vomica	Strychnos Nux vomica	Poison-nut	240

Term	Latin	English	Page
O			
Oil, Mineral- (Rock-)	**Petroleum,** Oleum petrae album	Crude Rock-oil, Mineral oil	245
Oleum petrae album	**Petroleum**	Crude Rock-oil, Mineral oil	245
Opium	**Opium,** Papaver somniferum	Garden-poppy, Poppy	243
Opium	Papaver somniferum	Garden-poppy, Poppy	243
Oxide of Aluminium	**Alumina,** Argila pura,	Pure Clay, Al_2O_3	62
Oystershells, Lime of	**Calcarea carbonica (Hahnemanni)**	Carbonate of Lime	102
P			
Papaver somniferum	**Opium**	Garden-poppy, Poppy	243
Paris, Plaster of	**Calcarea sulphurica**	Sulphate of Lime, Plaster of Paris, Gypsum, CaSO4	108
Pepper, Spanish (Cayenne-)	**Capsicum,** Capsicum annuum	Cayenne-Pepper, Spanish Pepper	116
Petroleum	Oleum petrae album	Crude Rock-oil, Mineral oil	245
Phosphate of Iron	**Ferrum phosphoricum**	$FePO_4$	161
Phosphate of Lime	**Calcarea phosphorica**		105
Phosphate of Magnesia	**Magnesia phosphorica**		220
Phosphate of Potassium	**Kali phosphoricum**	KH_2PO_4	197
Phosphoric acid	**Phosphoricum acidum**		247
Phosphoricum acidum		Phosphoric acid	247
Phosphoricum acidum		Phosphoric acid	247
Phosphorus		Yellow Phosphorus	250
Phytolacca	Phytolacca decandra	Poke Root	253
Phytolaca decandra	**Phytolacca**	Poke Root	253
Picric Acid	**Picrinicum Acidum,** Trinitrophenol	$C_6H_2(NO_2)_3(OH)$	255

Term	Latin	English	Page
Picrinicum Acidum	Trinitrophenol	$C_6H_2(NO_2)_3(OH)$, Picric Acid	255
Plaster of Paris	**Calcarea sulphurica**	Sulphate of Lime, Gypsum, CaSO4	108
Platinum	Platinum metallicum	**Platinum**	257
Platinum metallicum	**Platinum**	**Platinum**	257
Plumbago	**Graphites**	Blacklead	171
Plumbum		Lead	260
Podophyllum	Podophyllum peltatum	May Apple	262
Podophyllum peltatum	**Podophyllum**	May Apple	262
Poison Hemlock	**Conium maculatum**		144
Poison Ivy	**Rhus toxicodendron,** Toxicodendron quercifolium	Poison Ivy, Shrub	270
Poison Ivy	**Rhus toxicodendron,** Toxicodendron quercifolium	Shrub	270
Poison-nut	**Nux vomica,** Strychnos Nux vomica		240
Poke Root	**Phytolacca,** Phytolacca decandra		253
Poppy	**Opium,** Papaver somniferum	Garden-poppy	243
Potash	**Kali carbonicum**	Carbonate of Potassium	194
Psorinum		Nosode from human scabies vesicle	264
Pulsatilla	**Pulsatilla,** Pulsatilla pratensis	Wind Flower	267
Pulsatilla pratensis	**Pulsatilla**	Wind Flower	267
Pure Flint	**Silicea**	H_2SiO_3, Silica	276
Q			
Quicksilver	**Mercurius solubilis,** Hydrargyrum	Mercury	225

Term	Latin	English	Page
R			
Rattlesnake	**Crotalus horridus**	Brazilian Rattlesnake	148
Red onion	**Allium cepa**		58
Rhus toxicodendron	Toxicodendron quercifolium	Poison Ivy, Shrub	270
Roasted Sponge	**Spongia, Euspongia officinalis, Spongia marina tosta**		279
S			
Salt, Common (Sea Salt)	**Natrum muriaticum,** Natrum chloratum	Common Salt, Sea Salt, Chloride of Sodium, NaCl	230
Sb_2S_3	**Antimonium crudum**	Black Sulphide of Antimony	69
Sb_2S_5	**Antimonium sulphuratum aurantiacum**	Golden Sulphuret of Antimony	71
Sea Salt	**Natrum muriaticum,** Natrum chloratum	Common Salt, NaCl, Chloride of Sodium	230
Sepia	Sepia officinalis	Cuttlefish (ink-bag)	273
Sepia officinalis	**Sepia**	Cuttlefish (ink-bag)	273
Shrub	**Rhus toxicodendron,** Toxicodendron quercifolium	Poison Ivy	270
Silica	**Silicea**	H_2SiO_3, Pure Flint	276
Silicea	**Silicea**	H_2SiO_3, Silica, Pure Flint	276
Silver, Nitrate of	**Argentum nitricum,** Lapis infernalis	Lunar Caustic, AgNO3	77
Socotrine Aloes	Aloe socotrina	**Aloe**	60
Soda	**Natrum carbonicum**	Carbonate of Sodium, $NaCO_3$	228
Sodium Sulfate	**Natrum sulphuricum**	Sulfate of Soda, Glauber's Salt, Na_2SO_4	233
Solanum dulcamara	**Dulcamara,** Amara dulcis, Dulcis amara	Bittersweet	153

Term	Latin	English	Page
Southernwood	**Abrotanum,** Artemisia Abrotanum		47
Spanish Fly	**Cantharis,** Cantharis officinalis, Lytta vesicatoria		114
Spanish Pepper	**Capsicum,** Capsicum annuum	Cayenne-Pepper	116
Spanish Spider/Tarentula	**Tarentula hispanica,** Tarantula fasciiventris Lycosa hispanica	Spanish Tarentula	298
Spiritus nitri acidus	**Nitricum acidum**	Nitric Acid	235
Sponge, Roasted	**Spongia,** Euspongia officinalis, Spongia marina tosta		279
Spongia	Euspongia officinalis, Spongia marina tosta	Roasted Sponge	279
Spongia marina tosta	**Spongia,** Euspongia officinalis	Roasted Sponge	279
St. Ignatius Bean	**Ignatia,** Ignatia Amara, Strachnos Ignatii		185
St. John's Wort	**Hypericum,** Hypericum perforatum		183
Stannum		Tin	281
Staphisagria	Delphinium staphisagria	Stavesacre, Louse Wort	283
Stavesacre	**Staphisagria,** Delphinium staphisagria	Louse Wort	283
Strachnos Ignatii	**Ignatia,** Ignatia Amara	St. Ignatius Bean	185
Stramonium	Datura stramonium	Thornapple	287
Strychnos Nux vomica	**Nux vomica**	Poison-nut	240
Strychnos Nux vomica	**Nux vomica**	Poison-nut	240
Sulfate of Soda	**Natrum sulphuricum**	Sodium Sulfate, Glauber's Salt, Na_2SO_4	233

Term	Latin	English	Page
Sulphate of Lime	**Calcarea sulphurica**	Plaster of Paris, Gypsum, CaSO4	108
Sulphate of Potassium	**Kali sulphuricum**	K_2SO_4	199
Sulphur		Brimstone, Sulphur	290
Sulphuric acid	**Sulphuricum acidum**		293
Sulphuricum acidum		Sulphuric acid	293
Surucucu	**Lachesis**, Lachesis muta	Bushmaster	204
Syphilinum	Luesinum	Nosode from luetic ulceration	295
T			
Tarantula fasciiventris	**Tarentula hispanica**, Lycosa hispanica	Spanish Spider, Spanish Tarentula	298
Tarentula hispanica	Tarentula fasciiventris Lycosa hispanica	Spanish Spider, Spanish Tarentula	298
Tartar Emetic	**Antimonium tartaricum**, Tartarus stibiatus, Tartarus emeticus	$(C_4H_4O_6 (SbO) K)_2 + H_2O$	72
Tartarus emeticus	**Antimonium tartaricum**, Tartarus stibiatus	Tartar Emetic, $(C_4H_4O_6 (SbO) K)_2 + H_2O$	72
Tartarus stibiatus	**Antimonium tartaricum**, Tartarus emeticus	Tartar Emetic, $(C_4H_4O_6 (SbO) K)_2 + H_2O$	72
Thornapple	**Stramonium**, Datura stramonium	Thornapple	287
Thoroughwort	**Eupatorium perfoliatum**	Boneset	156
Thuja	Thuja occidentalis	Arbor Vitae	301
Thuja occidentalis	**Thuja**	Arbor Vitae	301
Tiger Lily	**Lilium tigrinum**	Tiger Lily	210
Tin	**Stannum**		281
Tinctura acris sine Kalio	**Causticum**	Hahnemann's Tinctura acris sine Kalio	122

Term	Latin	English	Page
Toxicodendron quercifolium	**Rhus toxicodendron**	Poison Ivy, Shrub	270
Trinitrophenol	**Picrinicum Acidum**	$C_6H_2(NO_2)_3(OH)$, Picric Acid	255
Tuberculinum		Nosode from expectoration of tuberculosis	305
U / V			
Uragoga ipecacuanha	**Ipecacuanha**	Ipecacuanha Root	190
Vegetable Charcoal	**Carbo vegetabilis**		119
Veratrum album	Helleborus albus	White Hellebore	308
Vitis alba	**Bryonia**, Bryonia alba, Vitis diaboli	Wild Hops, White Bryony	99
Vitis diaboli	**Bryonia**, Bryonia alba, Vitis alba	Wild Hops, White Bryony	99
W / Y			
White Arsenic	**Arsenicum album**	As_2O_3, Arsenic Trioxide	83
White Bryony	**Bryonia**, Bryonia alba, Vitis alba, Vitis diaboli	Wild Hops	99
White Hellebore	**Veratrum album**, Helleborus albus		308
Wild Hops	**Bryonia**, Bryonia alba, Vitis alba, Vitis diaboli	White Bryony	99
Wind Flower	**Pulsatilla**, Pulsatilla pratensis		267
Wolfsbane	**Aconitum napellus**	Monkshood	50
Wormseed	**Cina**, Artemisia Cina		135
Yellow Jasmine	**Gelsemium**, Gelsemium Sempervirens		166
Yellow Phosphorus	**Phosphorus**		250
Z			
Zinc	**Zincum metallicum**		311
Zincum metallicum		Zinc	311

Abrotanum
Artemisia abrotanum, southernwood (N.O. Compositae).

Generalities
Symptoms change places, i.e. various alternating complaints. Abrotanum needs an outlet, a valve; it needs discharges. Abrotanum is one of the main remedies for discharges that come easily and *exudations. Marasmus,* emaciation, especially in the lower extremities. Extreme weakness. Chilliness. Food assimilation is impaired. This disorder can best be studied in *marasmus* of the newborn. The neck of the infant is so thin and weak that its head falls to the side. The face looks old, young children look like old men. Their entire bodies are emaciated, wasting away. They seem to be suffering from malnutrition and their skin is wrinkled. *Exudates* and *ulcers* appear around the navel area. Disorders of glands and mucous membranes with a fever that is prolonged and stays high. Night sweats. Burning sensation in palms.

Mind and Emotions
Sad disposition with increasing anxiety and irritability. Angry, morose, sulky, cruel, brutal. Despondency. Agitation. Changing moods. Weak memory. Tired after mental exertion. Thinking is difficult, cannot understand what is going on. Delusion or fear of a softening of the brain. Children needing Abrotanum are irritable, stubborn and melancholic. Sometimes they isolate themselves from other children and avoid any close contact. They feel drowsy, sluggish. Slow comprehension.

Head
Headaches. Sensation of creeping along the convolutions of the brain, with tingling. Sensation of wind rushing from the right ear.

Cardiovascular System
Heart trouble, especially after suppression of *diarrhea* or rheumatism.

- **Respiratory System**
  Nosebleed. Dryness in the nose. Scratchy throat. Sensation of breathing hot air.

- **Digestive Tract**
  Emaciation despite having a good appetite. Difficulty swallowing, eructations, heartburn, *flatulence* and *colics* in the *abdomen*. Sharp and gnawing pain in the stomach, worse during the night. Sensation as if the stomach is hanging or floating in water, along with a peculiar feeling of coldness. Feeling that only holding the legs together tightly will prevent the intestines from protruding through the *anus*. Food passes undigested. Alternating *diarrhea* and *constipation*. Hemorrhoids (suppressed).

- **Extremities**
  Rheumatism with inflammation of the joints, which are painful or swollen and stiff with a prickling sensation. Pain is worse in the morning and improves with motion. *Paralysis* with numbness but no pain. Weak and tremulous. Neuralgic pain with great restlessness that is improved by motion.

- **Skin**
  Itchy skin. Vesicles filled with a watery fluid. White nodules on the forehead and cheeks. Purple spots with ill-defined margins. Veins are visible and purplish. Skin eruptions like flea bites. Itchy chilblains.

- **Modalities**
  Aggravation: After checking or suppression of discharges, especially *diarrhea*. Cold, cold air. Getting wet. During the night. Fog.
  Amelioration: During *diarrhea*. Motion.

- **Causation**
  Checking or suppression of discharges.

■ Indications

Colitis. Continuous fever. Eczema. *Erythema nodosum.* Failure to thrive. Helminthiasis. *Hemangioma.* Hemorrhoids. *Hydrocele. Lymphadenitis* with *gastroenteritis. Naevus flammeus. Ranula.*

■ Compare

Aethusa, Baryta carbonica, China, Kali bichromicum, Magnesia carbonica, Natrum muriaticum, Pulsatilla, Silicea.

Aconitum napellus

Aconitum napellus, monkshood, wolfsbane (N.O. Ranunculaceae). Grows in humid areas of almost all mountainous regions of Northern and Central Europe, especially in Jura mountains, Switzerland, Germany, and Sweden. Aconitum is highly poisonous! Don't use lower potencies (only 6x / c3 or higher).

■ Generalities

Oversensitivity of the nervous system. Violent symptoms that appear **suddenly** and with great intensity right from the beginning. All complaints, both acute or chronic, are accompanied by a fear of death or the feeling that death is imminent or near. **Panic attacks** with sudden *palpitations*, red face, numbness on one side of the body, sweats, trembling, *vertigo*, shortness of breath and fear of death. Sudden dry fever, chilliness during hot phase of fever. Heat is felt in the upper part of the body, external cold more in the lower part of the body. Sensitive to cold and cold wind (coming from the northeast).

■ Mind and Emotions

Marked oversensitivity of all senses; easily frightened; **restless;** hurry, impatience and terrible **anxiety. Fears death, agonizing fear of death.** Predicts the time of death. Fear of misfortune; constant fear for no reason. Fear of crowds, confined spaces, elevators, tunnels, being in the dark, accidents, earthquakes, airplanes, heart disease, stroke, etc. Panic attacks.

■ Head

Vertigo and frontal headache, worse from noise and light. Tendency to faint. Face red and hot when lying down, pale and livid (bluish) when sitting up. One-sided numbness of the face. *Vertigo* getting up. Sensitive to light. Eyes red; lacrimation. Sensitive to noise; ringing in the ears.

- **Respiratory System**

  Watery, acrid *coryza*; nosebleed, bright red; sensitive to odors. Cough coming from the *larynx*, painful, dry and hoarse. Stitches in chest. Worse from breathing out. Sudden shortness of breath.

- **Cardiovascular System**

  Heart trouble. Strong and rapid pulse. *Tachyarrhythmia*. *Palpitations* and hot flushes.

- **Digestive Tract**

  Dryness in mouth and throat; white coated tongue. **Intense thirst for cold drinks**. Choking and vomiting with cold sweat. Sharp pain in stomach. Tenderness of *abdomen*. Slimy, green or bloody stool.

- **Urinary Tract and Reproductive system**

  Urination difficult and painful. Fear of death during pregnancy or labor. Child and mother suffer from retention of urine after delivery.

- **Extremities**

  Skin is hot and dry, red spots. Cold with chill and shivering. Numbness in hands and feet. Limbs are achy, stiffness, weakness. Pain in muscles. Soreness in hip joint area. Knees turn to jelly.

- **Sleep**

  Disturbed sleep with nightmares and waking up with a fright.

- **Modalities**

  Aggravation: In the evening and during the night, especially around **midnight;** heat, cold; motion, touch, fright, vexation, cold/dry. **Amelioration:** After onset of perspiration; stillness, open air.

- **Causation**

  Fright, shock, life-threatening event; cold, **cold and dry wind** (easterly); suppressed discharges.

■ **Indications**

Angina pectoris. Appendicitis. Bronchial asthma. Blepharitis. Bronchitis. Fever in common colds and inflammatory conditions. *Gastritis.* Headache. *Laryngitis. Neuralgia. Neuritis. Otitis media.* Panic. *Pharyngitis. Pleurisy. Pneumonia.* Pseudocroup. *Rhinitis. Tachyarrhythmia. Tachycardia.* Retention of urine.

■ **Compare**

Arsenicum album, Belladonna, Bryonia, Ferrum phosphoricum, Phosphor, Rhus toxicodendron, Stramonium, Sulphur.

Aethusa cynapium
Fool's parsley (N.O. Umbelliferae).

■ Generalities

Violence of symptoms: vomiting, cramps, pain, delirium. Marked prostration and sleepiness. Tendency to get cramps. Frequent chills.

Fool's Parsley   Photo: DHU

Mind and Emotions

Nervous anticipation before exams; **fear of exams.** Fear of not waking up again before falling asleep or before anesthesia. Great anxiety and restlessness; irritability. Restless, anxious, weepy. Loner. Reserved, introverted and always distant; but strong emotions inside that cannot be expressed. Feeling that nobody understands, estranged from others, feels different. **Retreats from society, strong love for animals.** No contact with other people, but deep connection with animals. Passion for animals; has many pets, is very attached to them. Talks to animals, talks to self. During delirium, patient sees animals.

■ Head

Epileptic fits with eyes turned downwards. Eruptions (herpetic) on (the tip of) the nose. Wrinkled face; white, marked linea nasalis; bluish pallor around the mouth.

■ Digestive Tract

Aversion to and **intolerance of milk.** Milk is vomited soon after drinking; hungry immediately after vomiting. Violent vomiting in children; especially when intolerant of mother's milk or milk in general. Thirstless. Craving for salt and pasta; aversion to fat and fresh fruit.

Digestion disturbed from constant eating. *Diarrhea* in newborn children, they look worn out and have hippocratic face. *Diarrhea* after drinking milk. Stools contain undigested food, greenish or yellow and frothy. Violent vomiting and *diarrhea* with *dehydration*.

■ Sleep

Fear before sleep. When almost asleep, wakes up with a start, afraid of suffocating. Wakes up with shortness of breath, has to open a window. Sleeplessness due to fear of dying in sleep. Restless sleep, talking in sleep, somnambulism.

■ Modalities

Aggravation: Milk; frequent meals, after vomiting, after stool, teething; cold water; heat, warmth of bed; worse from hot weather; before and at the beginning of *menses*; during the summer; 3 to 4 am, evening, in the dark.

Amelioration: Walking in the open air; conversation; covering up.

■ Indications

Cholera infantum. Weak concentration. *Diarrhea.* Epilepsy. *Gastroenteritis.* Herpes. *Lactose intolerance. Pylorospasm.*

■ Compare

Antimonium crudum, Arsenicum album, Calcarea carbonica, Calcarea phosphorica, Magnesia carbonica, Natrum carbonicum, Natrum muriaticum, Nux vomica, Sanicula.

Agaricus muscarius

Amanita muscaria, fly agaric, bug agaric (N.O. Agaricaceae). Found in Europe, Asia and America in dry habitats, especially in pine tree forests.

■ Generalities

Extraordinary sensitivity to cold, tendency to catch colds. Profuse sweating from slightest exertion. Pains follow a diagonal pattern, i.e. in right shoulder and left hip. Children are awkward, clumsy, and timid. They appear slightly retarded.

Fly Agaric   Photo: DHU

■ Mind and Emotions

Extreme anxiety about health, especially **fear of cancer.**
Good-natured, naïve; weakness of will, often dependent on others (e.g. the doctor). Mood swings are extreme. Exaltation, **intoxicated** with increased self-confidence. No signs of exhaustion. Fearless, careless, reckless. *Retardation* (in talking and motoricity). Incoherent speech. Jumps from one idea to another, loquacity, exaggerated fantasies. Progressive weakness of memory, searching for words. Great irritability to the point of rage, in later stages patient is taciturn. Mental confusion, indifference (especially in the morning) and aversion to work. Full of anxiety and apathetic. Morbid ideas, e.g. certain places look like graves.

■ Children

Agaricus children can be retarded mentally and slow in learning how to walk and talk. Generally slow in learning. Overall intellectual development seems to progress slowly, thus many mistakes in speech and later on in writing. Weak memory. Comprehension is slow and they find it difficult to make a decision. They feel weak; very attached to their parents and dependent on them. Nervous hyperactivity with both mental and physical restlessness. Liveliness, laughing, singing, dancing and running around.

■ Head

Vertigo; *ataxia*. Headache in the forehead as if there were ice underneath the skin; worse from sunshine; Better after urinating. Head is constantly in motion. Cramps in the nape of the neck. Icy coldness on the scalp. Twitching in facial muscles, **grimaces.** *Chorea* and *convulsions* in children from scolding or insults. Eyes itchy and burning, twitching eyelids, *nystagmus*, double vision, defective color vision, nearsightedness. External ear red and burning.

■ Cardiovascular System

Irregular heartbeat, especially on waking. Better from motion, eructations, passing flatus or stool.

■ Digestive Tract

Oral mucous membranes are sore, bad breath, dryness and scratching in the *pharynx/esophagus*. *Fibrillation* of the tongue, articulation difficult. Paroxysms of ravenous appetite, increased thirst. Patient feels nauseated and bloated and has to vomit. Violent *flatulence*, cramps in the stomach. *Diarrhea* green and slimy.

■ Respiratory System

Coryza, nosebleed. Violent, spasmodic cough followed by sneezing, getting worse during the night and in the morning; worse from eating.

■ Urinary Tract and Reproductive system

Impaired urination with *incontinence*. Bed-wetting in children, especially after playing and excitement, also after getting cold. Scanty urine, dribbling.

■ Back and extremities

Backache with extreme tenderness in single vertebrae at the processus spinosus. **Involuntary twitching of muscles and choreic movements.** Hands and feet are red, burning and itching. Trembling hands and legs; impaired coordination. *Chorea* is better during sleep and worse after sex; sometimes in children after punishment.

■ Skin

Violent itch. Sensation of icy needles. Tenderness to touch.

■ Sleep

Sleep unrefreshing although patient is tired, frequent yawning.

■ Modalities

Aggravation: After sex; after eating; cold air; before a thunderstorm; pressure; touch; mental exertion; morning, during the day.
Amelioration: Gentle motion; evening, during sleep.

■ Causation

Epilepsy from suppressed eruptions.

■ Indications

Bronchitis. Frostbites. *Chorea minor. Enteritis*. Epilepsy. Hay fever. Headache. Hyperactivity. *Irritable bowel syndrome. Jactatio capitis. Multiple sclerosis. Nocturnal enuresis. Pavor nocturnus. Pertussis.* Phobias, especially pathophobia. *Postencephalitic conditions. Retardation*, psychomotor or mental. Speech defects. Sunstroke. Tics.

■ Compare

Argentum nitricum, Arsenicum album, Cuprum, Nitricum acidum, Rhus toxicodendron, Zincum.

Allium cepa

Red onion (N.O. Liliaceae).

- ## Generalities

Mucous membranes, especially of nose, eyes, *larynx* and bowels, suffer from increased secretion. Important remedy for *coryza*, allergic or as part of a common cold. After nerve injuries, pain as if from fine threads; phantom limb sensation after amputation.

Red onion　　　　Photo: DHU

- ## Mind and Emotions

Confusion of mind with extreme drowsiness and lethargy. Indolence. Great dullness of the mind, worse in the afternoon. Cold with **sleepiness** and lethargy in the evening. Anxiety. Confused, drowsy, not interested in anything. Indifference, forgetful of surroundings. Silly behavior.

- ## Head

Headache, better in the open air, worse in warm room. Dullness in head during *coryza*.

- ## Eyes

Red, burning; profuse, bland lacrimation. Sensitive to light.

- ## Nose

Acrid, violent and watery nasal discharge, *rhinitis* and hay fever with copious, bland lacrimation. Excoriating discharge from the left *nostril*, extending to the *right*. Adenoids.

- **Respiratory System**

  Upper respiratory infections and common colds extend downward to the *pharynx*, *larynx* and bronchi. Hoarseness; hacking and tickling cough. Sensation as if *larynx* were torn.

- **Digestive Tract**

  Craves raw onions, raw food and vegetables. Aversion to cucumbers, which don't agree with patient. Allergic to peaches. *Colics* in children after wet feet; worse from heat, better from motion. Heat and rumbling in the *abdomen*. *Diarrhea* with offensive flatus.

- **Modalities**

  Aggravation: Heat, warm room; evening.
  Amelioration: Open air.
  Side most often affected: Complaints start on the left side and move to the right.

- **Causation**

  Forceps delivery.

- **Indications**

  Bronchitis. Conjunctivitis. Diarrhea. Hay fever. Headache. Laryngitis. Neuralgia. Pharyngitis. Rhinitis. Upper respiratory infections.

- **Compare**

  Euphrasia, Gelsemium, Lachesis, Opium, Sabadilla, Sinapis nigra.

Aloe

Aloe socotrina, sococtrine aloes (N.O. Liliaceae).

■ Generalities

Phlegmatic, weary people. Great fatigue with sweating. Venous *congestion* all over the body caused by portal *congestion* and *plethora* in *abdomen*. Fullness in individual parts; dragging feeling; sensation of a plug. Heat, heaviness and fullness in *abdomen*, pelvis and *rectum*.

■ Mind and Emotions

Dissatisfied and angry at self, especially when digestion begins. **Hypochondriac; especially about stool.** Embarrassed and irritable because of involuntary stools. Alternating states: In the morning life appears to be nothing but a burden, in the evening patient is happy and content.

Aloe   Photo: DHU

Activity alternating with weariness. Aversion to mental work, which brings immediate fatigue.

■ Head

Congestive, pressing headache above the forehead, better from (ice-)cold applications; alternating with lower back pain.

■ Digestive Tract

Cannot control the use of the *anal sphincter*. Paralyzed feeling in *rectum*. Involuntary or unnoticed stool when passing flatus or while urinating. Even hard stools pass unnoticed. Spontaneous *diarrhea*, mixed with flatus. *Diarrhea* mostly in the morning (around 2 to 10 am), drives patient out of bed, accompanied by pain before and during stool, pain felt in the lower part of the *abdomen* and around the navel. Pulsating pain around the navel. In chronic, spastic *colitis,* the pain extends from the *abdomen* to different areas of the body, e.g. from sides to navel, from upper abdominal area to the chest. Stool: Mucus in gelatinous lumps or yellow and bloody. Sudden urge to defecate after eating or drinking. Rumbling in bowels just before stool. Pain and copious mucus in *rectum* after stool. Hemorrhoids protrude like dark red grapes; complaints improve after a cold bath; itching; very tender and sore. *Rectal prolapse* in children.

■ Back and Extremities
Lumbago, alternating with headache and hemorrhoids. Extremities are almost always cold, especially the feet.

■ Modalities
Aggravation: Summer, in warm weather, heat; after eating and drinking; morning.
Amelioration: Cool, open air; cold applications; cold weather; in the afternoon and in the evening.

■ Indications
Colitis. Diarrhea. Dysentery. Encopresis. Enteritis. Headache. Hemorrhoids. *Lumbago. Rectal prolapse.*

■ Compare
Aesculus, Natrum sulphuricum, Oleander, Podophyllum, Sulphur.

Alumina

Aluminum or oxide of aluminum, Al_2O_3, also called argila pura, pure clay.

■ Generalities

Dryness of mucous membranes and skin. **Slowness of body and mind. Sluggish functions. Mostly used in chronic conditions.** Lack of vital heat. Weak, emaciated and tired, has to sit down. Delicate children are prone to suffer from *coryza* and eructations after eating artificial baby food.

■ Mind and Emotions

Depressed, confused, hasty, in a hurry. Feels hurried inside though slow in execution and comprehension. Time passes slowly. Mood changeable, getting better as the day progresses. Answers slowly. The mind feels numbed. Unable to express ideas or feelings. Tired from talking. Confusion about identity. Everything seems unreal. Fear of knives; impulse to kill self at sight of a knife or blood.

■ Head

Stinging, burning pain in the head; with *vertigo*, worse in the morning, better after eating. *Vertigo* with *nausea*, better after breakfast. *Vertigo* on closing eyes; tendency to fall forward. Body starts swaying when eyes are closed. Boils and pimples on the face. Twitching of lower jaw. Blood rushes to the face after a meal. Sensation as if the face is covered by cobwebs or egg white has dried on face. **Eyes:** Objects look yellow. Eyelids feel dry, burning and aching; worse in the morning. Chronic *conjunctivitis. Ptosis. Strabismus.* **Ears:** Ringing. Eustachian tube feels congested.

■ Throat

Dry, sore throat; food cannot pass; *esophagus* is too narrow. Feels as if a splinter is in the throat. Loss of voice, constant need to clear the throat.

- **Digestive Tract**
Mouth sore, bad breath. Teeth covered with sordes. Gums are sore and bleeding. Craves indigestible things, **dry food.**
Aversion: meat, **intolerance of potatoes.**
Lack of appetite; can only swallow a mouthful at a time. *Colics,* complaints in the left side of the *abdomen.* **Severe** *constipation.* Stool is hard, dry and lumpy; no urge. Patient must use fingers to help remove stool. Inactivity of the *rectum,* even soft stool requires straining. *Rectum* sore, dry, inflamed and bleeding. Itching and burning around the *anus.* Difficulty passing even soft stool, has to press hard. *Constipation* **in small children.** *Diarrhea* on urinating. Painful urge long before stool, stool is then passed with much straining.

- **Respiratory System**
Pain at bridge of nose. Sense of smell diminished. *Rhinitis.* Nasal membranes are swollen and distended. Nasal secretion is thick and adhesive. Cough; mornings soon after waking; worse from talking; caused by spices. Hoarseness, loss of voice; tingling in *larynx.* Wheezing and rattling breath. Soreness in chest, talking makes it worse.

- **Urinary Tract and Reproductive system**
Paralysis of bladder muscles, has to strain to pass urine; difficulty starting urination. *Leukorrhea:* acrid, profuse, running down to the heels, worse during the day, better from a cold bath. Exhausted in body and mind after *menses.*

- **Extremities**
Pains in limbs with numbness. Legs feel asleep and heavy. Soles feel numb. Pain in soles, shoulder and upper arm. Coordination difficult when walking; *ataxia.* Brittle nails.

- **Skin**
Restless sleep; anxious and confused dreams. Sleepy in the morning.

■ **Modalities**

Aggravation: Periodically; heat, warm room; afternoon; **potatoes; after waking in the morning; cold, dry weather;** winter; sitting; full and new moon; talking.

Amelioration: Open air; washing in cold water; evening and every other day; mild summer weather; damp weather; warm drinks, eating.

■ **Indications**

Atony of stomach and bowels. Blepharitis. Bronchitis. Constipation. Impaired coordination. *Diarrhea.* Eczema. *Laryngitis. Pharyngitis. Rhinitis.*

■ **Compare**

Baryta carbonica, Bryonia, Cocculus, Conium, Graphites, Helleborus, Nux moschata, Opium.

Ambra grisea
Ambergris is a secretion from the sperm whale that is found floating in the sea.

Generalities
More frequent in women; **prematurely old.** Burnout syndrome; the slightest nervous stress and all external impressions affect patient strongly and aggravate every complaint. Symptoms suddenly change location.

Mind and Emotions
Bashful, self-conscious and timid. Embarrassment and anxiety when in company. Loss of self-confidence after *failure* or having been insulted. Tries to please everybody; cannot say no. Dwells all day on past occurences. Sadness and tearful when listening to music. Anxiety with ineffectual urge to defecate. Fear of the night, of strangers. Great anxiety and worries. Does not want to talk about problems, wants to be left alone. Hasty, nervous and excited when talking. Silly and loquacious. Asks many questions without waiting for the answer; jumps from one subject to another. Aversion to smiling faces. Suspicious, delusion of being laughed at. Mental weakness; slow comprehension; forgetfulness; dreaminess. Depression alternating with temperamental outbursts.

Head
Vertigo in older people, worse in the morning, after sleep and after a meal. Headache, worse from blowing one's nose. Deafness. Blushes easily.

Digestive Tract
Coldness in *abdomen. Flatulence.* **Cannot have stool in the presence of other people.** *Constipation.*

■ **Respiratory System**
Nervous cough, violent and spasmodic, with eructations and hoarseness; triggered by fear, excitement and music.

■ **Urinary Tract and Reproductive system**
Unable to urinate if others are around. Spotting between periods, caused by slight exertion and pressing during defecation. Itching in the genitals.

■ **Back and Extremities**
Trembling. One-sided complaints together with numbness. Numbness of parts patient is lying on.

■ **Modalities**
Aggravation: Noise, music; company, conversation, talking, presence of strangers, embarrassment; reclining; Evening; Waking 5 to 9 am; warm milk; old age.
Amelioration: Cold drinks and water; moving slowly in the open air.

■ **Indications**
Alzheimer's disease. Bronchitis. Constipation. Chronic fatigue syndrome. Dementia. *Metrorrhagia.* Senility.

■ **Compare**
Baryta carbonica, Cimicifuga, Ignatia, Lachesis, Mercurius, Moschus, Natrum muriaticum.

Anacardium orientale

Marking nut. Tree is found in the mountainous areas of India.

- **Generalities**

Feeling of a blunt plug or a ball in different parts of the body. Individual parts feel bandaged. External numbness. Catches cold very easily; sensitive to cold and drafts. Periodicity of complaints. Weakness of senses.

- **Mind and Emotions**

Internal conflict; feeling of having two wills; contradictory will. **Feeling of having an angel on one shoulder and a devil on the other.** Lack of self-confidence, deep-seated **inferiority complex;** has to prove self; helpless, needy, insecure; blames self;

Marking Nut   Photo: DHU

hypersensitivity. Laughing at serious matters and serious about silly things. Anxious about being followed when walking in the open air. Anxious; feels constantly surrounded by enemies. Fears the future, imaginary dangers. Fear of exams with burnout syndrome. Everything appears as if in a dream. Maliciousness; cruelty; treachery; sadism; hatred; vindictiveness; hard-heartedness; insensitivity. Lack of moral feeling. Scolding; cursing or swearing; sighing. **Sudden loss of memory**; absent-minded; incapable of any mental work.

- **Head**

Headache as if from a bandage or plug; worse from mental work. Headache when fasting, better after breakfast.

- **Digestive Tract**

  Empty feeling in stomach that improves with eating. Vomiting of pregnancy, better when eating constantly. Abdominal pain as if a blunt plug were pressed into intestines. Violent urge to defecate without evacuation. *Constipation*; even soft stools pass with difficulty. Hemorrhoids.

- **Skin**

  Red eruptions with unbearable itch that drives patient crazy. Worse in the warmth of bed. Vesicular eruptions, especially around the navel, with horrible itching. Itch improved by hot water. Warts on palms.

- **Modalities**

  Aggravation: Cold; heat; initiating motion; morning; rubbing; mental exertion; empty stomach; vexation.

- **Amelioration**

  While eating or after a meal; walking about slowly; evening.
  Side most often affected: Symptoms move from right to left.

- **Causation**

  Ailments from vexation.

- **Indications**

  Behavior disorders. *Chronic fatigue syndrome. Constipation. Depression.* Eczema. *Gastric and duodenal ulcers. Gastritis.* Headache. Hemorrhoids. Inferiority complex. Schizophrenia.

- **Compare**

  Baryta carbonica, Hyoscyamus, Ignatia, Lycopodium, Medorrhinum, Nux vomica, Platina, Rhus toxicodendron, Staphisagria, Stramonium.

Antimonium crudum

Black antimony, antimony sulfide (Sb_2S_3). In nature the substance is found as a shiny, crystalline mass of grayish-black color. The powder is gray like iron. Water-soluble.

■ Generalities

Adiposity or emaciation; edematous swelling; depletion. Warm-blooded.

■ Mind and Emotions

Ill-tempered, morose, dissatisfied, pessimistic. Exceptional irritability; does **not want to be touched or looked at**; any attention given makes him angry; does not want to talk or be spoken to. Emotional; introverted; **romantic; moonlight brings sentimental mood**; crying in a solemn atmosphere; writes poetry, talks in rhymes. Sadness, tired of life, suicidal.

■ Head

Migraine that gets better as soon as some discharge occurs (e.g. *coryza*, vomiting, *diarrhea*). The *causation* for the onset of migraines is often found in the suppression of some kind of discharge or skin eruptions. Headaches alternating with stomach pain. Eyelids are red, *conjunctivitis*, cracks in canthi. Cracks in corners of mouth, painful.

■ Digestive Tract

Tongue has a furred, thick, milky-white coating, "like snow". Thirstlessness. Craves pickles and sour things. Sour food aggravates gastric disorders. **Digestion is disturbed from overloading the stomach.** Feeling in stomach as if overloaded. Frequent vomiting but no relief. Stomach disorders after grief. Cramps and spasmodic pain in solar plexus. *Diarrhea* alternating with *constipation*. Hemorrhoids with constant oozing of mucus.

- ## Respiratory System
Dry, hacking, spasmodic cough that makes the patient shake; worse in a warm room. Loss of voice from overheating.

- ## Skin
Skin eruptions with itch, especially in bed. Inflammation of the skin with *pustules* and vesicles. Thick, hard scabs and crusts, honey-like color; some break and discharge a green, purulent fluid that burns like red-hot coals; accompanied by great exhaustion. Cracks around nostrils and corners of the mouth. Warts on soles; multiple corns, painful. Extreme tenderness of soles; thick and callous skin with very tender, horny spots. Nails are thick, split, hard, horny, dry, and grow slowly.

- ## Modalities
Aggravation: Heat, radiant heat; moonlight; cold and damp weather, bathing in cold water; touch; after eating; summer; in the evening, on going to bed, at night.
Amelioration: Cool, open air; walking in the open air; during rest; after a warm bath.

- ## Causation
Ailments from unhappy, **disappointed love**, grief; complaints after being in the sun, sunstroke; after a cold bath; ailments after vaccination; bad effects from drinking wine, especially sour wine

- ## Indications
Adiposity. Bronchitis. Chronic fatigue syndrome. Corns. Depression. *Diarrhea.* Eczema. *Gastric and duodenal ulcers. Gastritis. Gastroenteritis.* Headache. Hemorrhoids. *Impetigo contagiosa. Laryngitis.* Migraine. *Pertussis.* Upper respiratory infections. *Varicella.*

- ## Compare
Calcarea carbonica, Calcarea phosphorica, Capsicum, Carbo vegetabilis, Chamomilla, Ferrum, Graphites, Ipecacuanha, Pulsatilla, Sulphur.

Antimonium sulphuratum aurantiacum

Golden sulphuret of antimony, Sb_2S_5.

■ Generalities

General malaise, tiredness, weakness with *nausea*.
Burning feeling inside the head, especially with eye problems. Wakes at night with dull headache. Onset of blindness.

■ Digestive Tract

Doughy taste in mouth in the morning. Loss of appetite. *Nausea* and weakness. Feeling of pressure in *abdomen*, bloating, area around navel feels tender. *Constipation* with hard stool. Frequent flatus with sudden urge to defecate; followed by bright yellow, soft stool; violent *colics* at the end.

■ Respiratory System

Nosebleed while washing. Loss of sense of smell. Copious mucus from nose and throat; viscous mucus in bronchi and *larynx*. Tickling in *larynx*. Difficulty breathing. Rattling noise in respiratory tract; difficulty expectorating mucus. Winter cough. Dry, hard cough with no expectorate.

■ Skin

Itchy hands and feet. *Pustular* acne.

■ Indications

Acne. Bronchitis. *Constipation. Cough. Diarrhea. Epistaxis. Pneumonia. Rhinitis.*

■ Compare

Antimonium crudum, Arsenicum album, Ferrum metallicum, Mercurius sulphuricus, Tartarus stibiatus, Sulphur.

Antimonium tartarium

Tartarus emeticus, tartarus stibiatus, tartar emetic, $(C_4H_4O_6 (SbO) K)_2 + H_2O$.

■ Generalities

Great exhaustion and rapid wasting, cardiovascular weakness, hippocratic face. Sleepiness with tremulous feebleness and profuse, cold sweats. Massive obstruction of respiratory tract along with distinct rattling noise; too weak to expectorate. *Cyanosis* in respiratory tract disease, especially about the lips. Frequent in children and old persons.

■ Mind and Emotions

Irritable, morose, anxious and discouraged. Aversion to touch; wants to be left alone or fear of being alone. Children are very stubborn; don't want to be touched or looked at. *Stuporous* dizziness and irresistible urge to sleep; frequent yawning. Patient is completely self-absorbed and only leaves *stupor* to utter some incomprehensible words.

■ Digestive Tract

Nausea and vomiting, which are exhausting, but do bring relief. Constant *nausea* with *agony* and intense depletion. Vomiting along with violent, very painful choking. This leads very quickly to a suffocative state with great anxiety, as if patient were going to die. Thick white coating on tongue. **Craves sour foods, drinks and apples,** but they aggravate patient's condition. *Abdomen* feels as if full of stones. Exhausting diarrhea.

■ Respiratory System

Rattling of mucus in *trachea* with oppression, risk of suffocation and *cyanosis*. Mucus appears to be loose but cannot be expectorated due to weakness. Massive buildup of mucus in the respiratory tract. Much rattling but little *expectoration*. Cough is worse in the morning, when lying down; better when sitting up and from *expectoration*. Copious *expectoration*, whitish; mouthfuls of *expectoration*. Vomiting when coughing.

■ Modalities

Aggravation: Warmth; milk and sour foods; vexation; lying down; springtime, fall; humid and cold weather.
Amelioration: *Expectoration*; sitting up; fresh air; lying on the right side.

■ Causation

Bad effects of vaccination; staying in damp basements.

■ Indications

Asphyxia neonatorum. Bronchial asthma. Bronchitis. Bronchial pneumonia. Emphysema. Enteritis. Gastritis. Gastroenteritis. Pertussis. Pneumonia.

■ Compare

Antimonium crudum, Carbo vegetabilis, Ipecacuanha, Kali sulphuricum, Laurocerasus, Lycopodium, Stannum, Veratrum album.

Apis mellifica
Honeybee venom.

Generalities

Swelling, *edema*. *Edema* in extremities from kidney disorders. Effusions in serous membranes. **Burning, stinging pain;** as if from a beesting. Extreme tenderness. All symptoms appear suddenly and violently.

Honeybee   Photo: DHU

Mind and Emotions

Work mania, always busy doing something. **Pointless industriousness. Clumsiness;** drops things and laughs about it . Awkwardness; finds it difficult to express feelings. **Jealousy.** Erotic delusions and sexual mania. Irritable, easily vexed, nervous, hard to please; has a sharp tongue. Suffers from his own tantrums. Weeps easily, without a reason; discouraged, despondent. Indifference. Pretends to be happy even though actually feeling miserable; exaggerated cheerfulness; laughing at unhappy events. Absent-minded, cannot concentrate. Sleepiness. Premonitions of death.

Head

Meningitis or coma with shrill cries (cri encéphalique); spasms in one side of the body, the other feels as if paralyzed. Face swollen; eyelids appear to be filled with water; **swelling in** the upper and/or **lower lid** and in cheeks and lips. Conjunctiva swollen, red and burning.

- **Throat**
  Edamatous tonsillitis and inflammation of the *pharynx*. Uvula hangs down like a transparent sac. *Edema* of the *glottis*. Angioneurotic *edema*, Quincke's disease.

- **Digestive Tract**
  Thirstlessness, even during fever. Diarrhea; involuntary diarrhea at every motion; as if *anus* is wide open.

- **Respiratory System**
  Pneumonia or *pleurisy* with extremely violent pain when inhaling. Feeling that each breath could be the last. Cough, worse around midnight.

- **Urinary Tract and Reproductive System**
  Acute renal *failure*. *Cystitis* with burning pain. Scanty, milky urine with dark sediment like coffee grounds. Urinary *incontinence*, *albuminuria* after scarlet fever. Strong sexual desire. Cysts in ovaries; especially from suppressed sexual desire. *Abortion* between 2nd and 4th months.

- **Extremities**
  Puffy swelling of hands and feet, in lower extremities. Swelling and inflammation of joints, especially ankles. Inflammation of the knee-joint capsule. Clumsiness, awkwardness, impaired coordination. Weakness, *paralysis*.

- **Skin**
  Very sensitive. *Edema* of the skin resembling *Erysipelass* or *urticaria*. *Urticaria*; worse at night; after physical exertion. Pink, waxy-transparent swelling.

- **Sleep**
  Shrill cries during sleep. Restless sleep. Dreams of flying or travelling to distant places. Strong desire for sleep; extreme sleepiness.

- **Modalities**
  Aggravation: Heat, warmth, closed rooms; pressure, touch; afternoon 3 to 6 pm; after sleep; suppression of sexual desire.
  Amelioration: Cold applications, **cold;** open air, motion.
  Side most often affected: Right.

- **Causation**
  Ailments from jealousy, anger, frustration, vexation, anticipation, bad news, fear, grief, sexual excesses, shock; suppressed skin eruptions.

- **Indications**
  Abortion. Allergy. Anaphylactic shock. Arthritis. Cystitis. Erysipelas. Exudative pleurisy. Glomerulonephritis. Herpes zoster. Insect bites. Meningitis. Nephritis. Nephrotic syndrome. Ovarian cysts. Pharyngitis. Pneumonia. Pyelonephritis. Quincke's disease. Synovitis. Urticaria.

- **Compare**
  Arsenicum album, Belladonna, Cantharis, Lachesis, Lycopodium, Nux vomica, Palladium, Rhus toxicodendron, Vespa, Zincum.

Argentum nitricum

Silver nitrate, lapis infernalis, lunar caustic, AgNO$_3$. In antiquity, silver nitrate was used to cure epilepsy, causing poisonings characterized by a typical lead-gray discoloration of the skin (argyria).

Generalities

Nervous symptoms like *vertigo*, vanishing of thoughts, weak memory, trembling of extremities, weakness, with a hasty disposition. *Ulcerations* of mucous membranes. *Mucopurulent* discharge from the inflamed and ulcerated mucous membranes. **Painful splitter**-like sensation in

Silver Nitrate   Photo: DHU

different parts of the body, especially in the fauces and aruond the *uterus*. Useful for business people, students. Hysterical, nervous persons. Persons who are "dried out" and prematurely old. Warm-blooded, one of the warmest remedies!

Mind and Emotions

Fearful character. Anxious, irritable, nervous, in a hurry. Anxious about health, hypochondriacal; phobias with **fear of heights** (impulse to jump from a high place), claustrophobia, **anticipation**, stage fright; anxiety when alone, better in company. Craves company. **Impulsive,** impulsive thinking, irrational impulses. High emotionality. Compulsive behavior, superstitious ideas and phobia. Easily impressionable. Compassionate. Time passes too quickly for this patient, who does everything in a hurry. Has the delusion that parts of the body are expanding (e.g. head during headache, leg when suffering from *sciatica*). Dreams of snakes.

Head

Vertigo (this symptom is almost never absent where this remedy is indicated), frequently accompanied by buzzing in the ears.
Pale, aged look. Headache predominantly of *congestive* type, with violent throbbing, appears very often in intellectual workers after prolonged work or continuous mental excitement; in this state you will accompanied by the sensation that the brain is expanding, as if the skull were going to explode. The patient tries to relieve this sensation by exerting pressure on the head. Headache often appears as a right-sided *hemicrania* which may end in bilious vomiting. *Conjunctivitis*, small bright red spots the color raw meat on the eye, with copious *mucopurulent* discharge.

Throat

Splinter-like pain in throat. Hoarseness, chronic hoarseness with tickling cough. Chronic *laryngitis* in singers, cough at high notes; has to clear throat frequently. Papilloma and warts on throat or *larynx*.

Chest

*Palpitation*s, worse when lying on the right side, worse from exertion and emotional agitation.

Digestive Tract

Cravings: Sweets, which are not tolerated; salt and sugar. Stomach pain with frequent, **loud eructations** like a machine gun with pain extending to both sides. Frequent **flatus,** *meteorism*; loud rumbling in *abdomen*. Eructations and flatus don't bring relief. **Diarrhea from anticipation,** from emotions.

- ## Urinary Tract and Reproductive System
  Sex is painful, followed by leaking blood. Impotence, worse when thinking about it.

- ## Modalities
  Aggravation: Heat; sweets; during *menses;* at night and in the morning; mental work; lying on the right side.
  Amelioration: In the open air; wind blowing in patient's face; **cold**, cold bath; strong pressure.
  Side most often affected Left.

- ## Causation
  Anticipation, Fear. Eating ice cream. Masturbation and sexual excesses. Sweets. Tobacco (in boys).

- ## Indications
  Angina pectoris. Anxiety. *Apoplexy. Arrhythmia. Ataxia. Chronic fatigue syndrome. Colitis.* Compulsive behavior. *Conjunctivitis.* Connective tissue diseases. Depression. Epilepsy. *Gastritis. Gastroesophageal reflux disease.* Headache. *Hepatitis. Hypertension.* Impotence. *Irritable bowel syndrome.* Laryngeal *polyps. Laryngitis. Multiple sclerosis. Orchitis. Parkinson's disease. Pharyngitis.* Phobias. *Tabes dorsalis. Tremor. Ulcerations in the throat. Vertigo.*

- ## Compare
  Agaricus, Apis, Carbo vegetabilis, China, Iodium, Lac caninum, Lycopodium, Phosphorus, Pulsatilla, Sulphur, Zincum.

Arnica montana

Leopard's bane, fall herb (N.O. Compositae). Arnica montana is found in both low and high mountain regions in Europe.

■ **Generalities**

Shattered feeling with weakness and exhaustion; entire body aches as if bruised. Extreme sensitivity of the whole body, such that the bed feels too hard, causing the patient to move constantly; sensitive to touch. Discharges have a foul smell. Bleeds easily. Head and face are hot, the rest of the body is cold. Remedy for all kinds of **injuries.**

Leopard's Bane   Photo: DHU

■ **Mind and Emotions**

Wants to be left alone; says there is nothing wrong; claims to be in good health despite severe disease. Stubborn; contradicts; irritable, morose, easily frightened. **Fear of being approached, touched** (including approach to touch), instant death, heart disease. *Agoraphobia.* After an accident, fear remains at night; patient wakes frightened from horrible dreams. Absent-minded and dazed. During delirium, patient is convinced of being well; sends the doctor home. When answering questions, patient sinks into *stupor* and cannot finish what he was about to say; or answers correctly and relapses into coma. Stupefied state with involuntary stool and urination.

■ **Head**

Congestion going to the head with heat, while nose and the rest of the body remain cold. Concussion; head injuries; blunt injuries to the eye.

Migraine/*meningitis*/epilepsy/*vertigo* after head injury. Dull and pressive headache with the feeling that the pillow is too hard.

■ Digestive Tract

Eructations and diarrhea smelling of rotten eggs. Toothache after dental surgery or tooth extraction. Bloated *abdomen*; offensive flatus; *colic* pains in *abdomen*. Diarrhea with *mucopurulent*, bloody stools. Involuntary stools in sleep at night.

■ Respiratory System

Hoarseness or cough after straining the voice. Cough after crying. Whooping cough; dry, violent, very painful; child screams before coughing spell as if in pain. Cough with *expectoration* of bright, foamy, clotted blood. Whooping cough with bruised feeling, as if ribs were broken.

■ Chest

Stitches in chest. Sudden cardiac pain; pain feels like being squeezed or struck.

■ Urinary Tract and Reproductive System

Constant dribbling after delivery; or retention of urine, also from overexertion or accident. Danger of *abortion* after shocks etc. Great sensitivity of genitals.

■ Back and Extremities

Acute sprains, dislocations; contusions; muscle aches, especially after overexertion. *Arthritis* with tender and stiff joints; worse from cold and damp.

■ Skin

Symmetrical eruptions. Blue bruises after slightest pressure; *hematoma*. Livid discoloration of the skin; crush wounds; *petechiae*. Numerous small, extremely painful boils. Boils appear one after another.

■ **Modalities**

Aggravation: By slightest **touch** or pressure; **motion**; injury (blunt trauma, shock, commotion, overexertion, labor, sprain); in the evening, at night; damp.

Amelioration: Stretching out horizontally with head low; **lying down, rest;** cold bath.

■ **Causation**

Physical and psychological trauma, (blunt) injuries, contusion, wounds, concussion, accident; shock; overexertion and fatigue.

■ **Indications**

Acne. *Angina pectoris. Apoplexy. Arthritis. Brain concussion. Ecchymosis. Erysipelas. Furuncles. Hypertension.* Injuries and trauma. *Meningitis.* Migraine. *Pertussis. Pneumonia.* Post-traumatic headaches. Varicose veins.

■ **Compare**

Aconitum, Baptisia, Bellis perennis, Bryonia, Hypericum, Opium, Rhus toxicodendron, Ruta, Symphytum.

Arsenicum album

Arsenic trioxide, white arsenic, As_2O_3. Strong poison (Arsenic and Old Lace). The substance is used in horses, to make the coat shine. Arsenic is not poisonous in homeopathic dilutions (starting at 3x).

- ## Generalities

Anxiety, restlessness, exhaustion. Lack of vital heat, chilliness. Periodicity. Alternation of symptoms. Ulceration; **burning** pains; *edematous* swelling, *ascites*; acrid, thin, foul but scanty discharges; prone to malignancies.

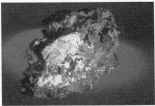

Arsenic Trioxide   Photo: DHU

- ## Mind and Emotions

Deep-rooted insecure feeling; great need for security and control. Patients depend on other persons, desire company, domineering in relations with close friends and in material matters, miserly, greed. Egotistical. Tidiness, pedantry; **conscientious about details**; compulsive cleanliness, compulsive washing. Perfectionism. Criticizes others and self, censorious.

Dissatisfaction. Irritability, especially in the morning. *Hypersensitivity;* sensitive to touch, light, smells, noises, untidiness. Restlessness; **anxious;** together with weakness. Panic attacks. **Fear** of being alone; robbers; disease, especially cancer and **death;** fear that he is going to kill people. Anxiety about health, hypochondria. Exhaustion, despair, loathing of life. Sadness, depression. *Suicidal.* Suspicious. Paranoid states. *Anorexia nervosa.*

■ **Head**

Face shows *agony*: pale, puffy, waxy and yellow, cachectic; *edema* around and under the eyes. Patient looks prematurely aged. Body is cold, periodic headaches that improve warmth. Epileptic fits, deathlike unconsciousness in later stages of disease; tetanic rigidity. Fainting in the morning.

■ **Respiratory System**

Chronic cough and asthma, worse when lying down, from smells, laughing, talking and turning over in bed; improved by sitting up. Asthma attack after *coryza*. *Dyspnea* with anxiety, restlessness, exhaustion, *cyanotic* face and sweats.

■ **Digestive Tract**

Cravings: Fatty and sour foods, snacks, bread and alcohol.
Aversions: Pasta, foods that trigger bloating (peas and beans), meat and fat on meat, butter and sweets. **Thirsty for little sips of cold water.**
Burning stomach pains, as if from scalding hot coals. *Nausea*, vomiting; aggravated by getting/sitting up. Stomach pain; better from (sweet) milk. Anxiety is felt in pit of stomach. Tendency to get *gastroenteritis*, **food poisoning**. *Nausea* at the look, smell or even the thought of eating. Tympanitic bloating of the *abdomen*. *Ascites*. *Peritonitis*. Violent *colics* in *abdomen*. Offensive, burning, acrid stools, not too copious. *Diarrhea* from cold drinks, fresh fruit, ice-creme. Extreme exhaustion after stool.

■ **Skin**

Itching, burning, swelling. *Edema*; eruptions, papular, dry, rough, scaly; aggravation from cold and scratching. Itchy; must scratch until the skin bleeds. Intense itch on the skin without eruptions; appears after suppressed eruption. *Psoriasis*. *Epithelioma*. *Carbuncles*. *Petechiae*. Urticaria after eating cod.

■ Modalities

Aggravation: Untidiness; cold; fresh ocean air, after midnight, 1 to 2 am; also 1 to 2 pm; being alone.

Amelioration: Warmth, heat; gentle motion; head elevated, open air. Company.

■ Indications

Anemia. Angina pectoris. Anorexia nervosa. Bronchial asthma. Bronchitis. Colitis. Compulsive behavior. *Cystitis.* Depression. Eczema. Food poisoning. *Gastric and duodenal ulcers. Gastritis. Gastroenteritis.* Hay fever. Headaches. Hemorrhoids. *Hepatitis. Herpes zoster.* Influenza. Panic attacks. *Pharyngitis.* Phobia. *Pneumonia. Psoriasis.* Sleeplessness.

■ Compare

Aconitum, Agaricus, Bismuthum, Cannabis indica, China, Graphites, Hepar sulphuris, Kali arsenicosum, Lycopodium, Nitricum acidum, Nux vomica, Phosphorus, Rhus toxicodendron, Veratrum album.

Aurum metallicum

Aurum metallicum or foliatum, gold. Gold is not oxidized by air or common acids.

■ **Generalities**

Rushes of blood, *congestion*. Very sensitive to cold. Generally oversensitive; especially to pain, which drives patient to despair.

■ **Mind and Emotions**

Aurum patients invest everything in one goal, e.g. in society/religion/ family; mostly in financial terms. Great sense of duty and justice. Quick in working and thinking, workaholic. Does not show feelings, inner emotions die. Internal hurry and restlessness. Irritability; cannot tolerate contradiction. Quarrelsome and violent-tempered. Taciturn; talks to self. Serious, introverted; responsible, ambitious. Egotism. Idealism. **Fears:** heart disease, heart attack, robbers, people. Worried about the future. Fears bankruptcy and the complete loss of his professional and social position. Hypochondriacal. Desire to **pray**; doubtful of soul's welfare. Patient goes into deep depression when he cannot reach his goal in life, inconsolable, total hopelessness. Feels worthless; guilt, self-reproach. Loss of self-confidence. Depression, melancholy, gloominess, despair; longing for death, **wants to die**, **thinks constantly of committing** *suicide*. The mere thought of *suicide* is comforting. **Suicidal,** e.g. car accident, shooting self, jumping out of window, a crash while hang-gliding (violent and sudden).

■ **Head**

Congestion going to the head, visible throbbing in the carotids and temporal arteries. Headache from studying. Tearing pain in the occiput that extends to the front and the forehead. Hair falls out in young men.

■ **Ears**

Mastoiditis with violent pain, which can drive the patient to commit *suicide*. Sensitivity to noise.

■ **Eyes**

Hemianopia; can see only the lower half of an object. Sees sparks before eyes, worse from mental exertion. Inflamed eyes with lacrimation and *photophobia*; stinging eye pain. Sensitivity and pain around the eyes. *Glaucoma* attacks. *Iritis;* sees black spots before eyes. *Exophthalmos.*

■ **Nose**

Ulcerations; bloody-purulent discharge. Offensive smell in the nose when blowing nose. Red, nodular nose.

■ **Cardiovascular system**

Sensation that heart has stopped beating for 2 or 3 seconds and then restarted with a jerk, beating violently. Violent *palpitations*. Feels as if the heart is loose while walking. Paroxysmal pain at night behind the sternum. Blood vessels feel hot.

■ **Digestive Tract**

Cravings: Bread, milk, dainties, pastries, delicacies, alcohol, coffee. Aversion: Meat. Foul breath "like old cheese". Ravenous appetite and thirst or loss of appetite. Burning feeling in the stomach and eructations. *Constipation* with hard and lumpy stools. Diarrhea at night. Stool grayish white, like ashes. Warts around the *anus.*

■ **Urinary Tract and Reproductive System**

Urine cloudy, like buttermilk. Painful retention of urine. Sweating in the genital area. *Uterus* or testicles hard and enlarged. Increased sexual desire. Swelling and pain in the testicles. Undescended testis, inguinal *hernia*. Erections during the night and seminal emissions. Depression due to infertility. *Amenorrhea* with melancholy. *Leukorrhea* thick yellow/white, not smelly. Tenderness of *vagina*. Pain during childbirth can drive patient to despair. Jaundice during pregnancy.

■ Extremities

Pain in bones; tearing; as if bones were broken; worse in the morning; better from motion. Pain in the knee, as if tightly bound. *Exostosis.* Offensive, cold foot perspiration. Cold hands at night. *Edema* in the legs, worse at night. Trembling from anger or fright.

■ Sleep

Sleeplessness; depression on waking after only a few hours of sleep. Sighs, whimpers, sobs and cries out in sleep. Fearful dreams. The nights are horrifying, causing patient to fear the night. Sleep unrefreshing.

■ Modalities

Aggravation: Night; cold; emotions; alcohol; winter, cloudy sky, being in the house; *menses.*
Amelioration: Sunshine, open air; cold bath; walking; warmth; moonlight, **in the evening**; (sad) music; eating.
Side most often affected: Right.

■ Causation

Ailments from grief, sorrow, disappointment, mortification, unwanted responsibility, lovesickness, fright, financial losses, wounded pride, contradiction, suppressed frustration, vexation.

■ Indications

Alcoholism. *Angina pectoris.* Bone pain. *Cataracts. Chronic fatigue syndrome.* Depression. *Glaucoma. Hepatitis. Hypertension. Iritis.* Inguinal *hernia* (in children). *Mastoiditis. Orchitis.* Sleeplessness. *Sinusitis.* Suicidal disposition. *Uterine myoma.* Undescended testis. Valvular heart disease.

■ **Compare**

Aurum muriaticum natronatum, Ignatia, Mercurius, Natrum sulphuricum, Natrum muriaticum, Nux vomica, Platinum, Psorinum.

Baryta carbonica

Barium carbonate, $BaCO_3$.

■ Generalities

Mentally and physically **immature.** Dwarfism. Emaciation. Weakness. Mostly indicated for children or old people. Chilly. Frequent colds. Enlargement of lymph nodes, swollen glands, glandular cancer. Vascular sclerosis.

■ Mind and Emotions

Retarded development, dementia, idiocy. Mental inadaquacy; emotionally immature. Childish behavior. **Naïveté.** Needs recognition, easily influenced by others. **Lack of self-confidence. Inferiority;** feels small and worthless. Embarassment. Feels or is laughed at. Timidity. Hiding. Insecure; irresolute. Passivity. Prefers to stay at home. Aversion to company. Need for protection and loving care. Unable to think or act independently. Weak father figure: father retarded, weakling or father of a retarded child. Concentration difficult; bad memory. Anxiety. Fear/ feeling of being inadequate with the desire to be reassured. Fear about health and despairs of recovery. Anxiety neurosis. **Fears everything!** Fear of being alone, of the dark, ghosts, strangers, leaving the house/ staying at home alone, going insane, people, being laughed at, trying new things; fainting .... Fear of not looking good. *Agoraphobia.* School phobia. Fear for others. Fear of taking responsibility, e.g. does not want to have children of his own. Anger/despair/grief at trifles. Narrow-minded ideas about morality. Refuses to grow up. Denies self the right to lead an independent life and to grow as part of natural development. Unable to laugh. Easily frightened. Hypersensitive. Nervous nail-biting. Inhibited aggression. Blames self. Distrustful, careful, reserved, jealous, suspicious; criticism is not tolerated. Reticence. Delusions; paranoia; feels watched by others, criticized and laughed at.

■ **Head**

Vertigo. About to faint; at night, in a crowded room, after a meal. Hair falls out, *alopecia*. Itchy scalp. Brain feels loose. Headaches, especially in occiput and vertex. *Photophobia. Cataracts.* Hears noises in ears. Impaired hearing. Oversensitive hearing; pain in the brain at any noise. Swelling of nose and upper lip. Face: stupid look, mouth open. Redness. Feels as if face is totally covered by cobwebs. Half-sided *paralysis/sweats.*

■ **Throat**

Tonsillar hyperplasia and chronic/*recurrent tonsillitis.* Breathing impeded when lying down, due to enlarged tonsils. Hard swelling of cervical lymph nodes.

■ **Respiratory System**

Loss of voice, hoarseness. Catarrh in *larynx* and *trachea.* Copious mucus in upper respiratory tract. Asthma. Rattling noise when breathing. Impending *paralysis* of the lungs.

■ **Digestive Tract**

Cravings: sweet foods, eggs. Aversions: fruit, especially bananas and plums. *Salivation;* drooling in sleep. Weakness after eating. Bloated *abdomen* with emaciation. *Constipation* with hard stool.

■ **Cardiovascular System**

Aneurysm. Arteriosclerosis. Hypertension.

■ **Urinary Tract and Reproductive System**

Sex drive diminished or aversion to sex. Erectile dysfunction, impotence, *sterility*. Falls asleep during intercourse. *Hypertrophy of prostate* with induration in older men.
Loquacity during *menses.*

■ **Sleep**

Nightmares; wakes with a fright but cannot tell why.

■ **Modalities**

Aggravation: Slightest **cold** (does not apply to headaches); humidity; thinking about symptoms; lying on the painful side; after eating; washing affected parts of the body; company, pressure.

Amelioration: For headache: open air.

Side mostly affected: Right.

■ **Indications**

Adenopathy. Alopecia. Angina tonsillaris. Bronchial asthma. Common cold. *Constipation.* Enlarged prostate. *Enuresis.* Congenital deformity. *Hodgkin's disease.* Phobia. *Prostatitis. Mental retardation.* Sexual dysfunction. Slow development.

■ **Compare**

Alumina, Barium muriaticum, Bufo, Calcarea carbonica, Calcarea iodata, Dulcamara, Pulsatilla, Silicea.

Belladonna

Atropa belladonna, deadly nightshade (N.O. Solanaceae). Stramonium, Hyoscyamus and others belong to the same family. Sometimes it is difficult to differentiate between them. In ancient times women used belladonna to dilate their pupils, which has been proven to make a positive impression on men. This explains the plant's name, which means "beautiful lady".

■ Generalities

Symptoms are very intense and violent, appearing and disappearing **suddenly;** with heat, bright redness, burning, swelling and throbbing. High fever with dry skin, red face, red eyes, *dilated* pupils, hot head and cold extremities. Extreme *hypersensitivity* to noises, pain and vibrations.

Deadly Nightshade   Photo: Sertürner

■ Mind and Emotions

Vivid imagination. Children are lively, cheerful, intelligent, alert and experience everything intensely. They behave like angels as long as they are healthy and turn into devils when ill. Impatience with sudden tantrums, rage, anger and fury with screaming, hitting, biting, spitting, kicking, pulling hair and acts of violence. Fear of dogs, animals, imaginary things. Delirium (during fever) with tantrums, loquacity, horrible delusions and hallucinations with monsters, ghosts, dogs, wolves etc. Unconsciousness, interrupted by screaming.

■ Head

Heat flushes and *congestion*, burning sensation in head; **red face**. Migraine with pulsating, throbbing pain; worse from vibration, light and noise; aversion to light, loud noise and sun; better from cold applications, pressure, dark rooms and lying down. Aversion to light; **pupils** *dilated* **and flashing;** *convulsions* during fever. *Vertigo*, worse when turning the head, turning over in bed and bending forward.

- ### Throat

  Tonsillitis with pus, throat is bright red and swallowing difficult. Constricted feeling in the throat with dryness. Visible throbbing in carotids.

- ### Digestive Tract

  Dryness of mucous membranes with intense thirst or thirstlessness. Craves lemon, lemonade and cold water. Increased tenderness of the *abdomen*, provoked even by slight shaking of bed, worse from touching bedclothes. Cramps and cramplike pain in all hollow organs like stomach, bowels, gall bladder. *Constipation* with dryness in *rectum*.

- ### Respiratory System

  Cough dry, convulsive, paroxysmal, worse at night, around midnight with impending suffocation.

- ### Skin

  The skin is scarlet, smooth, glossy, moist, and is burning hot to the touch.

- ### Sleep

  Grinding of teeth and talking in sleep. Trembling, starting awake from sleep, jerking in sleep or when about to fall asleep. Sleeping on the *abdomen*. Nightmares. Dreams of falling, dogs. Feels sleepy but cannot sleep.

- ### Modalities

  Aggravation: Heat, sun, draft, vibration, motion, bending forward, noise, light, touch, when head gets cold, haircut; at night and in the afternoon around 3 pm; admonitions.

Amelioration: Warmth, being in a warm room; rest; lying on the *abdomen*; stretching backwards; pressure.

Side most often affected: Right.

■ Causation

Ailments from being in the sun; after washing hair; ailments from excitement, fright, fear, grief, disappointed love, vexation.

■ Indications

Angina tonsillaris. Arthritis. Bronchial asthma. Constipation. Convulsions during fever. Delirium. *Dysmenorrhea.* Epilepsy. *Erysipelas.* Fever. *Gastric and duodenal ulcers. Gastritis.* Headache. Heatstroke. *Hypertension. Mastitis. Meningitis. Migraine. Neuralgia. Otitis media. Pertussis. Pharyngitis. Pneumonia. Pyelonephritis.* Scarlet fever. *Sinusitis.* Sunburn. Sunstroke.

■ Compare

Aconitum, Apis, Bryonia, Chamomilla, Glonoinum, Hyoscyamus, Lachesis, Stramonium.

Bromium

Bromine. A viscous, corrosive substance, dark red or brown in color, that generates a highly irritating gas.

■ Generalities

Enlargement and induration of various glands, especially on the left side. **Better at the seaside.** Patients are intolerant of cold and catch colds easily. Tendency to obesity or emaciation. Weak and tremulous. Complaints frequently appear accompanied by *palpitations*. This remedy is suited to blond patients with blue eyes, especially children who have fine, pale, sensitive skin and very fair hair and eyebrows (dark hair may be found as well); lymphatic constitution.

■ Mind and Emotions

Nervousness and excitement. Cheerfulness alternating with sadness and silence. *Intoxication* with a dazed state, increased sense of adventure, euphoric mood, lack of inhibitions and discrimination. Craves mental activity. Weakness; aversion to any work at all, to reading. Forgetfulness, weak memory; unable to concentrate. No interest in household duties. Indifference. Tiredness. Sad and despondent. Crying and moaning. Anxiety. Restlessness and fear. Patient sense that someone is standing behind him though no one else is present.

■ Head

Sensation of cobwebs on the face; symptom occurs mostly when moving nostrils. *Vertigo* looking at running water; patient cannot cross a bridge without feeling dizzy. Faints easily. Headache after overheating. Heat in head, face red. Face as gray as ashes in chronic diseases. Noise in eara. Inflammations of the ear. Swelling and inflammation of the left parotid gland.

■ **Digestive Tract**

Generally better from eating. Gastric *ulcers*; coffee-ground vomit. Eructations. Stomach pain after hot food and hot drinks. Diarrhea with pain in the stomach from eating oysters. Does not tolerate anything sour, *diarrhea* after sour foods. Stool contains mucus and false membranes. Bloody stools like coffee grounds. Protruding, burning hemorrhoids, painful during daytime and at night.

■ **Respiratory System**

Nostrils flutter like a fan. Nosebleed. *Coryza* with frequent sneezing; nose congested, worse from sneezing. Burning and coldness in the nose. Nostrils are sore. Hoarseness with scraping und rawness in *larynx*. Hoarseness/loss of voice after overheating.

Cough; dry; spasmodic; in the evening before midnight; attacks of suffocation; unproductive; worse when entering a warm room; when inhaling dust; improved by a sip of cold water. Every breath causes coughing. Rattling noise from mucus in *larynx* during fits of spamodic cough. *Expectoration* consists of whitish, viscous mucus. Tickling in *larynx* that provokes constant coughing. Constriction or spasm of *larynx*. Coldness in *larynx*. Shortness of breath with intense sweating. Feels as if air passages are filled with smoke. **Asthma: Better at the seaside; aggravated in sailors on going ashore.**

■ **Urinary Tract and Reproductive System**

Frequent flatus from *vagina*. Suppressed *menses*. Constant dull pain in left *ovary* with swelling and hardness. Swelling and induration of left testicle.

■ **Extremities**

Increasing weakness; legs are weak, trembling and ice-cold extremities.

■ **Modalities**

Aggravation: Heat; after a common cold during warm weather, in the evening before midnight.

Amelioration: At the seaside; riding on a horse or in a car; motion.
Side most often affected: Left.

■ **Indications**

Acne. *Adenopathy. Angina tonsillaris. Bronchial asthma. Bronchitis.*
Diphtheria. *Dysmenorrhea.* Induration of glands. Headache. *Laryngitis.*
Orchitis. Parotitis. Pertussis. Pharyngitis. Tuberculosis.

■ **Compare**

Conium, Iodium, Medorrhinum, Spongia.

Bryonia

Bryonia alba, vitis alba, vitis diaboli. White bryony, wild hops (N.O. Cucurbitaceae). Bryonia is found mostly near hedges or fences. The mother tincture is derived from the root of the fresh plant before it blooms.

■ Generalities

According to Vithoulkas, the central idea of Bryonia is **dryness** on all levels. Extraordinary dryness of mucous membranes. Effusions in serous membranes (i.e. pleura, peritoneum) with stitching pains in the area of the diseased organ. **Sharp pain**. Acute diseases develop slowly. **Generally aggravated by motion.**

White Bryony   Photo: DHU

■ Mind and Emotions

Irritable and morose, angry; **wants to be left alone**, does not want to be bothered; worse from any interference by others. Intolerant of contradiction. Taciturn. "Dried out emotionally", shows hardly any emotions. Dissatisfaction; refuses things he has just asked for. Anxiety, discontent, despondency. Fear of death, impending disease, disaster, being alone; anxiety about the future. Businessmen with a materialistic and rational outlook. Patient is hardworking, busy and works fast. Great fear of poverty; miserly. Talks constantly about business and financial problems. During delirium, talks nonsense about the business or wants to go home even when already there.

- **Head**

  Headache on the left side, above left eye, extending to occiput; worse from coughing and motion.

- **Digestive Tract**

  Very **thirsty** for large quantities of cold water. Craves warm milk, soup, wine and coffee. *Nausea* and fainting when rising to stand. Pressure in stomach after eating as if from a stone. Pain in liver area, better when lying on the right side. Dull stitches in right groin. *Constipation* with very hard, dry, burned-looking stool.

- **Respiratory System**

  Coughing is very **painful,** patient has to hold his chest. Cries before coughing. Dry, hard cough. Choking and vomiting during cough. Cough is aggravated by heat, warm room.

- **Urinary Tract and Reproductive System**

  Pain in breasts with tense feeling during *menses*. Nosebleed or other *hemorrhages* instead of *menses*. *Mastitis*, especially when lactation ceases. Breasts are hot but still pale and hard as a rock. Feeling of heaviness; the slightest motion is so painful that breasts have to be immobilized by binding.

- **Back and Extremities**

  Lumbago with violent, stitching, tearing or drawing pain that is worse when walking. Inflammation of the joints, which are red, swollen, hot and stiff. Inflammatory swelling of joints with paleness of surrounding tissue.

- **Sleep**

  Sleeping position: On left side. Starts awake when falling asleep and during sleep. Dreams of past events, work, business and household affairs.

■ **Modalities**

Aggravation: Motion; touch; heat, **warmth;** around 9 am and 9 pm, from 3 am to 9 pm; morning; dry food, bread and food causing *flatulence*, after eating; cold drinks; cold and dry weather; cold wind; overheating in warm, stuffy rooms; emotional states (excitement, vexation, anger, fright, insults, disdain, contempt).

Amelioration: Rest; hard **pressure;** lying on painful side; cold drinks and cold applications (except for stomach complaints); sweat and other discharges; walking in the open air.

Side most often affected: Right.

■ **Causation**

Ailments from emotional states like anger, fright, scorn, insult, contempt, grief, disappointment, haste, violent behavior.

■ **Indications**

Appendicitis. Arthritis. Bronchial asthma. Bronchitis. Cholecystitis. Constipation. Gastritis. Gout. Headache. *Hepatitis. Lumbago. Mastitis. Meningitis.* Migraine. *Pericarditis. Peritonitis. Pertussis. Pleurisy. Pneumonia.* Rheumatism. Sciatic pain.

■ **Compare**

Apis, Belladonna, Calcarea carbonica, Calcarea fluorica, Chamomilla, Chelidonium, Nux vomica, Rhus toxicodendron, Sepia, Spigelia, Stellaria media, Veratrum album.

Calcarea carbonica

Calcarea carbonica Hahnemanni. Carbonate of lime. The remedy is made from the snow-white inner layer of oyster (Ostrea edulis) shells (N.O. Acephala).

■ Generalities

Weakness and **exhaustion. Chilly;** especially cold feet, covered with dank and sticky sweat. Sweating in sleep around the nape of the neck. Body secretions have a sour smell. Lymph nodes enlarged. Prone to infections. Tendency to obesity. Sluggishness, clumsiness, flabbiness/induration. Trembling after mental or physical exertion. Belladonna is the complementary remedy in acute diseases (it grows in chalky soil). Tuberculinum follows well.

Lime of Oystershells   Photo: DHU

■ Mind and Emotions

Apprehensive. Fear of: darkness; ghosts; thunderstorms; heights; mice; dogs; contagious diseases, death, etc.; **losing her mind; people watching and noticing her confusion. Despairs of recovery; overwhelming anxiety about health and fear of cancer.** Worried about soul's welfare; about the future. Compulsive thoughts about trifles. Vexed at trifles. Aversion to work; gives up on work because of excessive fatigue. Indolence, sluggishness, lethargy, but also works stubbornly on one task. Peaceable nature. Stubborn, obstinate. Irritability, vexation, agitation. Easily offended. Depression, despondency, melancholia, whining, self-pity. Jumpiness. Delusions; horrible visions on closing eyes.

■ Head

Vertigo **in high places.** Fainting spells. All kinds of headaches; starting in the morning, worse from mental work, alcoholic drinks and physical exertion. *Congestion* going to the head: Head is hot and heavy while the face is pale. Alternately, patient feels icy-cold in and around the head. Burning sensation on top of the head while forehead is cold. Fontanelles close late. Chronic *hydrocephalus*. Profuse head sweat, especially at night. Itchy scalp. Cradle cap in children breast-fed babies. Teething delayed and difficult. Chronic *dilation of the pupils*.

■ Digestive Tract

Cravings: **Sweets;** soft-boiled **eggs;** indigestible things like chalk, coal, graphite, etc. Aversion to fats, meat and cooked foods. The entire digestive tract is sour: sour taste, sour eructations, sour vomit, sour stools. Milk is not tolerated, child vomits milk, which looks curdled. Ravenous hunger with a weak stomach. Frequent eructations, generally sour. Feeling of emptiness, queasy feeling in stomach; heavy feeling. Bloated *abdomen*. Obstinate *constipation*; children feel better as long as they are constipated. Diarrhea with stools containing undigested matter.

■ Back and Extremities

Overall weakness and tiredness in limbs. Feeling of coldness in feet, knees and the lower legs as if from "cold, damp socks". Bony deformities, especially in the spine and the long bones. *Exostosis*. Brittle nails. Painful suppuration near the nail bed. Weak muscles; children are late in learning how to walk. Cramps in calves at night. Rheumatic complaints. Twitching, trembling, cramps, *convulsions*.

■ Modalities

Aggravation: Cold and wet weather; cold, dampness, any exertion; after sex; full moon; evening and early morning; when climbing upward; during teething; pressure of clothes; milk and smoked meat.

Amelioration: Dry weather; touching and caressing affected part of the body; lying down quietly in the dark.

Side most often affected: Right; except in the case of muscular complaints in the throat, chest problems and *sciatica*. These symptoms appear mostly on the left side of the body.

■ Causation

State of exhaustion after physical or mental exertion; excessive worries and duties. Bad effects of: alcohol; loss of vital fluids; sexual excesses; masturbation; overexertion; injury from lifting; suppression of perspiration, skin eruptions or *menses*. Ailments from anger, grief, rudeness, fright, worries, exaggerated need for admiration, bad news.

■ Indications

Abscess. Adenopathy. Adiposity. Acne. Allergy. *Angina tonsillaris.* Anxiety. *Arthritis. Arthritis psoriatica. Bronchial asthma.* Backache. *Bronchitis. Canker sores. Chronic fatigue syndrome.* Common colds. Leg cramps. Connective tissue diseases. *Cholecystitis. Constipation. Dentitio difficilis.* Depression. Eczema. Epilepsy. *Goiter. Gout. Hypertension. Hypothyroidism.* Headache. *Infectious mononucleosis.* Influenza. Systemic lupus erythematosus. Malignant degenerations. *Metrorrhagia. Migraine. Multiple sclerosis. Muscular dystrophy. Nephrolithiasis.* Nightmares. *Osteogenesis imperfecta. Otitis media. Pharyngitis. Premenstrual syndrome. Rheumatoid arthritis. Rhinitis.* Sciatic pain. *Scleroderma. Scoliosis. Sinusitis. Uterine myoma. Varicose veins. Vertigo.* Warts. Whitlows.

■ Compare

Antimonium crudum, Baryta carbonica, Bromium, Calcarea bromata, Calcarea fluorata, Calcarea muriatica, Calcarea phosphorica, Calcarea sulphurica, Capsicum, Graphites, Kali carbonicum, Phosphorus, Pulsatilla, Rhus toxicodendron, Sanicula, Silicea.

Calcarea phosphorica

Phosphate of lime.

■ General Characteristics

Tall and skinny. Chilly. Weakness and feebleness. Sensitive, hypersensitive, sentimental, delicate, frail. Sensitive to noise, cold, draft, humidity, change of weather and thaw. *Convalescence* slow or difficult after an acute disease. Lymph nodes/tonsils enlarged. **Childhood:** Physical abuse; intimidating, frightening surroundings; emotional abuse: child's main caregiver is domineering, violent-tempered or excessively controlling.

■ Mind and Emotions

Very sensitive persons whose feelings are easily hurt. Sensitive to the slightest criticism. Low self-esteem. Anxious and embarrassed. Fear of rejection, separation, the dark, being alone, thunderstorm, dogs and cats; anxiety about others, about health. Longing, **fantasy world,** romantic, daydreamer. **Feels discontented,** uncomfortable, inner emptiness, moody, morose, irritable, angry. **Desire to flee; desire to travel;** homesickness; restlessness, impatience. Sighing, lamenting, **whining;** demanding. Grief, disappointment, sees self as a victim. Indignation and outrage. Intolerant of contradiction. Suppression of negative feelings, passive aggression. Aggravated by consolation. Patient does not persevere, fatigue comes quickly, sluggish, indifferent. Concentration difficult, forgetful, aversion to mental work. Stupefaction, confusion. Scholten: "The worst thing would be for others to think I'm stupid." They are afraid that others might think they are not good at school or making friends, or think they are stupid or silly.

■ Sleep

Sleepy in the morning. Children sigh in their sleep.

- **Head**

  Migraine. Headache in schoolchildren. *Vertigo.* Late teething, caries. Delayed closure of fontanelles.

- **Digestive Tract**

  Cravings: Smoked meats, spicy, salty, sweet foods; fish, cold drinks, milk. Aversions: Salt, fish, milk. Heartburn, vomiting, stomach pain, pain in the *abdomen, flatulence,* diarrhea.

- **Urinary Tract and Reproductive System**

  Before *menses:* Breasts are tender, sleep is disturbed, depression, irritability, mentally slow, *constipation,* pain in lower *abdomen* similar to labor pains, nymphomania. **During** *menses:* diarrhea. Metrorrhagia; *menses* too early, menstrual cycle only 2 weeks in some cases.

- **Back and Extremities**

  Tension in throat area, chronic stiff neck, worse from draft/wind. Rheumatic pain. Stiffness of joints. Tingling, feeling numb and cold. Trembling; cramps. Growing pains. Late in learning to walk.

- **Modalities**

  Aggravation: 3 to 9 pm. Damp and cold weather, change of weather, draft, easterly winds, **snow melt.** Motion, walking. Thinking about complaints, mental exertion.

  Amelioration: Travel. Summer; dry and warm weather; lying down.

- **Causation**

  Poor nutrition, bad news, bad weather. Exertion.

- **Indications**

  Adipositas. Arthritis. Backache. *Carpal tunnel syndrome. Chronic fatigue syndrome. Dentitio difficilis.* Depression. *Diarrhea.* Growth pains. Headache. Hemorrhoids. *Otitis media. Scoliosis.*

- **Compare**

Calcarea carbonica, Calcarea fluorica, Kali phosphoricum, Sanicula, Tuberculinum.

Calcarea sulphurica

Calcium sulphate, plaster of paris, gypsum, $CaSO_4$.

■ Generalities

Tendency to **suppuration,** wounds don't heal; suppuration lasting months or years. Discharges are yellow, thick, clotty, crusty, creamy, purulent and continual; pus thick and bloody. *Fistulas.* Obesity. Lack of reaction. Sluggishness, fatigue, tiredness.

■ Mind and Emotions

Extreme jealousy. Strong personality. Quarrelsome and domineering. Heightened sense of importance; has a marked need for admiration but hides it. Hates those who don't agree with him. Whining and lamenting because he feels he is not appreciated. Discontent; irritable; irascible; malicious. Mood swings; sadness on waking, cheerful and happy in the evening. Anxious about the future, about health, about soul's welfare. Fear of misfortune, death, birds. Fears appear mostly at night when in bed. Mental dullness, confusion; sudden loss of memory.

■ Head

Chronic and periodic headache, often in the forehead. Pernicious acne; entire face covered with crusts; pimples and *pustules* on the face. Inflammation of the eyes, discharging thick yellow pus. *Otitis media* with persistent suppuration.

■ Digestive Tract

Abscessed teeth and gums with purulent discharges. Craves green, unripe fruit and alcohol. Indigestion, cramp-like pain in *abdomen, colic,* flatus. Painful *abscesses* around the *anus; fistulas* discharging constantly yellowish pus.

■ Respiratory System

Catches cold easily especially after a draft. *Coryza* thick, yellow, lumpy, often streaked with blood. Nasal discharge on one side only. Wheezing with a sensation of suffocating. Dyspnea. Persistent hoarseness, better in the open air. Catarrh with profuse mucus in the respiratory tract and copious *expectoration*.

■ Skin

Skin affections that are purulent, burning and itching. *Abscesses, furuncles*, acne, *fistulas* with chronic suppuration. Violent burning and itching of soles.

■ Modalities

Aggravation: Heat; change of weather, after air gets cooler, draft, cold and wet weather; exertion, motion; touch.
Amelioration: Open air, walking in the open air; eating.

■ Causation

Ailments from suppressed perspiration.

■ Indications

Abscess. Acne. *Adiposity*. Allergy. *Bronchitis*. *Conjunctivitis*. Eczema. *Fistulas*. *Impetigo contagiosa*. *Mastoiditis*. *Otitis media*. Pseudocroup. *Sinusitis*.

■ Compare

Hepar sulphuris, Medorrhinum, Pulsatilla, Silicea, Sulphur.

Camphora

Camphor; laurus camphora. The remedy is made from the camphor tree (Cinnamomum camphora), which grows in Japan.

■ **Generalities**

Weakness, exhaustion, wasting, **collapse**. Whole body is icy cold, with rushes of blood to the head and *congestion* in the chest. Skin ice cold, cold sweat, paleness and *cyanosis.* **Although very sensitive to cold, patient cannot tolerate any covers and throws them off.** Sensitive to touch. Prone to cerebral spasms and cramps in all muscles and hollow organs. Camphora acts as an antidote to almost all plant remedies.

Camphor Tree

■ **Mind and Emotions**

Unconsciousness, coma; delirum; anxious restlessness, nervous irritability, nervous agitation. Anxiety at night, especially when alone. Quarrelsome, enraged. Feels unloved by family, deserted and isolated. Delusions, illusions, hallucinations; e.g. being alone in the world; being a devil.

■ **Head**

Pulsating headache, especially in occiput. *Vertigo* that causes patient to sway. Fainting. Violent *convulsions.*

■ **Digestive Tract**

Unquenchable thirst for small quantities of cold water, which are vomited immediately after drinking. *Nausea* and vomiting with collapse; coldness in mouth and breath, contorted face and squeaky voice. Coldness or burning in *abdomen*. Diarrhea with great weakness, cold sweat and collapse.

■ Respiratory System

Sudden *coryza* with generalized coldness, nasal congestion and sinus headache. Persistent nosebleed, especially with gooseflesh. Breath feels cold.

■ Urinary Tract and Reproductive System

Burning sensation and pain when urinating. Retention of urine; although bladder is full, urine is not evacuated.

■ Modalities

Aggravation: Cold air, cold; motion; at night; suppressed body secretions.
Amelioration: Thinking about complaints; heat; drinking cold water; sweating.

■ Causation

Cold, from suddenly catching a cold; bad effects from shock such as injury, surgery, infection, sunstroke; bad effects from measles.

■ Indications

Bronchitis. Cholera. Chronic fatigue syndrome. Cystitis. Dysentery. Epilepsy. *Gastroenteritis.* Headache. *Nephritis. Pneumonia. Rhinitis. Septicemia.* Sunstroke.

■ Compare

Arsenicum album, Carbo vegetabilis, Cuprum, Laurocerasus, Opium, Phosphorus, Secale cornutum, Veratrum album.

Cannabis indica
Indian hemp, hashish (N.O. Moraceae).

- ## Generalities
Great fatigue, weakness, lack of sensation. Alternating symptoms.

- ## Mind and Emotions
All kinds of **delusions.** Panic attacks with *agony* and mental confusion; afraid of losing control or losing his mind. Anxiety about health; fear of insanity, death, darkness. Exuberant loquacity; constantly asking questions, excessive **theorizing.** Gullible. Laughs at slightest thing, laughing fits. Confusion; incoherent thoughts. Everything seems to be unreal; hallucinations, illusions, mental delusions, clairvoyant; sensation of floating; forsaken feeling; feeling of leaving body. Marked forgetfulness; begins a sentence and forgets what he was about to say. Unable to remember any sentence or particular event because mind is filled with other thoughts; cannot focus on one thing. Absorbed, daydreaming. Distorted and confused sense of time; time seems to move too slowly. *Apathy,* indifference; sleepiness; unconsciousness.

- ## Head
Cramps from excitement or mental exertion. Chronic *vertigo*, feels as if floating away. Feels as if skull were opening up and closing again. Dull, heavy, throbbing headache. Violent headache with hallucinations. Frequent, involuntary shaking of head.

- ## Digestive Tract
Increased thirst, accompanied at times by an aversion to drinking. Ravenous hunger that is not relieved by eating huge amounts of food. Empty eructations. Pain around stomach entrance that improves with pressure.

- **Urinary Tract and Reproductive System**
  Burning pain in urinary tract before, during and especially after urination; dribbling. Kidney pain keeps patient awake at night; worse from laughing or any other vibration of the body.
  Strong sexual desire. Painful erections at night. Swelling of prepuce.
  Menstruation very painful, like during labor pains.

- **Modalities**
  Aggravation: Darkness; overexertion; alcohol, tobacco; tight clothes.
  Amelioration: In the open air, walking in the open air; taking a deep breath; washing with cold water; rest; coffee.

- **Causation**
  Ailments from hashish or marijuana.

- **Indications**
  Behavior disorders. *Chronic fatigue syndrome. Cystitis. Delirium tremens.* Depression. *Dysmenorrhea.* Headache. *Nephritis.* Phobia. *Psychosis.*

- **Compare**
  Agaricus, Arsenicum album, Belladonna, Cannabis sativa, Hyoscyamus, Lachesis, Nitricum acidum, Nux moschata, Phosphorus, Stramonium, Sulphur.

Cantharis

Cantharis officinalis or lytta vesicatoria, Spanish fly. In folk medicine it is used as an aphrodisiac.

- ■ **Generalities**

  Burning, cutting, stinging, tearing, agonizing pain. Sudden, violent inflammation. All conditions are intense and destructive.
  Periodicity: every fourth day.

- ■ **Mind and Emotions**

  Hot temper. Restlessness, nervousness, irritability, discontent. Intolerant of touch or being approached by someone. Cheerfulness alternating with

  Spanish Fly   Photo: DHU

  sadness. Increased sexual desire. Fear of water, mirrors and shiny objects. Fear at night. Rage, anger; enormous temper tantrums. Raging delirium with cries for help.

- ■ **Head**

  Temper tantrums with *convulsions*. Burning headache as if the brain were on fire or full of boiling water.
  Inflammation of the eyes after a burn. Xanthopia.

- ■ **Throat**

  Anger when throat is touched. Sore throat burning like fire. Viscous mucus or small blisters in the throat.

- ■ **Digestive Tract**

  Burning thirst but aversion to drinks. *Colicky* pain and burning pain in *anus* during stool. Diarrhea with greenish or bloody mucus.

- **Urinary Tract and Reproductive System**

  Cystitis with violent, burning pain before, during and after urination. **Constant desire to urinate;** urine passes drop by drop. Urinary tract infections with bloody urine. Patient must cry out while passing urine because of the strong pain. Severe *tenesmus,* improved by cold applications. Increased sexual arousal. **Strong sexual desire with** frequent, strong, prolonged and painful erections, worse at night. Young boys pull at their penises. Menstruation with black blood, too early and too heavy.

- **Extremities**

  Feeling of dryness in the joints.

- **Skin**

  Burning skin with or without blisters. Gnawing pain in the skin when touched. 1st- and 2nd-degree burns; scalds and burns with blisters, sunburn. Mosquito bites with unbearable itching.

- **Modalities**

  Aggravation: Touch; urinating, sound of running water; drinking cold water or coffee; bright/shiny objects; heat; night.
  Amelioration: Rubbing, warmth, lying down, rest, cold or cold applications.
  Side most often affected: Right.

- **Indications**

  Burns. *Colitis. Cystitis.* Eczema. *Encephalitis. Gastroenteritis. Herpes zoster. Meningitis. Pharyngitis. Pleurisy. Priapism. Pyelonephritis.* Sexual disorders. *Urethritis.*

- **Compare**

  Apis, Arsenicum album, Belladonna, Mercurius corrosivus, Nux vomica, Platinum, Sarsaparilla, Stramonium.

Capsicum

Capsicum annuum, cayenne pepper, Spanish pepper (N.O. Solanaceae). The plant is found in Central America and in India. The remedy is prepared from the fresh, ripe pods.

■ **Generalities**

Chilly, *adiposity*, indolent, lacking drive; sluggishness. **Burning pain** as if the affected parts have been sprinkled with red pepper. Feeling of constriction. Coldness in different parts of the body, sensitivity to cold.

■ **Mind and Emotions**

Phlegmatic personality; obese people, who lack ability to react; easily exhausted; indolent, avoid any physical exertion; friendly people who get excited about trifles. Children prefer not to go out into the open air, they are always chilly; stubborn/obstinate, clumsy, obese, dirty,

Spanish Pepper   Photo: DHU

awkward, not inclined to work or think. **Homesickness** (in indolent, melancholic people), longing for the past, silent discontent with the present situation; their cheeks are red and they cannot sleep. Great sleepiness during the day. Obstinate, irritable, patient sees the negative side of everything. Fear of criticism. In a bad mood when body gets cold. Suicidal.

■ **Head**

Bursting headache as if the skull were about to shatter into pieces, worse from coughing, from motion, while walking and sitting. Eyes look red, burning in the morning and lacrimation. Pressing pain in the eye as if from a foreign body. *Mastoiditis*; painful swelling behind the ear, extremely painful and tender. Chronic *otitis media* (perforata). Sensitive to noise during feverish chills. Herpes labialis. Nosebleed. Dry lips with cracks. Face/cheeks/nose are red but cold.

Respiratory System

Fetid breath, at exhalation but also during fits of explosive coughing. Cough with pain in distant parts of the body like the head, bladder, knees or legs etc. Nervous, convulsive cough that comes in sudden fits; feels as if the chest will burst from coughing. *Pertussis.* Cough; better in the evening, while lying down. Viscous mucus. Hoarseness in singers and preachers. Patient expects that taking a deep breath will relieve all worries. Shortness of breath that seems to come from the stomach. Feeling of constriction with pain as if the chest were tied up; pain gets worse even at slight motion. Asthma.

Digestive Tract

Cravings: stimulants, especially alcohol (alcoholics!), coffee (which is not tolerated); hot spices, especially pepper and salt. Base of the tongue greenish. Burning pain at the tip of the tongue. *Stomatitis (aphthosa).* Increased *salivation*, foul taste and offensive breath. Often thirsty. Heartburn; acid and burning eructation. *Flatulence* with *colic.* Dysentery: diarrhea with frequent small stools, which consist of mucus and are sometimes mixed with blood, *tenesmus.* Thirsty after every stool, shivers after drinking. Stinging pain while passing stool. Hemorrhoids: bleeding with burning pain in the *anus.*

Urinary Tract and Reproductive System

Burning in bladder, urine burns, stinging and cutting pain in *urethra*, especially when not urinating. Acute *cystitis*; urine only comes in drops. Retention of urine after exertion. White discharge, like whole milk, e.g. later stage of *gonorrhea.* Coldness in *scrotum.* Multiple complaints during pregnancy.

- **Extremities**

  Rheumatism; aggravation in the morning and after rest, from cold; improved by moving.

- **Modalities**

  Aggravation: Damp cold, in the open air; removing covers; draft, at slightest draft even when warm; cold air; water; humidity, bathing; cold; empty swallowing; after eating; alcohol; gentle touch.
  Amelioration: While eating; **heat;** sustained motion.
  Side most often affected: Left.

- **Indications**

  Adiposity. Alcoholism. Backache. *Bronchitis. Colitis.* Depression. *Gastritis.* Hemorrhoids. Headache. *Mastoiditis. Pertussis. Urethritis.*

- **Compare**

  Antimonium crudum, Calcarea carbonica, Ferrum, Graphites, Sulphur.

Carbo vegetabilis
Vegetable charcoal, charcoal.

Generalities

The vital force is nearly exhausted, complete collapse. Extreme weakness. Entire body is **icy cold,** especially extremities: nose, hands, feet and knees. The skin is cold. Even breath is cold. Internal burning while cold externally. Burning pain. *Anemia* after severe, exhausting diseases. Foul-smelling discharges. Passive bleeding from mucous membranes. **Desire to be fanned.**

Charcoal   Photo: DHU

Mind and Emotions

Indifference, listlessness, *apathy*. Sluggishness, slowness, passivity. Aversion to mental work. Irritability; violent temper. Weak concentration. Unable to come to a decision. Loss of memory comes and goes. Fixed ideas. Monotony. Mental lethargy/confusion. Fear of the dark, especially when in bed at night; fear of ghosts, of illness, anxiety about health. Hypochondriacal irritability. Weepy mood. Easily frightened.

Head

Face cyanotic, elongated and thin.

Cardiovascular System

Progressive *cardiac* weakness; the surface of the body becomes increasingly blue, more *cyanotic*. Recurring feeling of oppression with difficulty breathing. Impaired, slowed-down circulation; heat flushes. Pulse is weak, soft or hardly palpable.

- **Respiratory System**

  Fear of not getting enough air; marked weakness; symptoms improved by fanning. Hoarseness; aggravated by humid air; in the evening. Burning sensation in the chest as from red-hot coals, weakness and fatigue. *Expectoration* has an unpleasant smell.

- **Digestive Tract**

  Gums puffy, bleeding easily. Aversion to foods containing **fat** and **milk**. Semi-solid foods are not tolerated. Intolerance of alcohol. Burning sensation in stomach. Excessive *epigastric flatulence*, extreme tension in *epigastrium* with spasmodic and constricting pain extending to the chest, along with difficult breathing. Digestive problems and flatulence; improved by eructations and flatus.

- **Extremities**

  Cold sweat in limbs. Blue, cold, *ecchymosis*. Cold from knees down. Improved by putting feet up.

- **Modalities**

  Aggravation: In the evening; fatty foods like butter and milk; alcohol; warm and damp weather; cold; during the winter; between 4 and 5 pm; lying down.

  Amelioration: Eructations, passing flatus; being fanned; cold.

- **Causation**

  Ailments after shock, e.g. accidents or serious disease.

- **Indications**

  *Adiposity. Agony. Anemia. Bronchial asthma. Bronchitis. Chronic fatigue syndrome.*Collapse. Comatose state. Eczema. *Esophagitis.* Fainting. *Flatulence. Gastric and duodenal ulcers. Gastritis.* Headache. Hemorrhage. Laryngitis. Pertussis. Pneumonia. Ulcers.

■ **Compare**

Argentum nitricum, Calcarea carbonica, Camphora, Carbo animalis, China, Lycopodium, Nitricum acidum, Sepia.

Causticum

Tinctura acris sine kalio. According to Hahnemann's prescriptions, this caustic substance is obtained from freshly burned lime derived from marble and bisulphate of potash.

■ **Generalities**

In early stages, marked *hypersensitivity* and hyperactivity; in later stages, weakness that creates a peculiar state of depression mixed with nervous excitement. Weakness is often accompanied by trembling. *Paralysis* in individual parts, mostly on the right side (face, tongue muscles, *pharynx* etc.). *Paralysis* with pain like electrical

Causticum Hahnemanni   Photo: DHU

shock. Burning pain. Burning and **soreness** in mucous membranes. Great sensitivity to drafts and cold; chilliness.

■ **Mind and Emotions**

Has a sense of social justice; does not tolerate injustice or repression \ for self or other people. Idealistic anarchist. In conflict with authority. Radical, brutal; provocative, quarrelsome; ambitious, competitive; critical, suspicious. Religious fanaticism. Revolutionary. Fighting for a better world; helping the poor and oppressed. Extremely sensitive, easily aroused; does not tolerate criticism. Irritability, vexation; anger, rage; opinionated, arrogant. Intensely **sympathetic;** cannot stand for anyone to suffer. Placid and modest. Whiny mood; cries at every opportunity. Hopeless sadness from worries, grief and suffering; cries a lot. Exhausted and depleted, "washed out". Premonitions that something bad will happen to self or family. Fears: darkness; being alone, especially at night; dogs. Restlessness, especially in the evening and at night.

Stuttering when excited or vexed. Weak memory and concentration; feeling that he has forgotten something. Inattentive, distracted, absorbed. Passive idiocy during the final stage.

■ Head

Sensation of an empty space between brain and forehead. Dry eyes with *photophobia*; feeling of sand in the eyes though there is none. Heaviness and paralytic feeling in upper lids.

■ Digestive Tract

Cravings: salt, smoked meats. Aversions: sweet foods. Sensation of unslaked lime in stomach, generating a lot of gas. Stools are evacuated more easily when standing up, including involuntary stools. *Constipation* with violent, unsuccessful urge. Patient bites cheeks while chewing or speaking.

■ Respiratory System

Prone to hoarseness; *aphonia* or hoarseness, especially in the morning or after overexertion; *paralysis* of the vocal cords. Hay fever with internal and external itching around the nostrils, sneezing in the morning on waking, viscous mucus in *pharynx*, nose stuffed up when lying down, especially at night. Deep-seated cough, hollow, with **raw** feeling in the chest and viscous mucus in lower part of *trachea*. Patient has to hold chest while coughing. Cough is improved by drinking cold water.

■ Urinary Tract and Reproductive System

Involuntary urination during cough, while walking, sneezing and sleeping. Marked weakness of bladder neck. Retention of urine when straining bladder muscles.

■ Extremities

Muscles jerk, writer's cramp, spasms, *convulsions*. Spasmodic pain. *Paralysis* which appear gradually, with coldness in affected parts.

Nervous restlessness in legs, especially when lying in bed. Staggering, tottering, reeling gait; stumbling. Coordination problems. Children are late in learning to walk. Painful varicose veins.

■ Skin

Warts, especially in the face and fingers. Skin eruptions; dry; around the nose; improved by cold water; worse from heat. *Fissures*; *rhagades* on lips, in corners of the eye and around the nose. *Paresthesia*. Slow healing of scars, or scars reopen after a burn, a scald or an old injury.

■ Sleep

Wakens at 2 to 4 in the morning and cannot go to sleep again due to restlessness. Restless sleep, full of dreams; starting awake out of sleep. Very drowsy during the day. Irresistible sleepiness after a meal; patient even falls asleep while standing, walking or talking. Sleepnessness arising out of compassion for others, e.g. night watching.

■ Modalities

Aggravation: Dry and cold weather; cold air; extreme temperatures; riding in a car; after getting wet or after taking a bath; 3-4 am; evening.
Amelioration: Damp and rainy weather; heat, warm air; drinking cold water.
Side most often affected: Right (face); **left.**

■ Causation

Burns and scalds; sleeplessness; getting wet; suppressed skin eruptions; lead poisoning. Ailments from annoyance, anger, vexation, worry, grief, sorrow and compassion.

■ Indications

Acne. Alcoholism. *Apoplexy. Arthritis. Ataxia.* Backache. *Bronchial asthma. Bronchitis. Chorea.* Constipation. *Dysphagia.* Eczema. *Enuresis.* Epilepsy. *Facial nerve paralysis*/Bell's palsy. Gout. Hay fever. *Herpes zoster.* Impotence. *Laryngitis. Multiple sclerosis.* Rheumatism. Sexual dysfunction. *Sinusitis. Torticollis.* Urinary *incontinence. Varicose veins.* Warts.

■ **Compare**

Calcarea phosphorica, Cocculus, Ignatia, Natrum muriaticum, Nux vomica, Phosphorus, Plumbum, Sepia, Staphysagria, Tuberculinum.

Chamomilla

Matricaria chamomilla, common camomile.

■ Generalities

Extreme oversensitivity. especially to pain. Unbearable pain, driving patient to despair, often with numbness; pain appears suddenly and in paroxysms. Soles burning and hot. Remedy frequently used for children with teething problems.

■ Mind and Emotions

Irritable, cross, angry, quarrelsome, nasty, ill-mannered, impolite, unhappy; it is impossible to get along with these patients or to please them. They ask for things which they then refuse to accept. Aversion to being touched or spoken to. Violent rage. Grumbling. Restlessness. Fear of wind. Wants to be carried and rocked gently. The child can only be quieted by being carried. Impatient from pain; pain makes them furious, cross and aggressive.

■ Head

Hot, sticky sweat (or cold and damp) on forehead and scalp. Redness and burning heat in face, especially cheeks, often just one cheek while the other is cold and pale.
Otitis media in children.

■ Digestive Tract

Teething painful; problems while teething. Neuralgic toothache. Aggravated by warm food. Intense thirst. Unbearable pain in *abdomen*, in the morning at sunrise; flatulent *colic. Diarrhea* during teething. Very painful diarrhea with *flatulence*; stool looks like spinach, green and full of mucus, or like scrambled eggs with rotten-egg smell.

■ Respiratory System

Asthma from vexation, agitation. Dry, violent cough, aggravated at night. Catarrh in children while teething.

- **Urinary Tract and Reproductive System**
  Incredible pain during *menses* with shivering, vomiting, diarrhea and fainting. Menstruation comes too early, is copious and extremely painful. Blood is black with clots. *Colic* with pressing feeling that moves upwards. Bad mood before *menses*. Spasmodic, agonizing, unbearable pain during labor.

- **Modalities**
  Aggravation: Vexation, anger, temper tantrums, mental exertion; coffee, warmth, heat, warm food, eructations; touch; wind; *menses;* in the evening and at night, from 9 pm to noon, or from 9 am to 9 pm, or at 9 am or 9 pm.
  Amelioration: Being carried, riding in a vehicle; mild weather; sweating; cold applications and cold drinks; fasting.
  Side most often affected: Left.

- **Causation**
  Anger, temper tantrums; teething; common cold; coffee, drugs or anesthetics.

- **Indications**
  Bronchial asthma. Bronchitis. Dentitio difficilis. Diarrhea. Dysmenorrhea. Infantile colic. Neuralgia. Otitis media. Premenstrual syndrome. Toothache.

- **Compare**
  Antimonium crudum, Calcarea phosphorica, Cina, Coffea, Colocynthis, Hepar sulphuris, Nux vomica, Rheum.

Chelidonium

Chelidonium majus, greater celandine (N.O. Papaveraceae).

■ **Generalities**

Important remedy for liver and gallbladder. Jaundice. *Nausea* and perspiration during pain.

■ **Mind and Emotions**

Domineering, opinionated, strong will, pragmatic. Would like others to follow his advice and wants to rule other people's lives. Anxiety about others. Suspicion, skepticism. Deep depression for minor reasons.

Greater Celandine   Photo: DHU

■ **Head**

Headache and neuralgia on the right side extending to the teeth and upwards to the eye, with extreme lacrimation. Icy cold feeling coming from occiput extending to the nape of the neck. *Vertigo* with tendency to fall forwards.

■ **Digestive Tract**

Tongue yellow, showing imprint of teeth. Pain in the right upper *abdomen* extending to lower angle of right scapula. Craves very hot drinks, milk, cheese, vinegar and sour foods. Aversion to cheese. Feeling of emptiness in stomach. *Constipation* with very hard stool; hard, round balls like sheep dung. *Constipation* alternating with diarrhea. Diarrhea painless, liquid, bright yellow or white. Violent itching around *anus*.

■ **Respiratory System**

Pneumonia on right side, involving basal lung segment, complicated by liver symptoms. Spasmodic, violent cough caused by a tingling in the throat, the sensation of dust in *trachea* or under sternum; patient coughs violently until tears come.

Back and Extremities

Pain beneath right scapula. Joint pain on the right side; pain in the knees, aggravated by walking. The right foot is icy cold while the temperature in the left foot is normal. Fingertips icy cold.

Modalities

Aggravation: Cold and rough weather, change of weather; motion; touch; 4 am, in the morning after waking.
Amelioration: In a warm room; eating and warm drinks; rest; evening after 8 pm.
Side most often affected: Right.

Indications

Arthritis. Cholecystitis Cholelithiasis. Gastritis. Hepatitis. Hepatopathy. Jaundice. Migraine. *Neuralgia. Pertussis. Pneumonia.*

Compare

Bryonia, China, Dulcamara, Lycopodium, Nux vomica, Podophyllum, Sanguinaria, Sepia, Sulphur.

China officinalis

Cinchona succirubra. Cortex peruviana. Hahnemann proved cinchona bark on himself after translating a materia medica. In this text, he was struck by the similarity between symptoms of cinchona bark poisoning and malaria.

- **Generalities**

  Weakness due to discharges that exhaust the patient, from loss of blood. Periodic fever; **periodicity** of symptoms. Chilly at slightest cold or draft. *Hypersensitivity* of all senses.

- **Mind and Emotions**

  Nervous erethism. Hypersensitive. Sensitive, easily hurt, easily offended. Extremely irritable; moody. Critical; pessimistic. Discontentment, disappointment. Envy, greed. Serious, taciturn, introverted; suspicious. Full of worries. Discouraged, dispondent, sad, cheerless. Loathing of life; suicidal with fear of death. Aversion to company. Patient

China officinalis

imagines that he has been left alone and is unhappy. Exhaustion. Vivid imagination. At **night** when going to bed, patient indulges in fantasies and **imagines self as hero**. During the night they build castles in the air; waking up to reality in the morning brings disenchantment. Fear of animals; dogs; misfortune; killing somebody; suffocating at night. Great anxiety; also from trifles or about the future.

- **Head**
  Throbbing headache, aggravated by slight touch, improved by hard pressure. Pale and yellow face, sunken eyes with dark rings around them. Hypersensitive to odors.

- **Respiratory System**
  Difficulty breathing with rattling of mucus and gasping for air; **wants to be fanned**. Asthma; humid weather, worse during the fall. Spasmodic, suffocating cough; caused by cold; worse from talking; laughing and lying flat on the bed. Spitting of blood. Coughing up blood.

- **Digestive Tract**
  Desire for sweets, highly seasoned foods.
  Loss of appetite or ravenous hunger. Everything patient eats seems to be transformed into gas. *Abdomen* distended by gas; no relief from eructations or flatus. Prone to *diarrhea,* especially after eating fruit. Stools are watery, yellow, brown or light-colored; painless and undigested stools accompanied by violent flatus. Chronic liver conditions with pain in right *hypochondrium.* Gallstones.

- **Modalities**
  Aggravation: Slightest touch; cold; draft; vibrations; noises; night, often around midnight; loss of body fluids; every third day; at a certain time of day.
  Amelioration: Strong pressure; bending double; open air.
  Side most often affected: Left.

- **Causation**
  Loss of body fluids like blood, milk, saliva, *leukorrhea*, semen, strong suppuration, prolonged *diarrhea* etc.; windy and stormy weather; getting soaked.

■ Indications

Anemia. Arthritis. Bronchial asthma. Bronchitis. Cholecystitis. Chronic fatigue syndrome. Colitis. Diarrhea. Fever. Flu. *Gastric and duodenal ulcers. Gastritis.* Headache. *Hemorrhage. Hepatitis.* Malaria. *Sciatic pain.* Sleeplessness. *Vaginitis.*

■ Compare

Arsenicum album, Carbo vegetabilis, Chininum arsenicosum, Chininum sulphuricum, Ignatia, Lycopodium, Natrum muriaticum, Nux vomica.

Cimicifuga

Actaea racemosa, cimicifuga serpentaria, black snakeroot or black cohosh (N.O. Ranunculaceae).

■ Generalities

Mental and physical symptoms alternate. Mainly affects the nervous system. Women in particular suffer disturbances, especially during *menopause*, *menses* and after giving birth. The heavier the menstruation, the stronger the complaints. Weakness and exhaustion after caring for the sick. *Hypersensitivity* to pain, labor pains and noises.

■ Mind and Emotions

Nervous types with a highly agitated nervous system, restlessness and an urge to move; desire to travel. Extroverted. Loquacity; changes subjects constantly. Sometimes averse to talking; at other times loquacious; answers in a rush without

Black Snakeroot   Photo: DHU

addressing the question. Sighing. Fear of injuries, rats, mental disease, death, being murdered. Changing moods, moody, irritable at trifles. Suspicious. Sad and melancholic as if in a dark cloud. *Apathy*; premonition of death; suicidal.

■ Head

Swaying sensation in the brain. Feeling of going crazy from headache; as if top of head were going to fly off. Headache with mental dullness and stiff neck.

■ **Urinary Tract and Reproductive System**

Pain around the *uterus*, shooting pain from side to side. The stronger the menstrual pain, the heavier the bleeding. Prolonged *menses* with violent backache, passing through the hips with heavy downward pressure extending to the thighs. Complaints during pregnancy: *nausea*, vomiting, shooting pain, sleeplessness, sadness, nervousness. Miscarriage during third month. This remedy can control contractions and ease delivery.

■ **Back and Extremities**

Pain and stiffness in the neck; very sensitive to draft. Lumbar pain. Pain in muscles, as if sore from exertion; causes sleeplessness. Trembling, jerking, cramps. Neuralgic and rheumatic pain in the entire body with a high sensitivity to cold, improved by warm wrapping. Violent, lancinating (shooting) pain in nerves or muscles. With rheumatism, abdominal muscles are particularly affected.

■ **Modalities**

Aggravation: Cold, damp and cold weather; draft; motion; touch; *menses* (suppressed); delivery; *menopause*; puberty; teething; morning; night; agitation, fright; after injury to the spine; alcohol.
Amelioration: Warmth; rest; eating.
Side most often affected: Left.

■ **Indications**

Arthritis. Chorea. Depression. *Dysmenorrhea.* Gestational psychosis. *Psychosis during menopause. Menorrhagia.* Migraine. *Neuralgia.* Phobia. Rheumatism. *Sciatica.* Sleeplessness. Soft-tissue rheumatism. Uterine inertia.

■ **Compare**

Argentum nitricum, Calcarea phosphorica, Caulophyllum, Ignatia, Lac caninum, Lachesis, Phosphorus.

Cina

Artemisia cina, wormseed (N.O.Compositae).

■ **Generalities**

Emaciation with ravenous hunger in children. Tenderness to touch. Periodicity; complaints always appear daily at the same time. Symptoms accompanied by yawning and stiffness. Cramps in all areas of the body.

■ **Mind and Emotions**

Restlessness, irritability, capriciousness. Obstinate, stubborn, cross, contrary, disobedient and capricious children. They want to be carried around and rocked, don't want to be looked at and refuse things when offered to them. Screaming, hitting and pinching. *Convulsions* from scolding and reprimands. Patient is not easy to please. Hypersensitive; does not want to be looked at. Notorious for constant bad mood, discontent.

■ **Head**

Tender scalp; aversion to touching of hair. Face alternating between red and pale color with dark rings around the eyes and pale or bluish discoloration around the mouth. Weak eyes; enlarged pupils; xanthopia.

■ **Digestive Tract**

Ailments from ascarides. Frequent swallowing. Alternating ravenous hunger and complete lack of appetite. Ravenous hunger shortly after a meal or vomiting. Spasmodic pain in pit of stomach. Stinging pain around the navel; navel area is very tender. Colorless stool. Ascarides in stool. Itching near *anus*.

■ **Respiratory System**

Constantly scratching, rubbing and picking nose. Itching in the nose. Coughing from feeling of suffocation. Spasmodic cough at slightest motion. Cough from anger or frustration, with pale face and stiffening before cough. Brings up whitish, viscous mucus at the end of paroxysms.

Urinary Tract and Reproductive System

Frequent urge to pass urine with profuse urination. Urinary *incontinence*. Milky urine.

Extremities

Cramps, twitching, trembling, spasmodic muscular twitching, *convulsions* worse from touch.

Sleep

Persistent, violent yawning. Restless sleep; child emits penetrating screams at night; grinds teeth, masticates, swallows and trembles in sleep. Moves on all fours during sleep. Child wakes with a fright before midnight.

Modalities

Aggravation: touch; worms, vexation; being looked at; pressure; cold; nights, during sleep, full moon; in the sun, during summer, in spring and fall; sitting; yawning.
Amelioration: Lying on *abdomen* or on hands and knees; sustained movement.

Causation

Ailments from worms.

Indications

Behavioral disorders. *Diarrhea. Enuresis.* Epilepsy. Helminthiasis, especially pinworms. *Otitis media. Pertussis.* Tooth-grinding in sleep.

Compare

Antimonium crudum, Antimonium tartaricum, Arum triphyllum, Bryonia, Calcarea phosphorica, Chamomilla, Medorrhinum.

Cocculus

Indian cockle; menispermum cocculus, anamirta cocculus (N.O. Menispermaceae). The ripe, dried fruits of this creeper are used to make the remedy. The plant grows in Sri Lanka, India, and on the Malayan Archipelago.

■ Generalities

Depletion of nervous system; *paralytic* weakness. Sentimental, romantic girls. Patient is too weak to hold up head, stand or even speak, especially during *menses*. Feeling of weakness or emptiness in various organs.

■ Mind and Emotions

Irritable weakness from lack of sleep, mental agitation or night-watches. Slow comprehension; slow on the uptake; *imbecility*. Confusion, dazed state. Very sad, brooding, morose, taciturn. Thoughts are fixed on unpleasant things. Intolerant of contradiction. Easily offended. Hasty speech. Anxious and nervous. Great anxiety about health of self and family.

■ Vertigo

Vertigo when riding in a car. Rotatory *vertigo* when sitting up in bed, which forces patient to lie down again. *Vertigo* with *nausea* and *palpitation*s.

■ Head

Migraine with *nausea* and vomiting. Feeling of emptiness in head.

■ Digestive Tract

Craves beer and mustard. *Nausea* and vomiting caused by riding in a car, train or boat: Travel sickness; seasickness, improved by closing eyes. *Nausea* when thinking about food or smelling food. Distension of *abdomen*; *colic* during *flatulence* as if *abdomen* were filled with sharp pieces of wood or sharp stones; often around midnight. Pain in liver and swelling of liver, worse from vexation and anger.

Respiratory System

Coryza with *congestion* on alternate sides.

Back and Extremities

Weakness of neck muscles, head feels heavy; muscles seem unable to support the head. Weakness in lumbar region, as if *paralyzed*; back pain. Paralytic stiffness of joints. Weakness in legs. Muscular *atony*. Coordination problems. Feet, hands and arms are numb or go to sleep. Trembling in arms, legs and the hands, worse from elevating hands.

Sleep

Sleeplessness from worries.

Modalities

Aggravation: Travelling by car, ship, train or plane; night watching, lack of sleep; anxiety; emotions; cold; noises; during *menses*; getting up from a horizontal position, stooping.
Amelioration: Resting on the side or sitting.

Causation

Lack of sleep, night watching, caring for the sick, overwork, worries, grief, vexation.

Indications

Chronic fatigue syndrome. Depression. *Dysmenorrhea*. Headache. Migraine. *Multiple sclerosis. Nausea.*

Compare

Alumina, Calcarea carbonica, Causticum, Conium, Gelsemium, Helleborus, Ignatia, Natrum muriaticum, Petroleum, Phosphorus, Phosphoricum acidum, Pulsatilla, Staphisagria, Tabacum.

Coffea

Coffee; coffea cruda or arabica. Fruit of the coffee tree (N.O. Rubiaceae).

◼ Generalities

Pathological hyperstimulation of all sense organs and the nervous system; with *hypersensitivity* to every pain, even the slightest. Any pain is unbearable for patient. Cannot tolerate the slightest pain without moaning and complaining. *Hypersensitivity* of all senses. Tenderness to touch. Aversion to

Coffee   Photo: DHU

and aggravation from being in the open air. Great exhaustion and weakness in oversensitive persons.

◼ Mind and Emotions

Extreme physical and mental activity. Great excitement and restlessness. Increased activity of the mind and heightened perception of noises or movements. Cheerful, boisterous, happy, lively. Euphoric states. Full of plans for the future; vivid ideas. Bright and witty; quick to act. Ambition; conscientiousness, pangs of conscience, feeling guilty. Hard-working, creative and productive; works for the good of others, so as not to feel isolated. Forsaken feeling. Charitable; compassionate, but refuses sympathy for self. Mood swings: weeping alternates with laughing. Crying for joy. Weeps, laments, agitated at trifles. Anxious, expects something terrible to happen; fear of the future.

◼ Head

Headache, one-sided with feeling as if a nail were being driven into the head or as if brain were being torn apart or shattered; often after mental overexertion, aggravated in the open air. Usually complaints start in the morning, get slowly worse, and finally become unbearable, so that patient moans and laments. Facial *neuralgia*; often due to bad teeth. Hearing very sensitive. Tendency to faint.

■ Chest

Strong *cardiac* activity with violent *palpitations*, aggravated by the heat of the sun.

■ Digestive Tract

Toothaches that are only tolerated by holding cold water in the mouth; pains extend to the fingertips. Spasmodic tooth-grinding. Pressure in stomach after eating; nervous hunger with greedy, hasty eating; *colic* with *flatulence*.

■ Urinary Tract and Reproductive System

Dysmenorrhea with extraordinarily painful *colic*; despair, crying, lamenting from pain. *Menses*: big, dark clots. *Hypersensitivity* of *vulva* and *vagina*. Labor pains intolerable, with fear of death. Complaints during *menopause*.

■ Sleep

Sleeplessness from excitement, nervous overstimulation, rapid flow of ideas, also after giving birth; caring for the sick. Wakes at every noise.

■ Modalities

Aggravation: Excitement, excessive joy; narcotics, coffee; strong smells; sensory impressions, noise; overeating; cold weather and cold air, open air; cold (but amelioration of toothache and pain in maxilla); touch; bright daylight, at night; *menopause*.
Amelioration: Heat; lying down, rest, sleep.
Side most often affected: Right.

■ Causation

Bad effects from joyful exaltation, excessive joy, pleasant surprise, from fright, conflict, vexation, excitement, fear of disappointed love, grief; abusing tobacco, alcohol and especially coffee.

■ Indications

Chronic fatigue syndrome. Dysmenorrhea. Headache. *Hyperesthesia.* Migraine. *Neuralgia.* Sleeplessness. Toothache.

■ Compare

Aconitum, Chamomilla, China, Ignatia, Kali phosphoricum, Lachesis, Natrum muriaticum, Nux vomica, Sepia, Staphisagria, Theridion.

Colocynthis

Citrullus colocynthis, cucumis, bitter apple or bitter cucumber (N.O. Curcurbitaceae). The plant is found in North Africa.

- **Generalities**

Colicky pain in all areas of body. Spasmodic, violent, tearing, *neuralgic* pain, relieved by strong pressure. Restlessness, especially during pain. Sensation of constriction as if by iron clamps.

Bitter Apple   Photo: DHU

- **Mind and Emotions**

Impatient, extremely irritable and easily vexed. Aversion to talking or answering. Anger with indignation.

- **Head**

Pressing headache. Neuralgic pain in the face; painful muscle spasms in the face.

- **Digestive Tract**

Colic due to anger and outrage. Sudden spasmodic pain in *abdomen* that occurs in waves, relieved by bending double, strong pressure, heat, after stool and passing flatus. *Infantile colic. Nausea* and vomiting at the peak of abdominal pain. Increased thirst. Greenish diarrhea after even the smallest quantity of food or drink.

- **Urinary Tract and Reproductive System**

Cutting pain in *urethra* and ovaries with restlessness that makes the patient double up. Menstrual pain improved by pressure and heat.

■ **Back and Extremities**

Painful muscle spasms. Shooting pain, as if electric shocks were going down the left side of one limb. Severe, spasmodic pain, together or alternating with numbness. Violent pain in hip joint, as if squeezed in a vise; improved by lying on the painful side and drawing up the leg.

■ **Modalities**

Aggravation: After meals; emotions, anger, vexation, grief; in the evening, at night, 6 am or 4 to 6 pm; stretching out; touch.

Amelioration: Pressure; bending **double,** drawing up the legs, lying on *abdomen;* coffee, starchy food, potatoes; rest, **heat,** bed warmth; gentle motion.

■ **Causation**

Bad effects of (suppressed) vexation, anger, insult, offense, indignation, excitement, fright, grief.

■ **Indications**

Arthritis. Cholecystitis. Dysmenorrhea. Gastroenteritis. Headache. *Infantile colic. Lumbago. Nephrolithiasis. Neuralgia. Renal colic. Sciatica.*

■ **Compare**

Chamomilla, Cuprum metallicum, Magnesia phosphorica, Nux vomica, Staphisagria.

Conium maculatum

Poison hemlock (N.O. Umbelliferae). Socrates was most probably poisoned with hemlock (see Plato's Phaedon).

■ **Generalities**

Weakness, in women during and after *menopause;* after acute diseases. Increased fatigue and muscular weakness in limbs with trembling, especially in legs; *tremors* in hands, *clonic* seizures. Weakness that forces patient to lie down. Ascending *paralysis* (poisoning of Socrates). Coordination problems when moving limbs, moving tongue (when speaking), of the eyes (double vision). **Induration of glands.** Lymph nodes are indurated and enlarged. Mammary glands and testicles are as hard as wood, especially in persons who have a predisposition to **cancer;** after

Speckled Hemlock   Photo: DHU

bruise or injury, occasional induration with burning pain. *Tumor formation* following bruise or blow; in malignant *tumors*, this remedy acts as *palliative.* Injuries of glands with induration and black *hematoma.* Perspiration during day and night; sweats when falling asleep or only on closing the eyes. Cold sweat on palms and fingers. Periodicity of two weeks.

■ **Mind and Emotions**

Patient feels he has to prove himself; fear of *failure*, feeling guilty. Idiocy, *imbecility.* Loss of memory. Weak concentration. Complete indifference. Sad, unhappy, depressed, anxious, sullen, weepy, narrow-minded, timorous, morose, bitter, emotionally closed and hardened. Aversion to company but still afraid of being alone. Listless and incapable of any mental work. Total *insomnia.* Fixed ideas, superstitious.

Materialist. Unable to think, with vanishing of thoughts and weak memory. Hypochondriasis with fear of people but also fear of being alone, in some cases due to sexual weakness or in old age. Anxiety/hysteria/sadness caused by suppression of sex drive.

■ Vertigo

Especially when turning over in bed; during gentle motion of the head or even just moving eyeballs; therefore patient has to keep head still; when turning the head to the left; in older women suffering from diseases of the *ovaries* or the *uterus*.

■ Eyes

Extreme aversion to light (*photophobia*) out of all proportion to the cause of the disease (e.g. strumose *ophthalmia* with slight inflammation); with no or only slight inflammatory signs around the eyes; *hyperesthesia* of *retina*; muscular *paralysis*, dysadaptation. *Ulcers* on cornea. *Ptosis:* eyelid appears to be pressed downwards as if by a heavy weight. Objects look red or rainbow-colored; poor *eyesight*.

■ Cardiovascular System

Violent *palpitations*, strong, accelerated pulse, or exceptionally slow pulse (*bradycardia* down to 30 beats per minute). Pulse is felt in the whole body. Weakness similar to fainting, skin cold and *cyanotic*, outbreak of cold sweat.

■ Respiratory System

Cough on lying down. Dry, painful, frequent or persistent cough, especially in the evening or at night, brought on or increased by horizontal position; hoarseness, pain in *larynx*, feeling of suffocation during cough; scanty, purulent, particularly difficult *expectoration*. Impossible to bring up mucus; swallows mucus; patient reports almost no coughing during the day. Violent, spasmodic paroxysms of coughing, caused by itching and tingling in chest or throat or a dry spot in *larynx*, also from taking a deep breath.

- **Digestive Tract**
  Cravings: **Salty foods**, sour food, coffee. Aversion: Milk, which is not tolerated. *Dysphagia.* Vomiting of dark chyme, like coffee grounds, with violent pain. Weakness and trembling after stool.

- **Urinary Tract and Reproductive System**
  Pauses during urination. Erectile dysfunction: despite desire, intercourse cannot be performed because erection fades during sex; impotence. Or the reverse: involuntary *ejaculation* when seeing or even thinking of a woman. Strong sex drive. *Prostate* conditions in older men. During each menstrual period, breasts become tense and painful; aggravated by walking or slightest vibration.

- **Modalities**
  Aggravation: At night and in the morning after waking; sleep, also siesta; when head is lowered; raising arms; looking at moving objects; before and during menses; prolonged sexual continence/suppression of sex drive; intercourse and loss of semen; alcohol (small quantities); physical and mental exertion; cold, while resting (pain in extremities); pressure from tight clothes; vibrations; dry, hot air; standing; during spring; old age.
  Amelioration: Moving; walking; warmth; pressure; in the dark. Stomach conditions and general state improved after eating. Fasting. Letting affected part of the body hang down. Stooping; walking bent over; sitting down. In the sun. Darkness.

- **Indications**
  Degeneration of central and peripheral nervous system. Eye diseases. *Facial neuralgia.* Glandular *tumors.* Hypochondriasis. *Multiple sclerosis. Myelitis acuta.* Prostate conditions. *Ptosis.* Stomach cancer. Tuberculosis. *Tumors* in female breast. *Vertigo.*

■ **Compare**

Agaricus, Anacardium, Carbo animalis, Causticum, Cocculus, Phosphoricum acidum, Sepia.

Crotalus horridus

Rattlesnake, Brazilian rattlesnake. Venom of the South American rattlesnake.

- ## Generalities

  Hemorrhages of dark, thin blood from all orifices; even sweat is bloody; blood does not coagulate. *Hemorrhagic diathesis.* Great depletion, sudden weakness, collapse, trembling. Jaundice. Tendency to *gangrene*, necrosis, *edema* and *septic* conditions with fever. Following bites, symptoms return regularly in circumscribed areas after long periods of time, especially in yearly intervals.

- ## Mind and Emotions

  Sadness, melancholy; weepy mood. Loquacity along with the desire to flee. Suspicion. Weak memory; cannot express self correctly. Anxiety and irritability; easily annoyed. Delirium with muttering, confused speech, trembling and weariness. Sleepy but unable to sleep. Unconsciousness.

  Rattlesnake   Photo: DHU

- ## Head

  Dull, throbbing pain in occiput that occurs in waves, worse from vibrations. Eyes yellow. *Retinal* bleeding. Dark *hemorrhages* from nose, mouth, etc.

- **Throat**

  Sensation of constriction in throat. Throat is dry, dark red and swollen, internally as well as externally. Pain in throat, worse from empty swallowing.

- **Digestive Tract**

  Severe swelling of the tongue. Unquenchable, burning thirst. Craves pork. Black or bilious vomit. Pressure of clothes is unbearable. Distended *abdomen*. Thin, black, coffee-ground stool.

- **Respiratory System**

  Cough with bloody *expectoration*.

- **Urinary Tract and Reproductive System**

  Dark, bloody, scanty urine.

- **Skin**

  Pale yellowish or blue-black discoloration. *Purpura* hemorrhagica, *ecchymosis*. Blood blisters. Old scars break open again. *Ulcers* with a tendency to develop *gangrene*. Skin is cold and dry. Swelling of skin all over the body.

- **Sleep**

  Wakes with a start from sleep. Terrifying dreams of murder, death and dead bodies. Sleepiness, but cannot sleep.

- **Modalities**

  Aggravation: Warm and damp weather; spring; falling asleep, sleep, in the morning after waking; lying on the right side; vibrations; alcohol. **Amelioration:** Light; motion. **Side most often affected:** Right.

- **Indications**

  Abscess. Angina tonsillaris. Carbuncles. Delirium tremens. Erysipelas. Gangrene. Hemorrhage. Hemorrhagic diathesis. Myocarditis. Nephritis.

Pharyngitis. Phlegmon. Purpura hemorrhagica. Pyelonephritis. Septicemia.

- **Compare**

Aceticum acidum, Baptisia, Elaps, Lachesis, Naja, Pyrogenium, Secale cornutum, Sulphuricum acidum.

Cuprum metallicum

Copper. The best conductor of electricity next to silver and gold.

- ### Generalities

Spasms and cramps in all areas. Periodicity of symptoms. Great tiredness, weakness from mental overexertion and lack of sleep.

Copper   Photo: DHU

- ### Mind and Emotions

Serious persons who are tense inside. Very closed; suppresses emotions, cannot show emotions. Insurmountable panic attacks. Fear of fire. Piercing cries; intense weeping, convulsive laughter. Shouting or screaming before *convulsions*. Changeable behavior; alternately yielding or obstinate; talkative, later melancholic; weeping alternating with strange antics. Children with behavior problems: hitting, biting, spitting; hold their breath when angry until they turn blue. Dullness and slowness of the mind.

- ### Head

Convulsions. Vertigo along with various complaints, better after passing stool. Headache at bridge of nose. During *convulsions* face is cyanotic and lips are blue. Involuntary grimaces. *Paralysis* of tongue; stuttering.

- ### Digestive Tract

Copper-like taste in mouth with *salivation*. Gurgles when drinking. Pronounced *nausea*. Strong feeling of pressure in stomach with spasmodic, paroxysmal pain. Miserable feeling in stomach. Violent *colic*. Copious diarrhea, like green water.

■ **Respiratory System**

Asthma with *nausea* and sudden vomiting, improves after vomiting. Persistent, violent, suffocating, spasmodic spells of coughing. Pauses between spells; patient appears to be dead. Cough improves with cold drinks. Attacks of suffocation, worse at 3 am.

■ **Urinary Tract and Reproductive System**

Cramps, jerking, muscle spasms, worse from sleep and sex. Severe cramps, with patient crying out loud from pain in lower extremities, especially in calves and soles. During fits, thumb is clenched inside fist. *Clonic* seizures starting in fingers and toes and extending to all parts of the body.

■ **Modalities**

Aggravation: Touch; hot weather; cold air, cold wind; at night; suppressed discharges; before *menses*; emotions, vexation.
Amelioration: Drinking cold water; sweating.

■ **Causation**

Suppressed skin eruptions, secretions, foot sweat.

■ **Indications**

Affective respiratory spasms. *Bronchial asthma*. Cholera. *Chorea. Convulsions. Encephalitis*. Epilepsy. *Gastroenteritis*. Headache. *Meningitis*. Migraine. *Pertussis*. Tics.

■ **Compare**

Agaricus, Bufo, Causticum, Cicuta virosa, Colocynthis, Ipecacuanha, Veratrum album, Zincum.

Dulcamara

Solanum dulcamara, amara dulcis, sulcis amara, bittersweet (N.O. Solanaceae).

■ Generalities

Complaints are caused or aggravated by humid cold or a change from warm to cold weather, therefore mostly during the fall. Sensitive to cold. Tendency to *adiposity*. Skin eruptions and rheumatic pain alternating with *diarrhea*.

Bittersweet   Photo: Sertürner

■ Mind and Emotions

Often mentally strong and emotionally weak. Ill-humored, quarrelsome. Impatience and restlessness. Strong will, domineering, obstinate, opinionated, egocentric; possessive toward family members. Anxiety about others. Suspicion. Despair over trifles. Anxiety about the future.

■ Head

Headache after suppression of catarrh. Skin eruptions on the face; facial *neuralgia* after suppressing it. *Ptosis.*

■ Respiratory System

Coryza; stuffy nose during rainy weather. Cough dry, hoarse and spasmodic with constricting pain in *epigastrium*. Asthma with loose cough and rattling from mucus.

■ Digestive Tract

Craves sweets. Intense thirst for cold drinks. Diarrhea with green, watery, mucous, sticky stool, sometimes with blood; preceded by cutting pain about navel; especially in summer when the temperature suddenly changes to cold or during fall, in cold, damp weather, or after some skin eruption has disappeared.

Urinary Tract and Reproductive System

Bladder catarrh caused by humidity or change from warm to cold. Catarrhal retention of urine, with milky urine in children who have been wading barefoot in cold water.

Back and Extremities

Back trouble after catching a cold. Joints are painful. Exhaustion and stinging in the whole body. Icy cold hands and feet. *Paralysis* in individual muscles, paralyzed parts are cold.

Skin

Skin eruptions caused or aggravated by cold. Crusty eruptions with *exudation*, generally accompanied by glandular swelling. *Impetigo*. **Flat warts.**

Modalities

Aggravation: Damp weather; humidity; damp cold; change from warm to cold; cold; at night.
Amelioration: Warmth; motion.
Side most often affected: Left.

Causation

Damp cold; change of weather from hot to cold; getting wet, bathing; injuries; suppressed skin eruptions; suppressed sweat.

Indications

Allergy. *Bronchial asthma.* Back pain. Facial nerve *paralysis* or Bell's palsy. *Bronchitis.* Common cold. *Cystitis. Diarrhea.* Hay fever. Headache. Herpes. *Hypertension.* Neuralgia. *Otitis media. Pneumonia. Sinusitis.* Warts.

- **Compare**

Arsenicum album, Baryta carbonica, Calcarea carbonica, Kali carbonicum, Natrum sulphuricum, Rhus toxicodendron, Silicea, Sulphur.

Eupatorium perfoliatum

Thoroughwort (N.O. Compositae) grows in North America near lakes and streams; it is called boneset in the vernacular.

■ Generalities

Painful, **exhausted feeling** throughout the body. Deep and violent pain in bones with fever; bones feel **as if broken**. Chills followed by high fever, especially 7 to 9 am. Periodicity of complaints. Scanty perspiration. Intense weakness during influenza. Jaundice.

■ Mind and Emotions

Restless and groaning because of pain.

■ Head

Head feels heavy, has to be held with hands. Throbbing headache improved after getting up. Bursting headache with cough. *Vertigo* with tendency to fall to the left side. *Coryza* along with sensitivity of eyeballs during headache or *coryza*.

■ Respiratory System

Hoarseness in the morning together with soreness in chest. Cough is so painful that patient has to hold chest. Cough improves by getting into a knee-elbow position.

■ Digestive Tract

Intense thirst for cold drinks; especially before or during chills. Craves ice cream. *Nausea* and vomiting. Bilious vomit after drinking or between chills and fever. Liver is sensitive to pressure.

■ Back and Extremities

Deep-seated violent pain in the back as if crushed, and in every bone and joint as if sprained. Stiffness and generalized aching when getting up. Chills start in lower back. Remedy can relieve the pain from an acute bone fracture.

- **Modalities**
  Aggravation: Cold air; motion; lying on affected part; coughing; smell or sight of food; at night.
  Amelioration: Vomiting (of bile); perspiration; conversation.

- **Causation**
  Bad effects of damp and cold weather or from being in damp areas. Alcoholism.

- **Indications**
  Bone fractures. Pain in Bones. Fever. Common cold. Influenza. Malaria.

- **Compare**
  Arnica, Bryonia, Chelidonium, Ferrum phosphoricum, Gelsemium, Natrum muriaticum, Nux vomica, Pyrogenium, Sepia, Symphytum.

Ferrum metallicum

Iron.

■ Generalities

Coldness throughout the body. Obesity. Parts of body that normally have a reddish color become white, anemic and puffy. Prone to *hemorrhages*; generalized weakness after *hemorrhages*. Great weakness, delicateness, often contrasting with glowing, healthy appearance.

Iron   Photo: DHU

■ Mind and Emotions

Sensitive and easily excited; quarrelsome, obstinate, arrogant, energetic, firm, courageous, dictatorial, opinionated, intolerant of contradiction. Irritability; annoyed by slightest noise. Desire for solitude; avoids any company, even of best friends. Anxiety of conscience as if guilty of a crime. Fears: of misfortune, evil, criticism, of being beaten; being in a crowd; crossing a bridge. Jumpiness; *hypersensitivity* to all sensory impressions, especially **noises.**

■ Head

Extremely pale with sudden, violent blushing at slightest pain, at slightest excitement or exertion. Hammering, throbbing, pulsating headache. *Vertigo*, swaying feeling when looking at running water, when crossing a bridge, looking down.

■ Chest

*Palpitation*s with accelerated pulse.

■ **Respiratory System**

Nosebleed. Hoarseness, cough, bloody *expectoration*. *Bronchial asthma.* Cough only during the day. Ameliorated by lying down and by eating.

■ **Digestive Tract**

Ravenous hunger alternating with complete loss of appetite. Craves tomatoes, sweet foods, soup, bread and butter. Intolerant of eggs, which cause vomiting or diarrhea. Vomiting immediately after eating, without *nausea*. Bringing up food at night, eructations or vomiting of foods that have remained in stomach during the day. While eating or drinking, diarrhea containing undigested food occurs. *Constipation*; back pain or spasmodic pain in *rectum* after stool; *rectal prolapse* in children; itching *anus* at night.

■ **Urinary Tract and Reproductive System**

Irritable bladder; urinary *incontinence* during the day. *Menses* too early, profuse, prolonged, pale, watery and exhausting; accompanied by bright red face and ringing in the ears.

■ **Back and Extremities**

Fear of touch on affected joints. Rheumatic pain in upper extremities, especially shoulders, when resting. Rheumatic pain in left deltoid muscle. Irresistible urge to bend the arm. Restlessness; must move limbs.

■ **Sleep**

Dreams of combat, battles, war.

■ **Modalities**

Aggravation: At night, after midnight; when sitting quietly; exertion; eating; eggs; loss of body fluids, during an outbreak of sweat; in winter; heat and cold; emotions (anger).
Amelioration: Walking slowly; after getting up; in summer; keeping busy.

- **Causation**

  Ailments from vexation, anger, contempt, annoyance.

- **Indications**

  Adiposity. Anemia. Arrhythmia. Arthritis. Bronchial asthma. Bronchitis. Chronic fatigue syndrome. Diarrhea. Enuresis. Epistaxis. Gastritis. Headache. *Menorrhagia.* Migraine. *Neuralgia. Pneumonia.* Rheumatism. *Vertigo.*

- **Compare**

  Antimonium crudum, Arnica, Calcarea carbonica, China, Graphites, Nux vomica, Pulsatilla, Sulphur.

Ferrum phosphoricum
Phosphate of iron, $FePO_4$.

■ Generalities
First stage of inflammation: fever, but no local or individual symptoms yet. Slightly elevated temperature, after inflammatory phase as well. High fever. Violent, local *congestions. Anemia.* Weakness; following recovery from a bowel infection; following *cystitis.* Chilly, sensitive to cold. *Hemorrhages* with bright red blood from all orifices. Contusion. *Hematoma.* Face alternately pale and red.

■ Mind and Emotions
Patient believe he must do his best to be allowed to study or keep his friends. Such patients do give their best and work hard. They have the feeling they must take care of their friends and siblings, defend their friends. Homesickness. Intense compassion. *Hypersensitivity,* sensitive to noise. Concentration is weak, forgetfulness. Discontentment, irritability. **Anxiety,** especially at night. Fears: death; thunderstorms; crowds; inexplicable fear of everything and anxiety about everything. Aversion to company.

■ Respiratory System
Intense feeling of oppression, breathing difficult along with stinging pain in chest when taking a deep breath. Short cough, cramp-like, dry, very painful, together with involuntary passing of urine. Cough gets worse when reclining. *Hemoptysis,* blood is bright red. *Pneumonia* when in stage of resolution.

■ Digestive Tract
Cravings: sour foods; seasoned foods, meat, fish, tomatoes. Thirsty for cold drinks. Aversions: eating, meat, milk, eggs. Sour eructations. Hiccups. Vomiting after a meal. Weak digestion. Painless diarrhea with stools that are often streaked with blood or bloody, containing

undigested food, especially in the morning and at night. *Enteritis* with fever in children.

■ **Urinary Tract and Reproductive System**

Menses, very heavy. *Dysmenorrhea* with fever and a red face.

■ **Modalities**

Aggravation: At night; 3 am, 4 to 6 am; motion, in the open air, cold air. Suppressed sweat. After eating. Standing.

Amelioration: Moving slowly, being alone.

Side most often affected: Right.

■ **Indications**

Anemia. Angina tonsillaris. Bursitis. Colds. Dysmenorrhea. Enteritis. Epistaxis. Fever. Gastritis. Common colds. *Hemorrhage. Otitis media. Pharyngitis. Pleurisy. Pneumonia.*

■ **Compare**

Aconitum, Belladonna, Gelsemium, Phosphorus.

Fluoricum acidum

Acidum hydrofluoricum, hydrofluoric acid is found in fluorite and cryolite.

■ Generalities

Excessive heat with the desire to be cool. Sensation as if scalding hot steam were coming out of the pores. Craves open air. Prefers a cold bath or shower. Sweat has an offensive smell; sour and sticky; also with reaction, feeling chilly and cold. Extreme energy.

■ Mind and Emotions

Disposition is characterized by a remarkable ambivalence. Happy in the morning and in a bad mood in the evening, pessimistic. Fearful premonitions with outbreaks of sweat. Dissatisfied, morose, irritable. **Restless mind, hasty, always in a hurry.** Impatient. **Energetic**, rigorous, impulsive and moody. Cannot tolerate contradictions or compromises. Very active. Overestimates self. **Materialistic**. Fear of death. Fear that something bad might happen. Restlessness with anxiety. Exhaustion. Forgets even little things in daily life, though normally the mind is very active and alert. Adventurous, but shuns work. Dislikes taking on responsibility. Condescending and irritable in criticizing others. Tendency to break up relationships. Aversion to own family. All reservations seem to be forgotten in private contact with strongly disliked persons. When speaking, makes mistakes from speaking too fast.

■ Head

Head is hot, headaches, pressure in the head, *nausea* and *vertigo*. Desire to urinate makes head symptoms worse. **Hair growth** (in certain areas). Hair is dry, brittle and matted. *Exostosis* between eyebrows. Facial muscles constantly in motion. Burning and itching eyes. When eyes are closed in the evening, patient sees flashes and sparks.

- **Respiratory Tract**

  Rhinitis with *constipation*. Aggravation when discharge stops.

- **Digestive System**

  Caries, decayed teeth. *Salivation*. Difficulty swallowing. Ravenous appetite, feels constantly hungry. Emaciation despite increased appetite. Eructations and flatus. Craves highly seasoned foods and cold drinks. Aversion to coffee, alcohol and fat. Cannot tolerate fat. *Constipation,* stools frequent and hard.

- **Urinary Tract and Reproductive System**

  Burning sensation when urinating. Offensive-smelling urine. Scanty, dark urine. Increased sexual desire, sexual excesses. Nymphomania. Acrid discharge. Violent and overwhelming erections and seminal emissions after sexual fantasies.

- **Extremities**

  Nails grow fast, brittle nails. *Whitlows*. **Strong urge to move, feeling of increased strength without fatigue.** Pain in joints and bones. Jerking, fibrillation and trembling in muscles. Inflammation and bone caries. Feels hot all over body, uncovers feet in bed. Sweaty palms.

- **Skin**

  Violent itching of the skin over whole body, better when cooled. Vesicles and *pustules*. Eczema in old age. Eczema gets worse even before the warm weather starts. Superficial blood vessels are *dilated*. Veins on back of the hand are pronounced. Varicose veins. *Ulcers* with hard edges and acrid discharges. Suppuration with *fistulas* and discharges that make the skin sore. Adhesions after inflammations and injuries. Red and tender scars surrounded by itching vesicles. Warts. *Hemangioma*.

- **Modalities**

  Aggravation: Heat. Full moon. At night, 3 to 5 am.
  Amelioration: Cold. Eating, after eating. Rapid motion.

■ **Indications**

Allergy. *Alopecia*. Caries. Eczema. Growth pains. *Hemangioma*. Hypercinesia. Graves' disease, *Naevus flammeus*. *Pharingitis*. *Rhinitis*. Sexual disorders. *Sinusitis*. Sun allergy. Sunburn. Swelling of glands. *Tenovaginitis*. *Thyroid cancer*. Varicose veins.

■ **Compare**

Calcarea fluorica, Coffea, Iodium, Medorrhinum, Nitricum acidum Silicea, Sulphur, Sulphuricum acidum.

Gelsemium

Gelsemium sempervirens, yellow jasmine (N.O. Loganiceae). Nux vomica, Ignatia, Curare and Spigelia are from the same family.

■ Generalities

Trembling. Important remedy in the Materia Medica for trembling; often going along with great exhaustion. Great weakness, relaxation of muscles together with partial or total *paralysis*. Mind is slow, stupid, awkward and apathetic. *Congestion* going to the head with dullness and numbness, sleepy from exhaustion. Adynamic fever (fever rises slowly, not above 101.6° F) with a dark red face as if drunk. Pulse slow, soft and weak; often considerable *hypertension* in old people. Insidious complaints that progress slowly. Symptoms of a cold appear

Yellow Jasmine   Photo: DHU

only a few days after exposure to cold. Skin is very hot, high temperature along with cold extremities. Fever with chilliness and shivering. Complaints are often accompanied by violent chill. Heaviness and tiredness in the whole body as well as in the limbs.

■ Mind and Emotions

Timid, sensitive, quiet, reserved. **Cowardice; stage fright**; ailments from **anticipation**, after fright, grief and following bad news. **Fears**: Being alone; thunderstorms; death; crowds; fear of falling; fear that heart could stop beating; exams. Little self-confidence, easily discouraged. Speaks as if in delirium, incoherent, silly and forgetful.

■ Head

Head is hot, crimson red, blotchy. Eyes glassy, pupils *dilated*. Difficulty keeping eyelids open (*ptosis*). Double vision. *Congestive* headaches.

Headache begins in the nape of the neck and settles later above the eyes. Normally worse in the morning, face red, speech impaired, thinking difficult, vision dim. Blindness precedes headache and subsides when headache sets in. **Headache** with *vertigo*. Migraine with depression and trembling; improved by profuse urination.

■ Respiratory System

Thin and acrid nasal discharges. Spasmodic cough. Soreness and catarrhal irritation in *pharynx* and *larynx* together with pain while swallowing, extending to ear.

■ Digestive Tract

Thirstlessness.
Stool: *diarrhea* from excitement; painless, watery, involuntary stools.

■ Urinary Tract and Reproductive System

Menses: Late and scanty; with *aphonia* during *menses* and violent, labor-like pains. Spasmodic pain in *uterus* extending to the back and hips. Suppressed *menses* with *congestion* going to the head and numbness. Cerebral irritation takes the place of labor pains.

■ Back and Extremities

Coldness of fingers and toes; feet icy cold up to the knee. Cold moving along the spine, going up to the occiput. Shivering as if ice were being pushed up the spinal column. Pain extends up the back. Chills wander up and down the back. Pain: violent; sudden; shooting; along nerves; worse from changing weather. Dull pain deep within the muscles. Cramps in extremities, fingers and toes clenched up, back muscles tense. Pain in the nape of the neck with stiffness as in *meningitis*.

■ Skin

Hot, dry, itching skin eruptions like in measles. *Erysipelas*.

- **Sleep**

  Sleeplessness due to nervous excitement, fright or bad news and after excessive smoking. Wakes suddenly with the sensation that "the heart would stop beating if he did not move about".

- **Modalities**

  Aggravation: Excitement, mental agitation, fright, anxiety, fear, thinking about complaints; before thunderstorm; downward motion, motion; around 9 or 10 am; heat of the sun; summer heat; sun; warm and humid or cold and damp; tobacco smoke.

  Amelioration: In the open air; alcohol and other stimulants; profuse urination; sweating.

- **Causation**

  Bad effects from fright, anxiety, sudden excitement, e.g. headache. Cramps and diarrhea after excitement, after exams or public appearance. Masturbation. Failure to recover from influenza.

- **Indications**

  Anxiety. *Diarrhea. Diplopia.* Fever. *Chronic fatigue syndrome.* Common cold/influenza. Hay fever. Headache. *Laryngitis.* Migraine. *Multiple sclerosis. Myasthenia gravis. Neuralgia. Paralysis.* Sleeplessness. *Tremors.* Upper respiratory infections. *Vertigo.*

- **Compare**

  Argentum nitricum, Laurocerasus, Lycopodium, Muriaticum acidum, Phosphoricum acidum, Sepia, Silicea, Stannum.

Glonoinum
Nitroglycerine or glycerol trinitrate.

■ Generalities
Intolerance of heat and aggravation by heat. Pulsating pain and pulsating sensation throughout body. Sudden paroxysms of pain. Surges of blood to head and heart; heat flushes upwards to the crown of the head. *Hypertension* in old age. Sudden and violent circulatory disorders.

■ Mind and Emotions
Intense nervous agitation. *Hypersensitivity.* Anxiety and fear with restlessness. Confusion. Gets lost in well-known neighborhoods. Fear of having been poisoned. Aversion to own family; does not recognize relatives. *Apathy* and indifference.

■ Head
Blood rushes to the head and violent *vertigo.* Waves of bursting, throbbing, pulsating headache with *congestion;* as if head were exploding. Headaches. Aggravation caused by vibrations of the head, sun, moving the body, ameliorated by putting pressure on the head. Headache instead of *menses.* Sunstroke and headache from sun; does not tolerate heat on head. Intolerant of anything on head; never wears a hat, keeps hair short. Burning heat on the vertex and on the nape of the neck. Head and brain feel enlarged. Chin feels elongated. *Convulsions* in children caused by cerebral *congestion.*

■ Chest
Nervous *palpitations* after strong excitement. *Palpitations* go along with visibly pulsating carotids. Blood rushes to the heart and chest. Pain in the heart spreading in all directions.

■ Digestive Tract
Craves cold drinks and nicotine. *Nausea* during *menopause.*

■ **Skin**

Old scars break open.

■ **Modalities**

Aggravation: In the sun; heat; motion; suppressed *menses, menopause*; alcohol, wine; stooping; moving, shaking and bending head backwards; while reclining.

Amelioration: Cold fresh air; cold, cold applications; pressure, when pressing the head or holding it upright with both hands; lying in the dark.

Side most often affected: Left.

■ **Causation**

Bad effects from sunstroke; agitation, fear, fright; accident; cutting hair.

■ **Indications**

Angina pectoris. Arrhythmia. Epilepsy. . Hypertension. Meningitis. Migraine. Ménière's disease. Palpitations. Sunstroke.

■ **Compare**

Belladonna, Ferrum, Lachesis, Melilotus, Natrum carbonicum, Pulsatilla, Sulphur.

Graphites

Black lead, plumbago. Carbon containing iron and other impurities like silicic acid, lime and manganese.

■ Generalities

Tendency to obesity, paleness, *constipation.* Sensitivity to cold. Oozing: "With Graphites everything oozes, skin and bowels". Discharges have an offensive smell (sweat, bad breath, stool and smell coming from skin).

Blacklead   Photo: DHU

■ Mind and Emotions

Slowness. Aversion to work; lazy, although very intelligent. Restless while working. Indifference; *apathy,* shyness. Laughs when reprimanded. Absent-mindedness, lack of attention, forgetfulness. Numbness. Despair over trifles. Exaggerated watchfulness, fearful. **Irresolute**. Sad; **weeps when listening to music**. Fear of death, thinks of death all the time; fears: misfortune; thunderstorms; work; insanity. Changeable or weepy mood. Irritability; easily offended. Sleeplessness from overabundance of ideas. Tiredness. *Vertigo.*

■ Head

Burning over the skull; in spots. Pain in occiput; as if contracting; extending to the neck. Cradle cap. **Eyes:** eczema on lids; with cracks. *Photophobia.* Dried mucus in eyelashes. In the morning, eyes are gummed up. **Ears:** impaired hearing, improved when riding in a car and when noises occur. Chronic discharges from ears.

- **Digestive Tract**

  Aversions: Warm and cooked foods; soup. Sweets, salt, fish, meat.
  Cravings: Beer and cold drinks. Chicken.
  Flatulence, salivation. Persistent *constipation* with no urge, hard lumps
  of stool covered with mucus. *Diarrhea:* Stool watery, brown, mixed with
  undigested matter, fetid.

- **Urinary Tract and Reproductive System**

  Strong sexual desire or no interest in sex. Sexual dysfunction; from
  excessive sex. Aversion to *sex. Dysmenorrhea.* Late *menses.*

- **Extremities**

  Burning; cramps; twitches. Feeling as if paralyzed/numb. *Paralysis.*
  Numbness.

- **Skin**

  Tenacious, honey-like secretions; behind ears; on eyelids; on genitals;
  on head; on face. Skin eruptions with acrid and offensive discharges.
  Fissures: in corners of mouth, on nipples, on fingertips, on toes, around
  anus. Skin dry, cracked, fissured with dry skin eruptions; near orifices
  (where skin and mucous membrane meet); calluses on palms and soles.
  Nails thickened, hard, jagged, brittle, ingrown and deformed.

- **Modalities**

  Aggravation: During and after *menses;* late onset of *menses.* Cold;
  drafts. Motion. Night.
  Amelioration: Warm wrappings.
  Side most often affected: Left.

- **Causation**

  Suppressed skin eruption. Ailments from premonitions, anticipation,
  fright, grief, music.

■ Indications

Abscess. Adiposity. Acne. *Alopecia. Arthritis. Bronchial asthma. Blepharitis. Conjunctivitis.* Connective tissue diseases. *Constipation.* Dementia. Eczema. *Erysipelas. Fissures. Gastric and duodenal ulcers. Gastritis.* Headache. Loss of hearing. Hemorrhoids. Herpes. Heat flushes. *Hordeolum. Impetigo. Keloids. Keratitis.* Malignant diseases. *Otitis externa. Otitis media. Photophobia. Psoriasis.* Sexual disorders. *Vaginitis. Vertigo.*

■ Compare

Antimonium crudum, Calcarea carbonica, Capsicum, Ferrum, Pulsatilla, Sulphur.

Helleborus niger

Christmas rose or black hellebore (N.O. Ranunculaceae). Plant grows in alpine regions. The remedy is made from the fresh sap of the rhizome.

- **Generalities**

Deadening of senses, dullness, numbness; sensory impressions weakened although sense organs not impaired. Indifference to pain. Sensitive to cold. Prone to internal bleeding. Generalized weakness of muscles, even complete *paralysis*. Tendency to *edema*.

Black Hellebore   Photo: DHU

- **Mind and Emotions**

Great despair and extreme, terrifying anxiety. Helplessness; patient pleads for help. Sadness, melancholy, downheartedness; indifference; irresolution. Idiocy, *apathy*. Answers slowly. Weak memory; forgets what he has just read or done. Mind is completely blank. Patient stares vacantly. Concentration difficult. Feelings of guilt and remorse; even suicidal thoughts because of total inadequacy. Delusions: she is doomed; everything appears new; she has made a mistake. Fear of imaginary things. Irritability; worse from consolation. Spontaneous sighing. *Meningitis* or *encephalitis* with numbness, unconsciousness; head rolls from one side to the other or tossed about; frowning, mouth moves as if chewing or speaking; burrows head into pillow, stares into space, cri encéphalique (piercing scream).

- **Head**

Pressing headache in occiput, improved by closing eyes. Empty feeling in head. Rolling head with sighing. Cramps alternating with numbness.

Vertigo. Head injuries with mental dullness and confusion. Furrowed brow, especially when trying to think.

■ Digestive Tract

Aversion to **apples**, vegetables, sauerkraut. Thirstlessness or intense thirst. Diarrhea during acute *hydrocephalus*, teething or pregnancy. Diarrhea slimy, bloody, gelatinous and watery.

■ Urinary Tract and Reproductive System

Urine is dark red, almost black, scanty, with a sediment like coffee grounds.
Suppressed *menses* after getting wet (feet).

■ Extremities

Muscles don't obey without total concentration. Clumsiness, awkwardness. Involuntary movements of one arm or leg. *Edema* in legs.

■ Modalities

Aggravation: 4 to 8 pm; from evening to morning; uncovering in bed; cold air; exertion; room filled with people.
Amelioration: Awareness, thinking about complaints, distraction; fresh air.

■ Causation

Ailments after head injuries, *meningitis, encephalitis,* concussion, stroke, fright, grief, suppressed skin eruptions.

■ Indications

Alzheimer's disease. Brain concussion. Colitis ulcerosa. Comatose state. *Cystitis.* Dementia. Depression. *Encephalitis.* Epilepsy. *Gastroenteritis. Meningitis.* Migraine. *Nephritis. Psychosis.*

■ **Compare**
Alumina, Apis, Arnica, Arsenicum album, Belladonna, Bryonia, Cicuta virosa, Cocculus, Mercurius, Opium, Phosphorus, Phosphoricum acidum, Zincum.

Hepar sulphuris

Hepar sulphuris calcareum or Calcarea sulphuratum Hahnemanni is made by heating equal weights of the white inner part of oyster shells and sublimated sulphur (flowers of sulphur) to white heat in a closed crucible.

■ Generalities

Hypersensitivity on all levels, especially to **pain**, cold air and touch. Stinging, splinter-like pain. Extremely sensitive to **cold**, cold air or the slightest draft; has to be covered completely, slightest uncovering makes complaints worse. Prone to **suppuration**; swollen glands with suppuration. All discharges are sour and smell like old cheese. Profuse sweats with no relief. Periodicity of complaints; every day, every month, every three months, always during winter.

■ Mind and Emotions

Easily hurt; fear of suffering, *hypersensitivity* to pain. Fear of bees, biting insects; syringes. Extreme irritability, over trifles. Impulse to kill at slightest insult. Pyromania; wants to set fires; delusion that world is on fire. Suicidal; desire to set self on fire. Discontentment, moroseness, lamenting, scolding, anger, rage, violent temper, vehemence, violence. Impatience, hurry; eating and drinking in a hurry, hasty speech. Weak memory and loss of memory, especially concerning names and sense of direction.

■ Head

Headache as from a nail. Inflammation of sinuses with yellow, acrid, offensive *coryza*, worse from cold. Purulent *conjunctivitis*. *Recurrent*, purulent and very painful *otitis media*; chronic discharge from ears.

■ **Throat**

Stinging pain in throat as from a needle or a splinter, extending to the ear when swallowing or yawning. *Recurrent tonsillitis* with pus formation.

■ **Respiratory System**

Croupy, retching, suffocating, dry cough, getting worse after exposure to cold wind, worse when any part of the body is not covered and in the morning; accompanied by hoarseness and rattling. Bronchial asthma from suppressed skin eruptions.

■ **Skin**

Minor wounds, slightest graze, even skin eruptions start to suppurate. Acne, extremely painful *abscesses*, *furuncles*, onychitis. Scar formation is slow. Skin is very tender to the touch, even just from clothes. Cracks in skin; deep *fissures* in hands and feet. Chronic or *recurrent urticaria*.

■ **Modalities**

Aggravation: Touch, pressure; cold, cold air, uncovering; dry, cold weather; at night and in the morning.
Amelioration: Warmth, in warm bed; humid and warm weather; warm wrapping, especially of the head.
Side most often affected: Right.

■ **Indications**

Abscess. Adenopathy. Acne. *Angina tonsillaris. Bronchial asthma. Blepharitis. Bronchitis.* Carbuncles. *Conjunctivitis.* Constipation. Eczema. *Furuncles. Impetigo contagiosa.* Headache. *Laryngitis. Neuralgia. Otitis media. Pharyngitis. Pleurisy.* Pneumonia. Pseudocroup. *Sinusitis. Urticaria.* Whitlows.

■ Compare

Aconitum, Arsenicum album, Calcarea carbonica, Calcarea sulphurica,
Graphites, Mercurius, Mezerereum, Nitricum acidum Nux vomica,
Psorinum, Silicea, Spongia, Sulphur.

Hyoscyamus niger

Henbane (N.O. Solanaceae). Belongs to the family of nightshades, along with Belladonna and Stramonium. During the Middle Ages it was used as a narcotic or a magic potion, or as an ingredient in some witches' ointments.

- **Generalities**

  Hyperesthesia. Impetuous, wild contractions of all muscles from head to feet; twitching, jerking, spasms. Restlessness.

- **Mind and Emotions**

  Jealousy. Anxious, irritable, tense. **Mistrust**, suspicion, fear of poisoning or intrigues, of being alone. General

Henbane   Photo: DHU

hydrophobia. Erotomania; exhibitionism in adults, obscene behavior and shamelessness; children play with genitals. Loquacity; loves to talk about feces, urine and genitals; cursing. Silly, ridiculous behavior. Numbness with violent outbursts during delirium. Fear of water and undressing/uncovering during fever delirium, along with playing with genitals or feces and urine. When in grief patient withdraws into himself, withdraws from others; feelings die, feels as if made of wood inside, no more emotions. Withdrawn, stays alone, tells silly stories; picks at the bed covers or counts imaginary money, muttering to himself or speaking with absent or dead people. Outbursts of violence, only when provoked. Desire to kill. Obsessive ideas, compulsive behavior; delusions, illusions, hallucinations. Numbness, unconsciousness.

- **Head**

  Clonic cramps. Facial grimaces. Crossed eyes.

- **Digestive Tract**
  Cramps in *esophagus* when looking at water; especially when hearing water run. Feeling of suffocation while swallowing, even liquids. Aversion to water and drinks. Dryness of mucous membranes of the mouth. *Hiccups.* Violent, *colicky* pain in *abdomen.* Sudden passing of stool; involuntary diarrhea, worse during or after emotional upheaval.

- **Chest**
  Palpitations and *arrhythmia* when lying down.

- **Respiratory System**
  Spasmodic cough with choking; caused by tingling in *larynx*; **worse when lying down;** patient must sit up. Coughing fits end in fluid and watery *expectoration.* Eating and drinking make cough worse; even touching throat provokes a coughing fit. Loss of voice following emotional excitement, especially anxiety and fear.

- **Urinary Tract and Reproductive System**
  Involuntary passing of urine. Increased sexual desire. Urge to masturbate in public. Nymphomania. Masturbation in young children.

- **Extremities**
  Restless hands; picking at bedcovers or clothing; gesticulating. Cramps in voluntary and involuntary muscular system; *tremors* and twitching. *Paralysis.*

- **Sleep**
  Going to sleep is difficult or impossible; twitching in muscles or shrieking when falling asleep. Talking, screaming and grinding teeth in sleep. Sleeplessness. Nightmares, lascivious dreams.

- **Modalities**
  Aggravation: At night, rest, sleep; touch; mental affects, jealousy, disappointed love; during *menses*; while reclining; after drinking; cold.

Amelioration: Stooping, bending head forward while sitting, sitting up; heat.

■ **Causation**

Jealousy, fright, suffering injustice, disappointed love, excitement.

■ **Indications**

Delirium (*tremens*). Cough. Dementia. Depression. *Encopresis. Enuresis.* Epilepsy. Mania. *Meningitis.* Nymphomania. *Pertussis. Pneumonia. Psychosis.* Schizophrenia. Sleeplessness. Sexual disorders. *Strabismus.*

■ **Compare**

Agaricus, Anacardium, Belladonna, Lachesis, Stramonium, Tarentula hispanica, Veratrum album.

Hypericum
Hypericum perforatum, St. John's wort (N.O. Guttiferae).

■ Generalities

Remedy for wounds in tissues rich in nerves (tips of fingers, toes, tongue, eyes, genitalia, coccyx), when pain is unbearable. Nerve pain after injuries and surgery, after concussion and trauma to the spinal cord. Great tenderness in injured parts.

St. John's Wort   Photo: DHU

■ Mind and Emotions

Agitation; depression; thinking is difficult. In low spirits, whiny; melancholy. Nervous depression after injury or surgery. Confusion; makes mistakes when writing; forgets what he was about to say. Feeling of being lifted up in the air along with fear of falling down. Sleeplessness or sleepiness.

■ Head

Blood rushes to head along with irration of cerebral nerves. *Convulsions* after trauma of head or spine. *Vertigo* with the sensation that the head is elongated; at night, desire to urinate. Tearing and pulsating headache. Pain after dental treatment.

■ Respiratory System

Asthma in foggy weather; improved by *expectoration*.

■ Back and Extremities

Injuries to spine with stinging, shooting pain. Pain is worse when moving arms or neck. Spine sensitive or tender to touch. Injuries to coccyx from a fall, bruise or childbirth. Phantom limb pain after amputation. Painful scars. Stab wounds and contusions of fingertips. Wounds from stabbing and biting. Shooting pain along the nerves. Weakness, stiffness, numbness, tingling.

■ **Modalities**

Aggravation: Injuries; exertion, motion, jolting; change of weather, fog, damp and cold weather, **cold air;** in a closed room.
Amelioration: Lying on *abdomen*; lying quietly; stretching backwards.

■ **Causation**

Bad effects of concussion to the back or spinal cord; nerve injuries; shock; bites.

■ **Indications**

Bronchial asthma. Coccyalgia. Brain concussion or contusion. Depression. Nerve injury. *Neuralgia. Neuritis.* Phantom limb pain.

■ **Compare**

Arnica, Calendula, Ledum, Natrum sulphuricum, Ruta, Rhus toxicodendron, Staphysagria.

Ignatia

Strachnos ignatii, ignatia amara, St. Ignatius bean. A plant indigenous of the Philippines and belonging, like Nux vomica, Gelsemium and Curare, to the Loganiaceae family.

Generalities

Physical and mental exhaustion from prolonged, silent **grief. Paradoxical, contradictory reactions**. Symptoms are only of superficial nature and change quickly from one spot another. Periodicity. Trembling, twitching of muscles. *Hypersensitivity* to pain.

Mind and Emotions

Romantic and realistic; conflict between romance or romanticism and reality leads to disappointment. Artistic; desire to travel. Contradictory; hypersensitive; introverted; easily offended. State of mind changes suddenly: Cheerfulness comes soon after grief, laughing after weeping. Silent grief. Aversion to consolation; consolation aggravates symptoms; aversion to company. Jealousy. Laughs spasmodically when in grief or after getting bad news. Hysterical weeping, sighing, yawning. Irritable, quarrelsome, angry. Intolerant of contradiction. Conscientous about details. Blames self. Hallucinations. Unconsciousness, especially after emotional excitement. Great anxiety and fear. Broods over everything, pessimistic about everything; great despair. *Suicide* by drowning. Dreams of water.

Head

Sweating predominantly or exclusively on the face. *Migraine*: Headache; as if from a nail driven into one temple; improved by passing large quantities of pale urine. Cramps, *chorea*. Ringing in the ears; improved by loud noise. When talking or chewing, patient bites into one side of tongue or the inner part of cheek. Toothache; improved by chewing, worse at rest.

■ **Throat**

Sore throat; improved by swallowing hard bits of food. Sensation of a lump in throat, which disappears while swallowing and is felt only when not swallowing. *Globus hystericus*. Formication in *larynx*.

■ **Respiratory System**

Nervous, spasmodic and tickling cough. Wants to take a deep breath. Aversion to tobacco smoke.

■ **Digestive Tract**

Cravings: cheese, salt, fruit. Aversions: **fruit.** Tolerates even near-indigestible foods, but cannot tolerate easily digestible food. Hunger and empty feeling in stomach around 2 am; not improved by eating. Weakness in pit of stomach. Stomach cramps from agitation. *Constipation*; worse from riding in a car. *Diarrhea* from emotions. Spasms in *rectum*. Violent stinging pain extending upwards into the *rectum*. Hemorrhoids improved by walking. Cramps in *esophagus*. Fits of hiccups.

■ **Urinary Tract and Genitals**

Strong sexual arousal accompanied by impotence. Absence of *menses* from grief.

■ **Modalities**

Aggravation: Grief, excitement, nicotine/tobacco smoke, alcohol, sweets, coffee, cold, touch, motion, strong smells, noises, light, morning.
Amelioration: Warmth, strong pressure, change of posture or position, swallowing, walking, lying on affected side, travelling, during rain.
Side most often affected: Right.

■ **Causation**

Loss, separation, death of a loved one, disappointed love, bad news, any disappointment. Emotional stress, emotional trauma, shock, **grief.**

- **Indications**

  Adiposity. Amenorrhea. Arrhythmia. Arthritis. Backache. *Bronchial asthma. Bulimia. Chorea.* Cough. *Chronic fatigue syndrome.* Depression. *Dysmenorrhea. Encephalitis. Gastric and duodenal ulcers. Gastritis. Globus hystericus.* Headache. *Hirsutism.* Migraine. *Rectal fissures. Rectal prolapse,* Rectal spasms. Spasms. Tics

- **Compare**

  Calcarea phosphorica, Causticum, China, Natrum muriaticum, Nux vomica, Platina, Sepia, Strychninum.

Iodium

Iodine is one of the chemical elements.

■ **Generalities**

Striking emaciation and debilitation progressing rapidly despite having a good appetite. Constant feeling of heat and fever along with restlessness. Sweating. Glands swollen and indurated.

■ **Mind and Emotions**

Excitation, unbearable, anxious **restlessness**; hurry; chaotic hustle and bustle; talkative. When resting, anxiety and frightening impulses and ideas, **improved by keeping occupied.** Fear of people and the doctor. Vexed, morose, sad; *suicidal*. Forgets what must be done or said. Constant feeling of having forgotten something, has to check again and again. Compulsive behavior.

■ **Head**

Pulsating, *congestion*, feels as if bound; *vertigo. Congestive* headache, worse when in warm air. Hair falls out.

■ **Throat**

Enlargement of thyroid, hard goiter along with a feeling of constriction.

■ **Chest**

Palpitation at slightest exertion. Sensation as if the heart were compressed or grasped by an iron hand.

■ **Digestive Tract**

Voracious appetite, eats frequently and large amounts, often thirsty; *continual* emaciation nonetheless. Always hungry; generally feels much better while eating or after having eaten. Hiccups; empty eructations, as if everything eaten turns into air. *Constipation*, improved by drinking cold milk. Foamy, watery diarrhea in the morning.

■ Respiratory System

Violent and acrid *coryza*, stuffy nose when indoors; runny nose in the open air. Dry, hacking cough, worse when the air is warm; grasps throat when coughing. Hoarseness. Pseudocroup. Breathing is wheezy and rasping. Shortness of breath and feels weak when climbing stairs.

■ Urinary Tract and Reproductive System

Shrinking of breasts with soreness. Profuse bleeding from *uterus*; cancer of *uterus*. Chronic, thick, yellow *leukorrhea* that is copious and caustic enough to make holes in underwear. *Testes* are indurated and swollen or *atrophic*. Hydrocele.

■ Modalities

Aggravation: Heat, warmth; exertion; fasting; rest; near the sea; morning.

Amelioration: Moving around in the open air and in cool air; **eating;** occupation, activity.

■ Indications

Adenopathy. Allergy. Anxiety. *Arrhythmia. Bronchial asthma. Bronchitis. Cachexia.* Compulsive behavior. *Diarrhea. Enlarged prostate. Goiter.* Hay fever. *Hydrocele.* Hyperthyroidism. Leukorrhea. Pneumonia. Pseudocroup. *Rhinitis.*

■ Compare

Argentum nitricum, Arsenicum album, Bromium, Conium, Fluoricum acidum, Lachesis, Lycopodium, Phosphorus, Spongia, Tarantula, Tuberculinum.

Ipecacuanha

Uragoga ipecacuanha, ipecacuanha root (N.O. Rubiaceae). This plant grows in the Brazilian rain forest.

■ Generalities

Ailments tend to recur periodically, especially attacks during the night, mostly every other day. Spasms. *Hemorrhages* with bright red blood from all orifices. All conditions are accompanied by constant *nausea* that is not improved by **vomiting**. Patient looks pale and exhausted. Warm-blooded.

■ Mind and Emotions

Ill-tempered, irritable mood; not easily satisfied; has many wishes, but does not really know what it is that he wants. Sadness.

■ Head

Headache, shattered feeling through the entire skull to the root of the tongue. One-sided migraine above one eye along with *nausea*.

■ Digestive Tract

Constant *nausea* that cannot be relieved, even by vomiting. Vomiting of white, profuse mucus similar to egg whites; no relief; afterwards patient feels numbed, but *nausea* stays on. Vomiting of bright red blood with *nausea*. Tongue is clean, sometimes just slightly coated with a whitish fur. Patient has to swallow constantly due to persistent *salivation*. Incontrollable vomiting during pregnancy. Thirstless. Exhausted, sunken and empty feeling in stomach, as if it were hanging down. Stomach disorders from fatty, indigestible, mixed foods. Abdominal cramps, *colic* and *tenesmus*. Stool is fermented, slimy, frothy; or grass-green, slimy or watery or sticky, or else diarrhea mixed with greater or lesser amounts of blood.

Respiratory System

Profuse mucus. Spasms, *obstruction*. Asthma attacks with great difficulty breathing, wheezy rattling and coughing attacks with difficult *expectoration* and gelatinous sputum as well as bluish discoloration of lips. Dry spasmodic cough with choking and vomiting. Bleeding from nose or mouth as in whooping cough. Children: suffocating cough, causing child to go blue in the face and stiffen. Nosebleed; coughing up blood.

Urinary Tract and Reproductive System

Profuse, gushing *hemorrhages* from *uterus*, bright red color; *menses* too early and too heavy; along with *nausea*. Weakness after *menses*.

Modalities

Aggravation: Variation in temperature, extreme temperatures; motion; humidity, damp heat, heat; in the evening, at night; vomiting; stooping.
Amelioration: Rest; fresh air.
Side most often affected: Right.

Indications

Bronchial asthma. *Bronchitis*. *Bronchopneumonia Enteritis*. *Epistaxis*. *Gastritis*. *Gastroenteritis*. *Hemorrhagic diathesis*. *Hyperemesis gravidarum*. *Menorrhagia*. *Metrorrhagia*. *Migraine*. *Obstructive bronchitis*. *Pertussis*. *Pneumonia*. Seasickness.

Compare

Antimonium crudum, Antimonium tartaricum, Arsenicum album, China, Cuprum, Kali carbonicum, Kali sulphuricum, Nux vomica, Pulsatilla, Sanguinaria, Tabacum.

Kali bichromicum

Potassium bichromate, bichromate of potash, $K_2[(CrO_2)(CrO_4)]$. Dark red crystals that are not affected by air, but dissolve in cold water.

Generalities

Extremely sticky, clinging, ropy, viscous, yellow discharges in the form of long strings; gelatinous mucus. *Ulcers* on the skin and the mucous membranes, extending deep into the tissue, as if from a hole punch. Great sensitivity to cold. **Pain in small areas,** tiny spots the size of a fingertip. Pain comes and goes suddenly. Obesity.

Mind and Emotions

Closed, serious, reserved, very correct, efficient, conscientious, exact, conservative, dogmatic, narrow-minded. Sticks to routine. Explanations are long-winded and elaborate. Materialistic. Avoids other people, afraid of people. Very irritable when disturbed; easily discouraged, sullen, easily offended, angry. Indifference. Sluggishness, aversion to mental and physical work. Weak memory and concentration.

Head

Headache on right side above the eyebrow. Before a migraine attack vision is disturbed. Pain in bones of skull and head. Headache during *sinusitis* that improves when discharge starts.

Digestive Tract

Sensation of a hair at the back of the tongue. During hot weather stomach problems get worse. Desire for sweets and beer, but intolerant of beer; *nausea* and vomiting after drinking beer. Stomach trouble alternating with rheumatism or asthma.

Respiratory system

Constant *sinusitis* with pain in facial bones in circumscribed areas, painful pressure above bridge of nose, loss of sense of smell together with huge quantities of secretions, which are extremely viscous, stringy, sticky, purulent and yellow-green with lots of bloody and crusty matter. Husky cough and hoarseness with viscous *expectoration* that does not dissolve easily.

■ Back and Extremities

Rheumatic pain improved by motion. Joint pain moving to different places in the body, coming and going suddenly. Diagonal pains. Creaking in joints. Rheumatic pain in fingers.

■ Modalities

Aggravation: Morning starting at 3 am, 2 to 3 am or **2 to 5** am, on waking; cold weather, cold; after sex; coffee, beer; motion; summer.
Amelioration: Warm and damp weather, warmth; bed warmth; rest; in the open air; during the day; bending forward; eating.
Side most often affected: Right.

■ Causation

Bad effects from drinking beer.

■ Indications

Adiposity. Allergy. *Arthritis. Bronchial asthma.* Backache. *Bronchitis. Gastric and duodenal ulcers. Gastritis.* Headache. *Laryngitis.* Migraine. *Neuralgia. Pneumonia.* Pseudocroup. *Rhinitis. Sciatica. Sinusitis.*

■ Compare

Bromium, Cinnabaris, Hepar sulphuris, Hydrastis, Mercurius, Phytolacca, Pulsatilla, Silicea, Thuja.

Kali carbonicum

Potassium carbonate, K_2CO_3, Potash.

■ Generalities

Generalized weakness, exhaustion, fatigue. **Stinging**, burning and tearing **pain.** Extremely prone to common colds. Sensitive to drafts, chilly; sweating. Proneness to *edema*. When a Kali carbonicum patient is suffering from a severe disease that has come on gradually, he sees the doctor late—often too late.

Carbonate of Potassium   Photo: DHU

■ Mind and Emotions

Conscientious, extremely correct, disciplined, **in control,** serious, tidy, persnickety, always on time, stingy, rigid, inflexible, dogmatic, conservative, intolerant. Rational person of rigid principles. Controlled by his intellect. Conception of the world: black or white, yes or no, right or wrong, good or bad. Professions like police officer, public prosecutor, translator, accountant. Denies feeling fear and other emotional states. Anxiety about health; fears in the dark: ghosts, being alone, the future, losing control, poverty. Extreme irritability while suffering from physical ailments. Very irritable when at home, discontented and quarrelsome. Loses temper over trifles. Impatient with own children. Dependent on family; desires company; but treats others badly. Talks to self. Easily frightened, especially by noises or touch; aversion to touch.

■ Head

Edema around the eyes; especially in the area **between eyebrows and upper lids.** Bags under eyes. Headache: pressing, tearing and stinging.

▪ Digestive Tract

Craves sweets. Sensation of water in stomach. **Fear is felt in stomach.** Anxious, cold, empty and frail feeling in stomach. *Colic* in upper *abdomen* extending to the back, improved by pressure. *Flatulence.* Alternately diarrhea or *constipation*. *Constipation* occurs especially before and during *menses*. Painful hemorrhoids, bleeding when stool is hard.

▪ Respiratory System

Dry, violent, paroxysmal and hacking cough together with stinging pain, choking and vomiting. Symptoms get worse when lying down. When coughing and during an asthma attack, patient has to sit up and bend forward using elbows and knees to lean on. Breathing difficult around 3 am. Respiratory diseases are accompanied by stinging pain in right lower part of the chest extending to the back.

▪ Urinary Tract and Reproductive System

Urge to pass urine when excited. Kidney conditions. Kidney stones along with stinging pain. Kidney *failure* together with edema.
Aversion to and aggravation from sex. Violent pain in lower back before and during *menses*. Period late or absent. Labor delayed, together with violent back pain. Proneness to *abortion* during early pregnancy; back pain after miscarriage.

▪ Back and Extremities

Back pain around 3 am, extending to buttocks and thighs; patient has to get up. Back pain and *sciatica* get worse when turning over in bed, to such an extent that turning is almost impossible. Weakness in back improved by lying flat on the back. Curvature of the spine. Inflammation in joints, including deformities.

▪ Sleep

Sleeplessness; wakes at 2 or 3 am and stays awake, or cannot fall asleep again before 4 or 5 am. Twitching when falling asleep. Screaming in sleep; starting awake from sound sleep at night. Dreams of ghosts, danger, robbers, falling or horrific creatures. Sleep unrefreshing.

■ **Modalities**

Aggravation: 2 to 4 am; cold, drafts; after sex; beginning of *menses* and during *menses*; touch; lying on the affected side.
Amelioration: Warmth; walking around; during the day.
Side most often affected: Right.

■ **Indications**

Abortion. Allergy. *Bronchial asthma. Bronchitis. Cardiac* insufficiency. *Cholelithiasis. Gastric and duodenal ulcers.* Headache. Hemorrhoids. *Hypertension.* Migraine. *Nephrolithiasis. Pertussis. Pleurisy. Pneumonia.* Renal insufficiency. *Sciatica. Sinusitis.* Sleeplessness. *Uterine myoma.*

■ **Compare**

Arsenicum album, Bryonia, Calcarea carbonica, Dulcamara, Lycopodium, Natrum muriaticum, Nitricum acidum, Nux vomica, Phosphorus, Sepia, Silicea, Stannum.

Kali phosphoricum
Potassium phosphate, KH_2PO_4.

▪ Generalities
Marked exhaustion, especially after mental exertion. Patients do not recover easily after a serious disease, surgery, chemotherapy or influenza. Fatigue, weakness, emaciation, *anemia*. Chilly. **Discharges of golden yellow color** with a foul or carrion smell.

▪ Mind and Emotions
Burnout syndrome causes loss of self-control and desire to be alone. Depletion of the nervous system due to overwork, strain. Outgoing. Desire for travel. Nervousness, irritability, impatience. Cursing at night. Perverted emotions: aversion to people he is close to, his own family. Cruel toward spouse. Mental fatigue, lethargy. Slightest task seems like hard work. Discontented, suspicious, sad, despondent, weary of life. Homesickness. Alternating moods. Anxiety. **Anxiety** about: being alone, sickness, death, the future. Sensitive to noise, *hypersensitivity* of all senses. **Jumpiness.** Sleeplessness. Weak memory. Confusion; delusions; sees dead people, shapes. Horrible visions. Essence according to Scholten: Patient is obliged to continue studies and preserve friendships.

▪ Head
Headache; worse from mental exertion. Eyelids droop, especially on the left side. After *sex* everythings looks hazy. Chronic acrid, purulent, offensive discharges from the ear.

▪ Digestive Tract
Cravings: Cold drinks and food, sweets, vinegar, salt and fish. Aversions: Bread, meat, salt and fish. Revolting bad breath, like rotten cheese. Dry mouth in the morning. Nervous feeling of emptiness in stomach. Gnawing stomach pain in the early morning. Flatus. Intestinal catarrh

along with painless, stinking diarrhea; aggravation in the morning; complaints are of nervous origin.

■ Urinary Tract and Reproductive System

Urine has a strong yellow color. *Menses* irregular. Offensive-smelling menstrual discharge or *leukorrhea*. Uterine inertia.

■ Extremities

Pain in joints; improved by motion and heat. Twitching in muscles and limbs. Cannot keep feet still. *Paralysis; hemiplegia.*

■ Modalities

Aggravation: Cold, winter; **sex;** at night; 3 am (2-5 am) and 9 pm; in the morning; mental exertion and emotional excitement, worries, mental fatigue; motion, walking/running.

Amelioration: Eating; cloudy weather; heat; slow movement; company; sleep.

Side most often affected: Right.

■ Causation

Ailments from: excitement; overwork; bad news, grief; persistent worries.

■ Indications

Anxiety. *Chronic fatigue syndrome. Diarrhea.* Headache. Indigestion. *Multiple Sclerosis. Neurasthenia. Vaginitis.*

■ Compare

Calcarea carbonica, Gelsemium, Phosphorus, Phosphoricum acidum, Picrinicum acidum.

Kali sulphuricum

Potassium sulphate, K_2SO_4.

■ Generalities

Warm-blooded. Cold hands and feet accompany all complaints. **Profuse yellow or greenish discharges,** especially from mucous membranes. A lot of sweating. Entire body pulsates. "Irritable Pulsatilla".

■ Mind and Emotions

Likes to help; delighted when are able to make others happy. Kind, gentle. **Stubborn, obstinate.** Great irritability. Always in a hurry; excited, impatient, impetuous. Lack of self-confidence; discouraged; unhappy with everything. Timidity. Self-pity. Irresolution. Mood swings. Crying. Consolation makes symptoms worse. Fears: in the evening when in bed; at night; when waking; at night: fear of death, falling, people. Startles at trifles. *Hypersensitivity* to noises. **Lazy and lethargic.** Aversion to work and company. Concentration difficult; confusion. Forgets what he was about to do or say. Essence according to Scholten: Patient feels she must bring love and joy to other people.

■ Sleep

Terrifying dreams of ghosts, death, robbers and murder.

■ Head

Headache; starting in the evening; violent, pulsating, boring; or stinging. Forehead feels hot. Bald spots; hair loss. Dandruff and cradle cap.

■ Ears

Watery, sticky, thin and yellow secretion causing soreness in the ear. Impaired hearing from syringitis.

■ Digestive Tract

Aversions: eggs, bread, meat, hot food and drinks.

Cravings: sweets, sour, cold food and drinks.
Aggravation: eggs. Burning thirst; *nausea* and vomiting. Eructations, bloating, feels full and heavy after eating. Empty feeling and coldness in stomach. Persistent *constipation*; alternating with diarrhea. Hemorrhoids. Violent itching around *anus*. Yellow-coated tongue.

■ Respiratory System

Thickening of mucous membranes with mouth breathing and snoring; also after *adenotomy*. Yellow, slimy *coryza*. Blocked nose; loss of sense of smell. Hay fever. Hoarseness. Cough is loose with rattling noise from mucus. Yellow, slimy *expectoration*. Cough wakes patient at 2 am.

■ Extremities

Rheumatic pain in joints or any other part of the body, characterized by changing and wandering nature. *Edema*. Heaviness. Cold hands and feet.

■ Skin

Flaking skin. Dry skin; burning and itching. Thin, yellow, watery fluid is discharged from *ulcers*. Inflammation along with pimples containing pus.

■ Modalities

Aggravation: Warmth, in warm room, in the evening; rest; exertion; overheating; drafts; after eating; 3 and 5 am.
Amelioration: In the open, in fresh air; walking.
Side most often affected: Left.

■ Causation

Suppressed skin eruptions.

■ Indications

Adenopathy. Allergy. *Alopecia. Angina tonsillaris. Arthritis. Bronchial asthma. Bronchitis.* Colds. Eczema. Hay fever. Headache. *Otitis media. Psoriasis.* Rheumatism. *Sinusitis.* Tuberculosis.

■ **Compare**
Calcarea sulphurica, Pulsatilla, Sanguinaria, Sulphur.

Lac caninum
Dog's milk.

▪ Generalities
Complaints switch sides; symptoms wander from one side to the other and back again; wandering complaints. Bleeds easily. Hypersensitive to noises, light and touch.

▪ Mind and Emotions
Heightened imagination and excitability of all senses; passion. **Fear of snakes,** fainting, death, diseases, dogs, spiders, storms. Nervous, extroverted, restless, sensitive, melancholic, hopeless. Feeling of being looked down on, insignificance. **Low self-esteem,** even self-contempt; little self-confidence. Aggression; maliciousness; hatred; anger; rage; swearing and cursing. Very forgetful and absent-minded. Makes mistakes when speaking or writing. **Floating sensation.**

▪ Head
Vertigo, feels as if floating in the air. Headaches starting at 2 am. Headache changes sides.

▪ Throat
Pain in throat that changes quickly from one side to the other. Pain moves to the ears and is improved by cold drinks. Diphtherial coating, shiny, lacquered appearance.

▪ Digestive Tract
Craves salt and pepper; warm drinks, whiskey. Intolerance of milk. Enormous hunger; as hungry after eating as before. Spasmodic pain in *abdomen,* improved by bending backwards.

▪ Urinary Tract and Reproductive System
Swelling and pain in breasts before and during *menses.* Breasts and throat are painful during the period; blood flows in gushes. *Mastitis*

along with great sensitivity and tenderness in breasts; worse from slightest vibration. Little milk in nursing women; *galactorrhea*. Definite intensification of sexual arousal when touching breasts and genitals.

■ Modalities

Aggravation: Cold; rest; morning; touch, vibration; before and during *menses*.

Amelioration: Warmth; motion; in fresh air; cold applications.

■ Indications

Allergy. *Angina tonsillaris*. Diphtheria. *Dysmenorrhea. Galactorrhea. Gastritis. Mastitis*. Migraine. *Pharyngitis*. Phobia. *Premenstrual syndrome. Vertigo*.

■ Compare

Argentum nitricum, Conium, Lac felinum, Lachesis, Phosphorus, Pulsatilla.

Lachesis

Lachesis muta or surucucu, bushmaster (N.O. Crotalidae). Snake native to Central and South America. The fresh venom discharged during its bite is used to make the remedy. The snake measures 3.6 m. Its bite is usually deadly. Hering proved the remedy on himself, which almost killed him and permanently paralyzed his left arm.

■ Generalities

Essence: overstimulation seeking an outlet. Extraordinary sensitivity to touch, especially near **throat** and waist. *Hypersensitivity* to heat and noise. Extreme loquacity. Great mental and emotional agitation that in many cases is relieved by endless talking. *Hemorrhages.* Blood coagulation is impaired. Crimson discoloration. Skin of the affected area is bluish-red, almost black, and

Bushmaster Snake   Photo: DHU

extremely tender. Complaints get worse before and after a night's sleep.

■ Mind and Emotions

The fundamental conflict exists between aggressive and sexual impulses on the one hand and the dictates of conscience on the other. The consequence is a *hypersensitivity* and hyperreflexia. Behind the sexual and aggressive excitement lies a primal fear. **Loquacity; jealousy,** envy, hatred, mockery, **sarcasm,** annoyance, quarrelsomeness, vehemence, anger, violence.

Overestimates self. Malicious, proud, insulting, suspicious, blames others, egotistical, passionate, intense, moralistic. Mental overstimulation. Vivid imagination, alertness. Workaholic, hurried, thinks and acts quickly. Lack of time, impatience. Desire to travel. Desire for entertainment. Intolerant of emotional excitement or any psychological pressure. Withdrawn and easily hurt. **Fear** of the unknown; dying in sleep; **snakes;** poison; poisoning; heart conditions; insanity; the future; anxiety about health; about spiritual welfare. Confusion, lack of concentration. Weak memory, but very good in the evening. Speech confused, hasty, incoherent, slow, strays from subject and changes subjects rapidly, speaks in a strange language; an eloquent speaker nevertheless. Sharp-tongued. **Hallucinations:** feeling of being under superhuman control; persecuted by enemies, being poisoned; guilt. Sadness, forsaken feeling on waking, melancholy, suspicion along with aversion to people, *apathy*, loathing of life. Sleeplessness. Alcoholism, drug addiction.

■ Head

Headache after being in the sun; face very pale. Bursting and pressing pain in temples, worsened by motion, pressure, stooping; heaviness and pressure on vertex. Sensation as if there were lead in occiput. *Convulsions; tetanic* rigidity; *paralysis.* Shaky and weak.

■ Throat

Left-sided *pharyngitis*; going from left to right. *Tonsillitis.* Sore throat: worse from swallowing, especially fluids or saliva, ameliorated when swallowing solid food. Sensation of a lump in the throat. Intolerant of tight collars, roll necks, necklaces. Aversion to being touched around the throat.

■ Cardiovascular System

Hypertension. Various heart problems. Feeling of suffocation when falling asleep. Hot flushes. *Palpitations* worse when lying on the left side, at night, in sleep. Tightness in chest. Varicose veins.

■ Digestive Tract

Cravings: pasta, oysters, spicy food, alcohol (whiskey), coffee; during *dysmenorrhea*. Aversions: wine.

Aggravation: alcohol. Coffee during *menopause*. Cold and warm food. Intolerant of tight clothes around the *abdomen*. Constriction around *anus*. Hemorrhoids: congested, incarcerated, crimson color.

■ **Sleep**

Respiration stops during sleep, causing patient to wake up in a fright, afraid of suffocating. Asthmatic breathing during or after sleep. Cannot lie on left side.

■ **Modalities**

Aggravation: After sleep, in the morning when waking; rest; slightest constriction; **warmth,** summer, warm room, warm bath; extreme temperatures; spring/fall; suppressed discharges; suppressed sexuality; before *menses,* during *menopause,* during pregnancy; wine, beer, tobacco.

Amelioration: All discharges (*menses, coryza* among others); fresh air; **motion.**

Side most often affected: Left; complaints that move from left to right.

■ **Causation**

Bad effects of disappointments, fear, grief, excitement, disappointed love, conflicts, jealousy.

■ **Indications**

Alcoholism. *Angina pectoris. Angina tonsillaris. Apoplexy. Arrhythmia.* Behavior disorders. *Cardiac* valvular diseases. *Claudicatio intermittens.* Colitis. *Diarrhea.* Diphtheria. Drug addiction. *Emphysema. Endometriosis.* Epilepsy. *Epistaxis.* Gastric and duodenal ulcers. *Globus hystericus. Hemoptysis. Hemorrhage. Hemorrhagic diathesis.* Hemorrhoids. *Hepatitis. Herpes zoster.* Hot flushes. *Hypertension.* Hypertensive crisis. *Hyperthyroidism.* Malignant diseases. Manic-depressive conditions. Menopausal complaints. *Metrorrhagia.* Migraine. *Myocardial infarction.* Nephritis. *Nephrolithiasis.* Otitis media. Ovarian *cysts.* Paranoia. *Pharyngitis. Polycythemia. Purpura. Retinal vascular bleeding. Sciatica.* Scarlet fever. *Septicemia.* Sleeplessness. *Thyroiditis.*

■ Compare

Apis, Cactus grandiflorus, Cimicifuga, Crotalus horridus, Hyoscyamus, Lac caninum, Medorrhinum, Naja, Phosphorus, Platina, Sulphur, Zincum.

Ledum

Ledum palustre, marsh tea, labrador tea (N.O. Ericaceae).

- **Generalities**

Generalized lack of vital heat; patient feels cold to the touch; symptoms are nevertheless aggravated by external heat and bed warmth. Affected limbs feel cold; yet pain is relieved by ice-cold applications. **Pain starts in lower extremities and ascends upward;** pain shooting upward. Left

Marsh Tea   Photo: Sertürner

shoulder and right hip joint are most often affected. Prone to bleeding. Night sweats with desire to remove covers. Bad effects of stab wounds.

- **Mind and Emotions**

Loner; aversion to company; fear of people. **Misanthropist.** Morose, sour; annoyed, irascible; sad.

- **Head**

Black eye after being struck, along with violent pain within the eye.

- **Urinary Tract and Reproductive System**

Red urinary sediment; the more sediment there is, the better the patient feels.

- **Extremities**

Rheumatism along with swollen, hot and pale joints. *Edematous* swelling and external coldness in joints. Pain and stiffness are worse at night when in a warm bed; improved when in cold water. Painful tenderness of soles. Hard nodes and deposits on ankles and later on wrists. Sensitivity to pressure in *periosteum* of fingers and toes. **Tendency to sprain ankles.**

■ Skin

Stab wounds, bites; insect bites or stings if the puncture is cold, swollen and mottled and is alleviated by cold compresses. Long-lasting discoloration of the skin after injuries. Eczema with violent inflammation of the skin. *Abscesses,* improved by cold applications. *Hematoma, purpura.*

■ Modalities

Aggravation: Warmth, bed warmth; at night; motion; wine and beer.
Amelioration: Cold, dipping painful limb in ice-cold water; rest.
Side most often affected: Upper left and lower right side.

■ Causation

Bad effects of injuries, especially stab wounds; chronic alcohol abuse.

■ Indications

Abscess. Arthritis. Bites. *Ecchymosis.* Eczema. *Erysipelas.* Gout. Rheumatism. Sprains. Stab wounds.

■ Compare

Apis, Arnica, Bellis perennis,
Bryonia, Hamamelis, Hypericum, Pulsatilla, Rhus toxicodendron, Ruta, Symphytum.

Lilium tigrinum

Tiger Lily (N.O. Liliaceae).

◾ Generalities

Lilium tigrinum has a strong effect on the pelvic organs. Pulsating, throbbing, fullness in the entire body. Pain in circumscribed areas, changing location quickly and suddenly. **Warm-blooded; burning palms and soles.** Mental symptoms alternate with physical symptoms.

Tiger Lily   Photo: DHU

◾ Mind and Emotions

Deep conflict between strong sexual desire and a marked moralistic/religious side. Fears eternal damnation. Worried about spiritual welfare. Torments self with religious ideas. Desperation about **religious matters** alternating with sexual arousal. Aversion to entertainment. Extreme irritability, anger, rage. Fearful, throws and strikes with objects. **Impatient,** nervous, saucy. Tearfulness. **Easily hurt;** consolation makes it worse. Alternating states: pleasure/guilt, anger/remorse; anger after sexual excitement. Constant restlessness as if from imperative duties that can't possibly be fulfilled. Harassed, **hurried;** fruitless and aimless hustle and bustle. Restlessness: **has to keep busy to suppress sexual desires.** Concentration difficult; confusion of ideas. Fear of impending disease, mental disease; that something is going to happen.

◾ Head

Wild sensation in head and *vertigo.* Blood *congestion* going to the head along with headache, better in the open air.

■ Chest

Nervous heart condition with anxiety. Violent, brief cardiac pain with intense *palpitations*. Sensation as if heart were being held or constricted by an iron ring, or as if grasped by an iron hand. *Palpitations*, worse when lying on the right side. Quickening of pulse, especially when in bed.

■ Digestive Tract

Craves meat. Feeling of bearing down and heaviness in the entire abdominal viscera. Constant urge to pass stool. Spasms in *anus*, frequently accompanying bladder conditions. Early morning diarrhea.

■ Urinary Tract and Reproductive System

Frequent urge to urinate. Sexual overstimulation. **Bearing-down feeling within female genital organs,** as if pelvic organs were about to come out through *vagina*; to prevent this she has to press her hand against her *vulva* or cross her legs. Menstrual blood flows only when walking; stops when standing or lying down.

■ Modalities

Aggravation: In a warm room, warmth; when lying on the right side, walking, standing up; between 5 and 8 pm, in the evening and at night; after *sex;* miscarriages; after anger or emotional agitation, consolation.
Amelioration: In the open air, walking in fresh air; motion, occupation, lying on the left side.
Side most often affected: Left.

■ Indications

Arrhythmia. Colitis. Cystitis. Depression. *Dysmenorrhea.* Headache. *Palpitations. Premenstrual syndrome.* Sexual disorders. *Uterine prolapse. Vertigo.*

■ **Compare**

Apis, Cactus grandiflorus, Helonias, Lachesis, Medorrhinum, Murex, Nux vomica, Platina, Sepia.

Lycopodium
Lycopodium clavatum, spores of club moss (N.O. Lycopodiaceae).

■ Generalities
Skinny person with an emaciated, furrowed face, rings round eyes and a yellowish complexion. Emaciation of the upper part of the body. Physical weakness coupled with strong intellect.

Spores of Club Moss   Photo: DHU

■ Mind and Emotions
Internal conflict between cowardice and egotism. **Lack of self-confidence; cowardice.** Feels inadequacy; but presents self as strong, competent and courageous; exaggerates and tells unbelievable stories. Ambition; love of power; arrogance; vanity; egotism. **Dictatorial and tyrannical, especially in familiar surroundings;** critical of others. Toady mentality, bows to those above and kicks those below. Afraid of new situations, of doing something new; anticipation; stage fright; fear of appearing in public. Fear of responsibility. Very irritable, irascible; intolerant of contradiction; depressed, melancholy. Sentimental. Fear in the dark, of ghosts. Fear of people and aversion to company, but afraid of being alone; prefers to have somebody in the room next door. Keen intellect; irony or even sarcasm. Anxiety about health; hypochondriasis. Striking loss of memory.

■ Head
Headache from overheating, improved by cold.

- **Throat**

  Constriction, cannot swallow either solid food or liquids. Ulcerative inflammation of tonsils along with stinging pain when swallowing. *Tonsillitis* starts on the right side extending to the left.

- **Digestive Tract**

  Craves sweets and warm drinks. Aversion to cold drinks. Ravenous hunger, satisfied after a few mouthfuls; extreme bloating immediately after eating even the smallest quantity. **Distension of** *abdomen* **from** *flatulence*; intolerant of onions and garlic. Improved by passing flatus and eructations. Liver disorders. Intestinal hypomotility. At first stool is almost always very hard and difficult to evacuate, becoming soft in the end. After passing stool, lingering feeling as if a major part of the stool hasn't come out yet.

- **Respiratory System**

  Fan-like flaring of nostrils. Blocked nose at night. Asthma; chronic irritable cough.

- **Urinary Tract and Reproductive System**

  Transparent urine with a sediment like red sand. Offensive-smelling urine. Burning in *urethra* when urinating. Kidney stones on right side. Promiscuity. Impotence from sexual excesses. Premature *ejaculation* or loss of erection during sex. "One-night stands" due to avoiding responsibility. *Frigidity*. Sexual disorders appear mostly within marriage.

- **Back and Extremities**

  Backache improved by urination. Burning heat between shoulder blades. Right foot is cold, left is warm. Painful tenderness of soles.

- **Skin**

  Cracks in heels. Eczema, *psoriasis*, warts.

■ Sleep

Sleeps on right side. Wakes at night from hunger. Wakes unrefreshed in the morning and wants to go on sleeping.

■ Modalities

Aggravation: 4 to 8 pm; warmth, muggy weather, in a closed room; after sleep; warm applications; pressure of clothes; presence of strangers.

Amelioration: In the open air; uncovering; cold applications; motion; warm drinks and meals.

Side most often affected: Right; symptoms move from the right side to the left.

■ Indications

Allergy. *Angina tonsillaris. Arthritis. Bronchial asthma. Bronchitis. Cholecystitis. Colitis. Constipation. Cystitis.* Depression. Eczema. *Chronic fatigue syndrome. Gastric and duodenal ulcers.* Gout. Headache. Hemorrhoids. *Hepatitis.* Hepatocirrhosis. *Hepatopathy. Hypertension.* Impotence. Migraine. *Nephrolithiasis. Neuralgia. Pharyngitis. Pneumonia. Psoriasis. Pyelonephritis. Sinusitis. Urethritis.* Warts.

■ Compare

Argentum nitricum, Arsenicum album, Aurum, Bryonia, Carbo vegetabilis, Chelidonium, China, Graphites, Magnesia muriatica, Medorrhinum, Natrum muriaticum, Nitricum acidum, Nux vomica, Phosphoricum acidum, Platina, Silicea, Staphisagria, Sulphur.

Magnesia carbonica
Magnesium carbonate.

■ Generalities
Fatigue and weakness; *failure* to thrive, slow in learning to walk and stand. *Adiposity.* **Acid,** corrosive **discharges; sour smell.** Periodicity: every three weeks. Chilly. Bolts of shooting, violent pain together with sweats. **Entire body is exhausted and aches, especially lower legs and feet. Children:** aggressive, annoying; very sensitive, nervous, easily exhausted, look pale and sick; headache in schoolchildren, also at night.

■ Mind and Emotions
Overwhelming nervous depletion. **Forsaken feeling.** Feels unloved by parents. Fear of aggression or violence. **Peacemaker.** Has the idea that aggression is either important for self-esteem, or else extremely detrimental. Extreme readiness for aggression, also auto-aggression, like hitting head against wall. Feeling of not being recognized. Ambivalence: very active/withdrawn and anxious; quarrelsomeness/fear of conflict. Anxiety, great fear of the future. Timorous, crazy, irritable, restless. Fear of being abandoned; disease; the doctor. Convinced he is suffering from an incurable disease. *Hypersensitivity*; sensitive to noise.

■ Head
Toothache: worse at night when resting.

■ Digestive Tract
Craves meat. Aversion to vegetables and salad.
Gastrointestinal disorders with pronounced hyperacidity. Weight loss despite eating a lot. **Intolerant of milk,** even mother's milk. In breast-fed children, milk passes undigested or is regurgitated. Distension of *abdomen.* Diarrhea: Stool green and frothy, like frog eggs on a pond. Cutting, colicky pain before passing stool, causing patient to double up.

Often, especially at night, this type of diarrhea is accompanied by a dry cough.

■ Urinary Tract and Reproductive System

Dysmenorrhea. Menstrual flow stronger at night or while reclining, or only in sleep, stops when walking. Short menstrual cycle, every 21 days. *Coryza* before and during *menses.*

■ Sleep

Waking at 3 am; sleepless 3 to 4 am. Unrefreshed on waking: more tired on getting up than on going to bed. Sleepy during the day.

■ Modalities

Aggravation: Milk. At night; 3 am or 3 to 4 am. Cold, drafts; change of temperature. Rest, bed warmth. Pregnancy. **Before and during** *menses.* **Amelioration:** Moving about in the open air.

■ Indications

Chronic fatigue syndrome. Colic. Constipation. Dysmenorrhea. Failure to thrive. Gastritis. Hepatitis. Lactose intolerance. Neuralgia. Premenstrual syndrome. Sleeplessness.

■ Compare

Calcarea carbonica, China, Colocynthis, Hepar sulphuris, Lycopodium, Magnesia muriatica, Rheum.

Magnesia muriatica

Magnesium chloratum, magnesium chloride.

- ## Generalities

Desires fresh air though chilly.

- ## Mind and Emotions

Pacifist who cannot bear any argument and always tries to make peace. Great need for care and security. Strong sense of responsibility and duty. Depressiveness; silent, sullen and morose; feels deserted by everyone. Delusion of having no friends. The essence according to Scholten: the idea patient's or mother's aggression leads to loss of maternal/parental care. **Fears at night in bed.** Restlessness, especially in the evening in bed. Sensitive to noise.

- ## Head

Bursting headache and *neuralgia* improved by warm wrapping and pressure. Head sweat. Acne before *menses*.

- ## Chest

Palpitations when patient is resting, improved by moving about. Stitching pain around the heart.

- ## Digestive Tract

Toothache; unbearable when food is touching teeth. Improved by warm food. Dry mouth along with almost unquenchable thirst. Craves sweets, fruit and vegetables, especially cauliflower and broccoli. Aversion to sweets and meat. Teething children cannot digest milk. Diarrhea or abdominal pain worse from milk, fruit or fatty foods. Pressing pain in the liver area; liver feels hard and enlarged; worse from lying on the right side. Flatus, distended *abdomen*. Stools hard and crumbly like sheep dung, difficulty passing stool. *Constipation* during teething.

- **Urinary Tract and Reproductive System**

  Menses very painful with violent cramps; improved by pressure on the back or by rubbing the back. *Menses* dark, in black clots. Great agitation during *menses*.

- **Sleep**

  Entire body is restless when going to bed in the evening and closing eyes; during the night, restlessness makes patient leave the bed and constantly walk around the room. Disturbed sleep. **Unrefreshing sleep,** still tired in the morning.

- **Modalities**

  Aggravation: Cold; 3 am; salt, fatty foods and milk; lying on the right side; touch; at the seaside; rest.

  Amelioration: Firm pressure; walking around in the **open air**; heat on affected parts.

- **Causation**

  Excitement; swimming in the ocean.

- **Indications**

  Chronic fatigue syndrome. Constipation. Dentitio difficilis. Diarrhea. Dysmenorrhea. Gastritis. Headache. Hepatitis. Hepatopathy. Hepatocirrhosis. Neuralgia. Sleeplessness. Toothache.

- **Compare**

  China, other Magnesia salts, Natrum muriaticum, Lycopodium, Pulsatilla, Sepia.

Magnesia phosphorica
Magnesium phosphate.

- **Generalities**

  Remedy for all kinds of pain:
  violent, cutting, boring, piercing
  radiating, shooting, stinging
  pain, coming and going in
  flashes, frequently changing
  location, neuralgic and
  spasmodic pain.

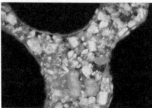

Phosphate of Magnesia   Photo: DHU

- **Mind and Emotions**

  Irritable, nervous,
  hypersensitive, sensitive, depressed, impulsive and passionate. Talks
  constantly about pain. Restless from pain. Many fears. Talks to self; sad
  taciturnity. Carries objects back and forth. Incapable of thinking clearly;
  sleepiness when trying to study. Essence according to Scholten: The idea
  that patient will lose all contact with friends if temper is displayed.

- **Head**

  Headache that starts in nape of neck or in occiput, extending to the
  entire head, settling above the right eye. Aggravation from 4 to 8 pm,
  improved by warmth and pressure. Headache in schoolchildren. *Vertigo*
  from overexerting eyes. Accommodation disorders during headache.
  Facial *neuralgia*.

- **Digestive Tract**

  Toothache; rapidly changes location at night. Worse from eating and
  drinking. Spasmodic hiccups; during hiccups, sensation of cold water
  being poured on him. *Colicky* abdominal pain, improved by warmth and
  bending double. *Colic* during *flatulence* accompanied by eructations
  that do not relieve symptoms.

- **Urinary Tract and Reproductive System**

  Constant urge to urinate when standing or walking; *enuresis*. Painful *menses*, improved by warmth and pressure. *Premenstrual* spasmodic pain that stops as soon as menstrual flow starts.

- **Back and Extremities**

  Cramps, especially in hands and fingers. Cramps in writers and musicians. Trembling hands. Right-sided sciatic pain.

- **Modalities**

  Aggravation: Cold; taking a cold bath, drafts; touch; at night; exhaustion; **motion;** teething.

  Amelioration: Heat, **warmth**, hot compresses, hot bath; **pressure;** bending double; rubbing.

  Side most often affected: Right.

- **Indications**

  Chorea. Colic. Dentitio difficilis. Dysmenorrhea. Infantile colic. Migraine. *Neuralgia. Nocturnal enuresis. Sciatica. Singultus.* Toothache. *Writer's cramp.*

- **Compare**

  Belladonna, Chamomilla, China, Colocynthis, Cuprum, Cyclamen, Dioscera, Drosera, Kali phosphoricum, other Magnesia salts, Nux vomica, Silicea, Zincum.

Medorrhinum

Nosode made from gonorrheal pus.

■ Generalities

Craves fresh air. Collapse along with the desire to be fanned. Sensitive to cold and dampness. *Gonorrhea* in patient's medical history or that of his family. Extreme discharges from all mucous membranes. Discharges have a fishy smell.

■ Mind and Emotions

Passionate people. Impatience, **hurry**, volatility; nervous, overstimulated. **Extreme** and exaggerated reactions. Pairing of opposites: extroversion/introversion; aggression, impulsivity and anger/ timidity and caution; fanatical love of animals/cruelty to animals. Egotism. Excessive sexuality. Very sensitive; lack of self-confidence; whiny mood. Irresolution. Internal anxiety and restlessness. Clairvoyance. **Fear of forthcoming events**, misfortune, fear that something is going to happen. Constantly washing hands. Nail-biting. Feels guilty. Sensation of being stared at. Fear that somebody is chasing him. Fear of darkness; of death. Night person who feels **better in the evening,** can work best in the evening. Morose during the day and cheerful at night. Feels that time passes too slowly. **Retreats into an inner dream world. Everything appears unreal.** Confusion. Lack of concentration. Extreme weakness of memory.

■ Head

Violent pain in head, driving patient crazy. Sensation of a foreign body under eyelids. Itching in the external auditory canal.

■ Respiratory System

Chronic *coryza* and *sinusitis*. Patient is constantly clearing throat to get rid of mucus which is stuck there. Asthma and cough improved by knee-elbow position or when lying on the *abdomen*.

■ **Digestive Tract**
Teeth feel loose. Desire for salt, fat, ice cubes, ice cream, sour fruit, oranges, unripe and green fruit, potatoes, (sweet) alcoholic drinks and other stimulants. Ravenous hunger, even right after a meal. Increased thirst. Violent, torturing pain in the entire *abdomen* along with cramps. Itchy *anus*.

■ **Urinary Tract and Reproductive System**
Chronic and *recurrent* infections of pelvic organs. Herpes and warts around the genitals. Children produce a fiery red, burning diaper rash. Extraordinary, violent sexual desire. Masturbation at an early age. Coldness of breasts, especially nipples.

■ **Back and Extremities**
Burning feeling along the spine, from the neck to the coccyx. Chronic rheumatism with pain in tip of left or right shoulder, deformation of finger joints and sensitivity in heels. Extreme restlessness in legs and feet. Tender soles, can hardly walk barefoot. Ankles swollen. **Burning, hot feet,** which patient has to uncover in bed.

■ **Sleep**
Sleeps on *abdomen*. Infants and children sleep while in **knee-elbow position.** Sleeplessness, especially after midnight and after 4 am.

■ **Modalities**
Aggravation: During the day, especially in the morning; when thinking about complaints; in the mountains; heat; thunderstorms; sweets and alcohol.
Amelioration: At the seaside; in the evening and at night; **lying on** *abdomen*, **knee-elbow position;** damp weather; discharges.

■ **Causation**
Bad effects from suppressed *gonorrhea*; suppression of discharges; ailments from anticipation.

■ **Indications**

Allergy. *Arthritis. Bronchial asthma. Cystitis.* Diaper *dermatitis.* Eczema. *Gastric and duodenal ulcers. Hypertension. Leukorrhea.* Migraine. *Neuralgia. Sinusitis. Urethritis. Vaginitis.* Warts.

■ **Compare**

Anacardium, Carcinosinum, Lachesis, Natrum sulphuricum, Nux vomica, Platina, Sulphur, Tarantula, Thuja, Tuberculinum.

Mercurius solubilis

Hydrargyrum, quicksilver, mercury. At room temperature, pure mercury is liquid and has a dull, silvery shine. In a test tube it moves constantly with a gentle motion, reacting strongly to every change in temperature (in the past it was used in thermometers). Amalgam fillings contain a high percentage of mercury. Long ago Paracelcus used it for his treatments.

■ Generalities

Essence according to Vithoulkas: Lack of reactive power coupled with instability or inefficiency of function. Main remedy of the syphilitic miasm. **Copious sweats** with every complaint; sweat aggravates symptoms. Great weakness and trembling from slightest exertion. *Ulcers* that spread quickly. Chronic suppurations.

■ Mind and Emotions

Hypersensitivity. **Emotionally unstable**; tears alternating with laughter. Restless, fidgety, anxious state of mind, lacking in self-control. Restless, hurried and inefficient. Hasty speech, makes mistakes when speaking. Stuttering. Introverted. Intolerant of contradiction. Discontented, suspicious, quarrelsome. Different impulses, e.g. to hit, destroy objects, to kill (self or others); when seeing a knife (murderer). **Most of the time patient is able to control destructive impulses.** Easily frightened. **Fears**: of robbers, mental illness, impending death; *suicide*. Extreme *hypersensitivity,* causing patient to see everybody as an enemy. Mentally slow; answers slowly. Difficulty in understanding. Memory weak. Unable to concentrate. Idiocy (compare with final stage of syphilis).

■ Throat

Strong swelling of tonsils; proneness to suppurations.

■ **Respiratory System**

Stinging pain in the area of lower right lobe of the lung.

■ **Digestive Tract**

Gums are swollen and puffy; bleeding gums. **Tongue is big and flabby and shows imprints of teeth. Profuse** *salivation*; wets the pillow while asleep. Metallic taste in mouth. Offensive breath. Mucous membranes detached (burning like fire). *Canker sores.* Violent thirst. *Dysentery*: stool is greenish and contains blood, with *colic* and fainting. *Tenesmus* before, during and after stool.

■ **Extremities**

Tremor; especially in the hands. Weakness. Heaviness. Rheumatism in joints; along with swelling and coldness. Cold, sticky sweat on thighs and legs at night. Parkinson's disease.

■ **Skin**

Itching in bed warmth. Almost always moist. Generalized tendency to sweat, without relief. Vesicular and pustular eruptions. *Ulcers*; unevenly defined, spreading; bleeding; accompanied by cutting pain.

■ **Modalities**

Aggravation: At night; extreme temperatures (heat as well as cold); bed warmth; lying on right side, motion, exertion, cold air, damp and rainy weather, change of weather; sweating; suppressed eruptions. **Amelioration:** Rest.
Side most often affected: Left.

■ **Indications**

Abscess. Acne. *Angina tonsillaris. Bronchitis.* Common colds. *Conjunctivitis.* Eczema. *Gastroenteritis. Parkinson's disease. Orchitis. Otitis media. Pharyngitis. Pneumonia.* Rheumatism. *Rhinitis.* Sexual disorders. *Sinusitis. Stomatitis.* Tooth-grinding (in sleep). Upper respiratory infections*Vaginitis.*

- **Compare**
  Alumina, Arsenicum album, Kali bromatum, Natrum muriaticum, Nux vomica, Plumbum, Pulsatilla, Silicea, Syphilinum.

Natrum carbonicum

Sodium carbonate, soda, $NaCO_3$.

■ Generalities

Ailments from overheating in the sun; great weakness from heat of the summer. The stomach is the organ most often affected; patient has stomach problems all his life. Chilliness, weakness and listlessness. Trembling when in pain. Delicate, frail, refined persons.

■ Mind and Emotions

Great depression; completely absorbed by sad ideas. Silent grief, forsaken feeling; feels estranged from family and friends. *Hypersensitivity* to noises, especially music; weeping when listening to music. Jumpiness. **Cheerful, funny; even when sad inside.** Nice, gentle, compassionate, selfless and ready to help. **Aversion to certain persons;** does not tolerate the presence of certain persons, in which case he withdraws. Aversion to company; but is afraid of being alone. Fear of misfortune, thunderstorms. Fear of the future. Incapable of thinking, slow in understanding, cannot concentrate; mental dullness.

■ Head

Headache from the sun and during thunderstorms. Headache, *vertigo*, numbness from mental exertion. Headache in temples. Headache alternating with digestive disorders.

■ Digestive Tract

Indigestion from certain foods. Aversion to milk, aggravated by milk. *Flatulence* and diarrhea after **milk.** Vegetables and pasta are also not well tolerated. **Digestion disturbed** from slightest dietary mistake. Empty feeling and ravenous hunger around 5 and 11 am and 5 pm. Stomach tender to the touch. Sunken feeling in *abdomen*.

- **Respiratory System**

  Chronic nasal catarrh extending to posterior nostrils and *pharynx*. Violent clearing of the throat and violent spitting of thick mucus, which always collects again.

- **Back and Extremities**

  Weakness of ankles; frequent sprained ankles.

- **Modalities**

  Aggravation: Mental exertion; **sunshine**; thunderstorms; milk; cold, drafts; in the morning.

  Amelioration: Motion, rubbing, massaging; after eating.

- **Causation**

  Heat and sunstroke; excessive joy.

- **Indications**

  Allergy. Food allergies and intolerance. *Gastric and duodenal ulcers. Gastritis.* Headache. *Intolerance of lactose. Irritable bowel syndrome. Pharyngitis. Sinusitis.*

- **Compare**

  Glonoinum, Lycopodium, Magnesia muriatica, Natrum muriaticum, Natrum phosphoricum, Natrum sulphuricum, Sepia, Silicea, Staphisagria.

Natrum muriaticum

Natrum chloratum, sea salt, common salt, sodium chloride, NaCl.

■ Generalities

Emaciation, especially of the neck, despite having a large appetite. Some complaints come and go depending on the course of the sun. Aversion to the sun. Sweat containing salty deposits. Discharges like egg whites. Symptoms appear periodically.

■ Mind and Emotions

Introversion in highly sensitive people after suffering emotional hurt and withdrawal from society, to the point of complete hardening ("pillar of salt"). Builds a protective wall around self. Major grief that cannot be expressed, **thus called silent grief. Unable to cry despite sadness. Consolation makes this state worse.** Hysterical reactions like involuntary crying or laughing at serious matters. Falls in love with unsuitable persons. Does not show feelings. Fear of being emotionally hurt, fear of rejection. Reserved, serious, closed. Aversion to company. Easily hurt or offended. Constantly remembering past, unpleasant occurrences; old grief is not forgotten; bears grudges. Hates those who hurt him. Sensitive to music. Great compassion and understanding for others. Responsible, punctual, perfectionist. Fear of robbers, anxiety about health, enclosed spaces. Depression with suicidal thoughts.

■ Head

Headache from the sun. Headache in schoolchildren. Pounding, bursting headache; worse 10 am to 3 pm, from motion, reading, light, noise, *menses*; improved by lying in a dark, quiet room and by pressure above the eyes. Sensitive to light. Hay fever. Oily skin. Herpes vesicles around lips. Dry, cracked lips; frequently one deep crack in the center of lower lip, especially in cold weather; *rhagades* in corners of mouth. Geographic tongue.

- **Digestive Tract**
  Craves salt, fish, pasta, sour and bitter foods. Aversion to fatty, slimy food, bread, chicken. Great thirst for cold drinks. Spasmodic abdominal pain, improved by tight clothes. Thin, watery stool at 11 am. Dryness of *rectum* along with *constipation*.

- **Respiratory System**
  Spasmodic tingling cough, worse when lying down. Asthma attacks often between 5 and 7 pm.

- **Urinary Tract and Reproductive System**
  Cannot urinate when others are present. Involuntary passing of urine when coughing. Burning pain in lower *abdomen* before *menses*. Dry *vagina*. Shamelessness when having sex. Aversion to sex due to grief.

- **Back and Extremities**
  Backache improved by hard pressure and lying on something hard. Stinging pain in lower back before *menses*. Restless feet.

- **Skin**
  Skin eruptions in bends of joints, near hairline and behind the ears. Skin eruptions from being overheated. *Urticaria* all over the body after exertion. Cracks in fingertips.

- **Sleep**
  Sleeplessness from grief or dwelling on past, disagreeable occurrences. Sleeping mostly on the left side. Dreams of thieves. Sleepwalking.

- **Modalities**
  Aggravation: Consolation, heat, **sun; at the seaside;** 9 to 11 am; exertion; near the end of *menses* or afterward, sex.
  Amelioration: Fresh air; sweating; **at the seaside;** fasting.

- **Causation**
  Grief, disappointment, lovesickness, humiliation, vexation.

■ **Indications**

Allergy. *Arthritis. Bronchial asthma.* Backache. *Chronic fatigue syndrome.* Colitis. Constipation. Depression. *Dyspareunia.* Eczema. *Gastritis.* Hay fever. Headache. Herpes labialis. *Irritable bowel syndrome.* Migraine. *Psoriasis. Sciatica. Urinary stress incontinence. Urticaria.*

■ **Compare**

Aurum, Ignatia, Lycopodium, Natrum carbonicum, Natrum sulphuricum, Phosphorus, Pulsatilla, Sepia, Staphisagria.

Natrum sulphuricum

Sodium sulfate, Glauber's salt, Na_2SO_4. Also used as a purgative.

■ Generalities

Extreme sensitivity to humidity. Aversion to damp weather; patient notices every change of weather from dry to wet. **Copious yellow and watery or thick, greenish-yellow, purulent discharges.**

■ Mind and Emotions

Realistic, objective, serious, matter-of-fact persons. Sense of duty. Feels responsible and guilty. Feeling of never having any success. Closed up. Strong emotional bonding with one partner. Grief, loathing of life and unable to function after separation or death of partner. **Sadness along with suicidal thoughts.** Fear of being left alone because he might commit *suicide*. Must exercise great control to keep from shooting self. **Does not commit *suicide* out of consideration for relatives/family.** Very sensitive to melancholy, moving music. Mental and emotional changes after head injury. Cheerful after stool.

■ Head

Headache, improved by fresh air and cold water. Headache after head injury. Sensitivity to light, especially during headache.

■ Digestive Tract

Tongue covered with a brown, bitter coat, turning greenish-yellow at the back. Craves yogurt and ice water. Aversion to yogurt. Liver complaints with soreness in right hypochondrium. The area is tender to the touch and painful when walking or at slightest vibration. Rumbling from flatus in right *abdomen*. Sudden diarrhea in the morning after getting up. Thin, yellow, watery stools that come out in gushes mixed with lumps. Stool accompanied by flatus.

■ Respiratory System

Bronchial asthma, worse in damp weather and in the early morning, wakes between 4 and 5 am from respiratory distress. Asthma in children. Loose cough with rattling, soreness and pain through right chest. Cough is so painful that patient jumps up in bed and has to press his hands against the painful side, or has to hold his chest.

■ Modalities

Aggravation: Dampness, damp weather, fog, at the seaside, near lakes; lying on the left side, rest; injuries; **morning, 4 to 5** am, late evening; warm damp weather.

Amelioration: Dry weather; fresh air; pressure; changing body position, after passing stool.

Side most often affected: Left.

■ Causation

Bad effects from a fall, injuries to head and spine.

■ Indications

Allergy. *Bronchial asthma. Cholecystitis. Colitis.* Craniocerebral trauma. Depression. *Diarrhea.* Headache. *Hepatitis. Jaundice. Pneumonia. Suicidal personality.*

■ Compare

Aurum, Colocynthis, Dulcamara, Kali carbonicum, Medorrhinum, Natrum muriaticum, Podophyllum, Sulphur, Thuja.

Nitricum acidum
Nitric acid; spiritus nitri acidus.

■ Generalities
Weakness of body. Weakness with trembling, so that the patient has to lie down. Chilly in a warm room or warm bed. Fears the cold. Fetid discharges, urine smells like horse urine. Night sweats, sour and offensive. **Sharp pain as if from splinters that comes and goes suddenly.** Pain occurs particularly in places where skin and mucous membranes meet. *Hemorrhages* with bright red blood from all orifices. Tendency to ulcerate with stinking, watery, acrid secretions.

■ Mind and Emotions
Anxiety about health. Fear of disease, cancer, death (even stronger than for Arsenicum album). Patient doubts that he will ever recover. Sees one doctor after another. Unforgiving, bears grudges, resentful, vindictive, unmoved by apologies. Nihilistic! Strong discontent with self. Irritable at trifles. Stubborn, sad disposition, weeps easily. Worried and full of anxiety. Fits of anger. Taciturn. Trembling when in a dispute. Egotistical; full of hatred; opinionated; malicious. Blames others and pities self. Mistrust. In later stages, hopelessness and despair, loathing of life. Presentiment of death, loss of memory. Sleep is severely disturbed.

■ Sleep
Sleep is unrefreshing, wakes at 2 am.

■ Head
Vertigo. Headache with sensitive scalp and sensation of a band around head, or as if head were tightly clamped, as in a vise. *Congestion.* Itching eruptions on the forehead at the hairline. Impaired vision. Impaired hearing and noises in ear. Deafness that is better from riding in a car or train.

- **Throat**
  Swollen lymph nodes.

- **Respiratory System**
  Flowing *coryza*, corrosive and offensive. Nosebleed. Warts and *fissures* in nostrils. Hoarseness. Irritable cough during the night, coughing in sleep. Copious *expectoration* with mucus and pus, bloody. Stitching pains in the chest, difficult breathing.

- **Cardiovascular System**
  Pulse is weak, irregular and frequent. *Palpitations* and anxiety. Throbbing in arteries, which can be felt all over the upper part of the body.

- **Digestive Tract**
  Cravings: herring, salt and fat, indigestible food (i.e. coal, soil). Aversions: milk, bread and meat.
  Herpes on the lips; cracks in corners of the mouth. Warts on the lips; putrid breath; mucous membranes are sore and ulcerated, as are the gums. Tendency to bleed, dryness and increased thirst. *Salivation* is increased, swallowing difficult. Jaw cracks when chewing. Loss of appetite. Intolerance of milk. Nauseated after eating. Stabbing abdominal pain. Offensive stool, painful evacuation. Violent pains for many hours after stool, even after soft stool. Perianal area painful, with cracks and ulcerations. Hemorrhoids extremely painful and bleeding.

- **Urinary Tract and Reproductive system**
  Urine is dark, offensive. Urine feels cold when passing, bloody and albuminous with cast. *Urethritis*. *Condylomata*. Itching in *vagina* after *sex*.

■ **Extremities**

Pain in joints and limbs, especially in the *tibia*, when the weather is changing. Profuse sweating of hands and feet. Patient feels as if walking on needles. Foot sweat acrid and excoriating.

■ **Skin**

Frequent inflammations of the skin; cracks, *rhagades, furuncles.* Severe acne. Warts.

■ **Modalities**

Aggravation: In the evening, **during the night**, after 2 am; touch; motion; change of weather; on waking; cold, in cold climate.
Amelioration: Passive motion like riding in a car; warm covering and hot applications; discharges from mucous membranes, which usually herald amelioration of complaints.
Side most often affected: Left.

■ **Indications**

Acne. *Anal fissures. Angulus infectiosus.* Anxiety. *Arthritis.* Backache. *Bronchial asthma. Bronchitis. Colitis. Enteritis. Gastric and duodenal ulcers. Gastritis.* Headache. Hemorrhoids. Herpes. *Impetigo contagiosa. Nephritis. Otitis media. Pharyngitis. Pyelonephritis. Rhinitis. Sinusitis. Stomatitis aphthosa. Urethritis. Vaginitis.* Warts.

■ **Compare**

Agaricus, Anacardium, Arsenicum album, Aurum metallicum, Hepar sulphuris, Lycopodium, Medorrhinum, Mercurius, Nux vomica, Sulphur, Thuja.

Nux moschata

Myristica fragrans, nutmeg (N.O. Myristiaceae).

■ Generalities

Disturbances of sensorium, mind and nerves. Any disease that is accompanied by **sleepiness or somnolence** or causes sleep. Affections of female organs. Chilliness. Dryness of skin and mucous membranes. Tenderness of body parts patient lies upon.

■ Mind and Emotions

Drowsiness, sleepiness and confusion. Overwhelming somnolence. Weakness or loss of memory. Idiocy and indifference. Thinks for a long time before answering. Fading thoughts when reading, talking and writing. Dreamy, clairvoyant states. Alternating moods; laughing at one moment and crying the next. Drowsiness, worse from *menses*. Pregnancy.

■ Head

Faints easily from pain, emotional excitement, sight of blood. Headache with accelerated breathing. Headache is worse when moving or after overeating. Dryness of eyes; eyes too dry to close.

■ Digestive Tract

Pronounced dryness of the mouth along with thirstlessness. Tongue is so dry that it sticks to the palate. Sensation of dryness though mouth is moist. Saliva is glutinous, thick like cotton. Desire for liquor, coffee, highly seasoned foods. Food allergies. Distended *abdomen* from *flatulence*, even while still eating. Flatus and fullness during pregnancy. *Constipation*; stool is soft but cannot be evacuated. Summer diarrhea with undigested, frothy stools; worse from cold drinks.

■ Urinary Tract and Reproductive System

Mental and physical complaints during pregnancy: personality changes with anger, agitation, anxiety, sadness, confusion, fainting; coughing, toothache, *nausea*, fullness, vomiting, heartburn, diarrhea and drowsiness. Tendency to *abortion*. *Menses*: dark, viscous, lumpy, prolonged; cramps during *menses*.

■ Modalities

Aggravation: Cold, windy, stormy, damp weather, change of weather; before and during *menses*; when riding in a car; fresh, cold air; getting wet (feet); emotional excitation, mental exertion.

Amelioration: Dry, warm weather; drinking hot water; warm bed.

Side most often affected: Left.

■ Causation

Ailments from shock, grief, disappointed love, stroke.

■ Indications

Allergy. *Constipation. Diarrhea. Dysmenorrhea.* Headache. *Hyperemesis gravidarum. Alzheimer's disease. Narcolepsy. Premenstrual syndrome.* Sjögren's syndrome. *Syncope.*

■ Compare

Allium cepa, Alumina, Cannabis indica, Cocculus, Gelsemium, Helleborus, Ignatia, Opium, Pulsatilla.

Nux vomica

Strychnos nux vomica, poison nut. Belongs to the N.O. Longaniceae, like Ignatia, Gelsemium, Spigelia and Curare.

- ### Generalities

Chilly; very sensitive to drafts. Great coldness along with heat and red face; catches cold from getting cold. *Hypersensitivity* of all senses.

- ### Mind and Emotions

Irritable, quarrelsome, ambitious, **"workaholic"**, demanding, **impatient**. Fussy; wants objects to be in their proper place. Sadness for the slightest reason, especially after a meal. Hypersensitive to external impressions, noise, smells, light or music.

- ### Head

Congestive headache along with *nausea* and retching. Spasmodic jerking and tearing pain in face. Photosensitivity, especially in the morning. Teeth sensitive to cold.

- ### Digestive Tract

Cravings: for spices, fat, fatty foods (which are not tolerated), alcohol, stimulants. Aversion to the usual **stimulants** and foods. *Nausea* with retching; hunger during *nausea*. *Gastritis*; indigestion; duodenal *ulcer*; sensation of a stone in the belly after overeating. Stomach sensitive to constriction and pressure. Fullness and distension after eating. Incomplete eructation, heartburn, *colic. Constipation*; **constant unsuccessful urge** to pass stool. Hemorrhoidal complaints.

- ### Respiratory System

Dryness of nose, itching *coryza*, improved in the open air. Nasal congestion in warm rooms. Hoarse, dry cough with odd sensations in *pharynx* and *larynx*.

- ## Urinary Tract and Reproductive System
  Cystitis with constant urge to urinate, but only drops pass. Heightened sexual desire. Pronounced sexual excitability from slightest cause, persistent erection in the morning; erectile dysfunction.

- ## Back and Extremities
  Back problems at night, stiffness and tearing between scapulae. Paroxysmal muscular cramps.

- ## Sleep
  Sleeplessness; wakes between 3 and 4 am after a few hours's sleep and cannot get back to sleep (until 6 pm).

- ## Modalities
  Aggravation: Cold, cold and dry wind; eating; alcohol; **early morning,** soon after waking, after mental exertion, motion, touch, sensory stimuli.
  Amelioration: Warmth; in the evening, during damp weather, strong pressure.

- ## Causation
  Bad effects from excesses, gluttony and overuse of stimulants; intoxications, alcohol, drugs, anesthesia.

- ## Indications
  Alcoholism. *Angina pectoris. Apoplexy. Arrhythmia. Arthritis. Bronchial asthma.* Backache. *Chronic fatigue syndrome. Colic.* Common cold. *Constipation. Cystitis.* Diseases of liver and pancreas. Dysmenorrhea. *Gastric and duodenal ulcers. Gastritis. Gastroenteritis.* Headache. Hemorrhoids. *Hypertension.* Impotence. Inflammatory bowel disease. Influenza. Irritable bladder. *Irritable bowel syndrome.* Migraine. Muscular rheumatism. *Nephrolithiasis. Neuralgia. Pertussis. Pharyngitis* and hoarseness after drinking alcohol. *Pyelonephritis. Pylorospasm in infants. Rhinitis. Sciatica.* Sleeplessness.

■ Compare

Anacardium, Asarum, Aurum, Calcarea carbonica, Carcinosinum, Chamomilla, Ignatia, Lilium tigrinum, Lycopodium, Medorrhinum, Sepia, Stramonium, Strychninum, Sulphur.

Opium

Papaver somniferum, garden poppy. Opium is obtained by making incisions in the green seed head of the poppy and drying the sap that oozes out.

■ Generalities

Complete lack of pain; absence of pain in conditions that are normally painful. Hypersensitivity of sense organs. All discharges like stool, urine, menses are diminished, but sweat (hot) is profuse. Skin is very warm and sweaty but not on lower limbs. Bed feels so hot that patient cannot stay in it and has to move in search of a cooler spot.

■ Mind and Emotions

Extreme **sleepiness;** falls asleep while talking, sitting etc. Intense flow of thoughts; vivid imagination. Patient does not complain, does not want anything, appears to be happy despite being ill. Content and happy in all situations. Indifference. Lacks sense of responsibility, tells lies. Hurried and impatient. Cannot judge a situation adequately any more; fearlessness, foolhardiness. Withdrawal into an inner world. Anxious; frightening hallucinations. Loss of consciousness, coma, delirium; speaks with eyes open during delirium. Imagines that he is not at home. Frightening images: memories of a survived trauma do not fade.

■ Head

Convulsions; *chorea,* trembling, jerking, *paralysis* and other neurological disorders; especially after a fright. Headache with pain in occiput, which feels very heavy. Dark red, puffy, hot, sweaty face; or red alternating with pale. Pupils contracted; eyes half closed.

■ Digestive Tract

Severe *constipation* with urge. Intestinal *atony,* especially after surgery and childbirth. Stool consists of hard, black lumps. Peristalsis reversed, with vomiting of huge amounts of feces or *paralysis* of entire digestive tract.

- **Respiratory System**

  Snoring. Respiration stops when going to sleep. Breathing difficult, slow, rattling, with interruptions; worse during/after sleep. Fits of suffocation when falling asleep or during sleep. Dry, hacking cough preceded and followed by yawning.

- **Sleep**

  Narcolepsy; gets into a deep, *stupor*ous sleep, hard to awaken. Vivid, beautiful dreams. Patient cannot get to sleep despite being tired; hears noises he normally would not take any notice of; or constant *somnolence.*

- **Modalities**

  Aggravation: During and after sleep; warmth; excitement, fear; alcohol; suppressed discharges.
  Amelioration: Cold food/drinks; cold; fresh air; walks.

- **Causation**

  Ailments from **shock, fright,** fear, disappointment, embarrassment, grief, humiliation, reprimands; head injury, surgery.

- **Indications**

  Apoplexy. Bedsores. Cheyne-Stokes respiration. Coma. Brain concussion. Constipation. Delirium tremens. Encephalitis. Epilepsy. Meningitis. Miosis. Narcolepsy. Paralytic ileus. Sleep apnea. Sleeplessness.

- **Compare**

  Aconitum, Allium cepa, Alumina, Arnica, Baptisia, Belladonna, Gelsemium, Hyoscyamus, Lachesis, Nux moschata, Nux vomica.

Petroleum

Crude rock oil, oleum petrae album. Mineral oil of dark brown color with a syrupy consistency. The homeopathic remedy is made from white petroleum; all matter with a low boiling point or that solidifies at room temperature has been removed.

■ Generalities

Various skin conditions and travel sickness with cold sweat, *nausea*, heavy pressure in occiput. Offensive sweat. Does not gain weight despite good appetite. Chilliness; generally aggravated **during winter.**
Complaints come and go suddenly.

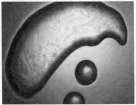

Crude Rock-oil   Photo: DHU

■ Mind and Emotions

Irritable, quarrelsome, easily offended, **irascible,** easily vexed, angry, sometimes violent, lively and passionate temperament; but on the other hand, timid, jumpy, whiny, irresolute. *Hypersensitivity* to noise. During delirium, patient he imagines someone is lying next to him or that one of his limbs is double. Confusion; disorientation in the street. Anxiety or delusion that death is imminent and he has to hurry up to get everything done.

■ Head

Vertigo when getting up; *vertigo* in occiput. *Vertigo* during rides in a car or boat travel. Headache in occiput as if from a lead weight.

■ Digestive Tract

Ravenous hunger, especially at night. Aversion to fatty foods and meat. Intolerant of cabbage, fatty foods, meat, beans and peas. Drawing stomach pain when stomach is empty, improved when eating. Diarrhea only during the day, hungry again after that. Stool is yellow and watery preceded by *colic. Nausea,* vomiting and sensation of a cold stone in stomach when riding in a car, improved by eating.

■ Chest

Cold feeling around the heart. Cough is worse at night with rattling in chest.

■ Skin

Rough skin with cracks, extremely dry; *rhagades,* deep, bleeding *fissures,* oozing and crusts. Itching is worse during the day. Skin folds, including the scalp, behind ears, nostrils, *anus* and *scrotum,* area between *anus* and buttocks, and the groin are affected. Painful, bleeding cracks on fingertips. Sensitive skin; even small wounds suppurate. Chilblains ooze and itch and burn in cold weather. Offensive sweat in armpits and feet.

■ Modalities

Aggravation: Winter, in cold air; before and during thunderstorms; travelling, riding in a car or in a train, sea voyage, air travel; fatty food and cabbage; during *menses;* in the morning and during the day; from vexation or fright.
Amelioration: In warm air, warmth, warm dry weather; eating.

■ Causation

Offense, travel, cabbage, suppressed skin eruptions.

■ Indications

 Bronchial asthma. Bronchitis. Chilblains. *Diarrhea.* Eczema. *Enteritis.* Headache. Herpes. *Herpes zoster. Psoriasis.* Travel and seasickness.

■ Compare

Cocculus, Graphites, Mezereum, Psorinum, Rhus toxicodendron, Sulphur, Tabacum.

Phosphoricum acidum
Phosphoric acid.

■ Generalities
Weakness in the emotional sphere, progressing into the physical and mental plane. Lack of reactions. **Exhaustion** with weakness and sweating or flushing. Prostration/collapse from grief, severe illness, taking drugs, drinking alcohol or suffering from fluid loss. Mucous membranes tend to bleed easily with striking weakness and sweating. Emaciation. Chilliness. Patient looks pale and in poor health. Complaints in young people who are growing too fast and suffering from many acute diseases.

■ Mind and Emotions
Indifference and *apathy*. Emotions come to a standstill or fade away. Ailments from silent grief, lovesickness. Exhausted and discouraged. Dwells on his condition. Dullness and indifference. Nothing interests him. Complete lack of reactivity. Deep dispair, hopelessness. Aversion to company. Does not want to speak, or speech is hasty.
Extremely forgetful. Dizziness; cannot marshal thoughts, searches for words and slow in answering. Comprehension difficult. Incapable of mental work. *Vertigo* from thinking. Sleepy during the day. *Stupor.*

■ Head
Hair falls out and turns gray in young people after grief. Headache as from a heavy weight on top of the head. Headache with *vertigo* and blood rushes to the head when moving the head, or from mental exertion. Headache from studying.
Dryness in nose and eyes.

■ Digestive Tract
Mouth is dry and has a bitter taste. Craves snacks, juice, fruit and cold milk. Very thirsty. Loss of appetite from grief. Cannot tolerate sour

foods. Distended *abdomen* making a rumbling and glugging noise. Painless diarrhea that does not exhaust patient, although it lasts for a long time. *Diarrhea* getting worse during the summer.

■ **Respiratory System**

Feeling of weakness in the chest when talking or coughing.

■ **Urinary Tract and Reproductive system**

Milky urine as if from flour or chalk. Phosphaturia. At the end of urination, urine looks like soured milk. Copious nocturia, urine is clear and watery. Has emissions during sleep and with stool. Backache and depression after sex. Impotence.

■ **Extremities**

Growing too fast; getting too tall. Exhaustion, Limbs feel weak. Gait is unsteady, stumbles easily. Tearing pain in bones as if *periosteum* were being scraped with a knife. Tearing pain in muscles and nerves. Formication.

■ **Modalities**

Aggravation: After sex, after mental exertion. During the night; cold and draft; worse from sensory impressions like light, noise, music.
Amelioration: Sleep; heat; motion.
Side most often affected: Right.

■ **Causation**

Ailments from grief, worries, shock, homesickness, bad news; Complaints starting after mental exertion; drug abuse; loss of vital fluids; following a disease; after sexual excesses.

■ **Indications**

Alopecia. Bronchitis. Chronic fatigue syndrome. Depression. *Diabetes mellitus. Diarrhea.* Headache. Impotence. *Periostitis.*

■ **Compare**

Aurum metallicum, Calcarea phosphorica, Carbo vegetabilis, China, Ignatia, Kali phosphoricum, Muriaticum acidum, Phosphor, Picrinicum acidum, Sepia.

Phosphorus

Yellow phosphorus. Fluorescent.

■ Generalities

Essence according to Vithoulkas: Diffusion. Weakness and exhaustion; **tendency to faint** and sudden prostration; but recovery and restoration of health come quickly. Proneness to *hemorrhages* with bright blood from all organs; small wounds bleed heavily; bluish marks after gentle bump. **Hemorrhagic** *diathesis.* **Burning** sensation (Sulphur, Arsenicum album); hands in particular. *Hypersensitivity* of all senses, particularly sensitive to smells and odors. Extremely ticklish. Ameliorated by being touched.

■ Mind and Emotions

Extroverted, open, friendly; sentimental; very **sympathetic** (cannot watch other people suffer), understanding. They radiate kindness and love, but are looking for love and contact themselves. Great desire for company; but they need periods of seclusion to regenerate. "Rather any kind of communication than none." Curiosity. Artists. Plenty of imagination, inexhaustible wealth of ideas, dreamy, absorbed in thoughts, daydreamer. Easily distracted, easy to impress, very suggestible. Jumpiness. Timidity. Quick to comprehend. Cheerfulness. Ready to help others. Full of **fears**; thunderstorms; being alone; dawn; dark; about others; death; ghosts and specters; future; illness; earthquakes; that something might happen, etc. Great restlessness. Mental exhaustion, confusion, delusions. Indifference. Melancholy, hopelessness, despair, loathing of life, *risk of suicide.*

■ Head

Headache: *congestive* headache along with burning pain in the head; heat appears to climb up the spine. Fits of migraine headaches lasting 1 to 3 days; pain seems to pass through the eye and leave the head

through the occiput. *Vertigo* and hot head from *congestion*.
Eye conditions.

■ Respiratory System

Nosebleed; during childhood. *Larynx* very painful. Hoarseness;
aggravated in the evening; even leading to *aphonia* (painless); along
with *hypersensitivity of larynx*. **Cough**: dry, burning, hacking,
spasmodic, sensation of a stinging tingling, "as if sore", with burning in
trachea and under the sternum. *Expectoration* very rare, often slightly
soluble; it may contain blood or pus, but mostly mucous; rust-colored,
viscous and sticky at times. During *bronchitis,* dry cough, in frequent
paroxysms; aggravation in the evening until midnight; when talking,
laughing, reading aloud, from change of temperature, lying on the left
side. Shortness of breath, especially when climbing stairs. In the case of
lung disease, oppression and feeling of heavy object on the chest,
especially during *pneumonia.*

■ Digestive Tract

Craves cold drinks and cold food, ice cream, chocolate, fruit, salads, fish,
salt, wine and highly seasoned foods. Hunger, especially during the
night, developing eventually into ravenous hunger. **Great thirst,**
particularly for cold water, which is taken in huge quantities. *Nausea.*
Stomach cramps, better from applying cold compresses. Burning pain in
stomach; better from cold drinks; but water is vomited as soon as the
gets warm in the stomach. Empty feeling all over the *abdomen.*
Diarrhea, sensation as if *anus* has remained open.

■ Sleep

Can sleep only on the right side. Sleep is refreshing; patient feels better
after sleep.

- **Modalities**

  Aggravation: Thunderstorms, sudden change of weather, windy and cold weather; mental and physical exertion; excitement; **lying on left side**; in the evening at dusk; cold; warm food.

  Amelioration: Rest and sleep, lying on right side; eating, cold food and drinks; rubbing, stroking, company.

  Side most often affected: Right.

- **Causation**

  Depleted state after exhausting diseases, after loss of body fluids like *hemorrhages*, breast-feeding, childbirth or growing (too) fast. Bad effects from strong feelings, emotions; excitement, agitation, anticipation; fright, fear, grief, sorrow; worries, vexation, anger.

- **Indications**

  Angina pectoris. Anxiety. Arthritis. Ataxia. Bronchial asthma. Bronchitis. Chronic fatigue syndrome. Diabetes. Eczema. Emphysema. Epistaxis. Gastric and duodenal ulcers. Gastritis. Gastroenteritis. Graves' disease. Headache. *Hemophilia. Hemorrhage. Hemorrhagic diathesis. Hepatitis. Hypertension. Laryngitis. Menorrhagia. Myocarditis. Nephritis. Optic nerve atrophy. Orthostatic syndrome. Osteomalacia. Pharyngitis.* Phobias. *Pneumonia. Psoriasis. Purpura. Retinal hemorrhage. Retinal detachment. Rickets. Tinnitus.* Tuberculosis. Typhoid fever.

- **Compare**

  Argentum nitricum, Arsenicum album, Causticum, Coffea, Medorrhinum, Pulsatilla, Rhus toxicodendron, Sepia, Sulphur, Thuja, Tuberculinum.

Phytolacca

Phytolacca decandra, poke root.

■ Generalities

Affinity with lymph nodes and **glands, such as** mammary glands, tonsils, parotid glands and testicles. **Very sore and washed-out feeling all over the body.** Patient feels need to move around but gets no relief. Pain changes location, shooting and stinging like electric shocks. Viscous, stringy discharges.

Poke Root   Photo: DHU

■ Mind and Emotions

Total indifference toward life; convinced of dying in the near future. *Apathy* and inability for mental work.

■ Head

Headache along with *nausea*; starting on the forehead extending to the back. *Vertigo*; fainting when sitting up.

■ Throat

Burning sensation in pharynx; cannot swallow anything hot. Violent throat pain extending to ears when swallowing. Back of pharynx is dark red; tonsils swollen, very red in the beginning of the infection, later with white spots that become confluent and form membranes as in diptheria. Tonsillitis with high fever, head and backache as well as a washed out feeling. Hard and painful swelling of cervical lymph nodes.

■ Digestive Tract

Irresistible need to grind teeth. Teething difficulty, or toothache ameliorated by clenching the teeth.

■ **Chest**

Mastitis; breasts are very hard and greatly swollen, hot and painful. When breast-feeding, the pain radiates all over the body. Cracks in nipples. Chronic discharges from the breast long after the nursing period. During *menses* breasts are swollen, hard and sensitive. Hard and painful nodes in breast.

■ **Extremities**

Rheumatic pain in muscles, joints and peripheral nerves, worse from motion and during cold and wet weather. Rheumatic complaints following *tonsillitis*; swellings in the joints, which are hard, tender and very hot. *Sciatica* where the pain extends down the outer side of the leg. Pain at tendon insertion points.

■ **Modalities**

Aggravation: Cold, **damp cold**; at night; motion, pressure, getting up from bed; swallowing, hot drinks.
Amelioration: Lying down (on the *abdomen*); cold drinks; rest; warmth; dry weather.
Side most often affected: Right

■ **Causation**

Bad effects from *tonsillitis*.

■ **Indications**

Angina tonsillaris. Arthritis. Dentitio difficilis. Galactorrhea. Headache. *Mammopathia fibrocystica. Mastitis.* Mumps. *Orchitis. Pharyngitis.* Rheumatism. Scarlet fever. *Sciatica. Sinusitis.* Toothache.

■ **Compare**

Apis, Belladonna, Bryonia, Conium, Hepar sulphuris, Kali iodatum, Lac caninum, Lachesis, Mercurius, Rhus toxicodendron, Silicea.

Picrinicum acidum

Picric acid, trinitrophenol, $C_6H_2(NO_2)_3(OH)$.

■ Generalities

Generalized burnout syndrome; collapse in the mental sphere. Mental, sexual, anemic weakness and exhaustion. Generally tired and weak, patient has to lie down. Exhaustion on the slightest exertion. Burning pains.

■ Mind and Emotions

Mental weakness and confusion after intellectual overexertion, e.g. students studying for exams, also fear of exams. Dullness. Cannot concentrate at all, or only for a very short period of time. Weak memory. Mental weakness. Indifference. Listlessness. Brain fatigue. Aversion to talking and thinking. Sleepy during the day; sleepless at night, especially after mental work.

■ Head

Headache on the slightest mental exertion, especially in overworked students, businessmen. Headache in people weighed down with sorrow. Headache in the occiput and in the nape of the neck, worse from mental work and better from putting a bandage around the head. Better in the open air or a cool place and lying down in a quiet place. Heaviness in eyelids, difficulty in keeping eyes open.

■ Urinary Tract and Reproductive system

Pronounced sexual excitability with *priapism* and many erotic thoughts. Tendency to masturbate. Strong sexual desire and violent erections are followed by weakness and impotence.

■ Back and Extremities

Severe and burning pain in legs. Back feels tired and painful, sometimes with a burning sensation. Fatigue that develops into an ascending *paralysis*. Writer's cramp or palsy.

■ **Modalities**

Aggravation: Exertion, especially mental exertion, anxiety, grief and sorrow; heat, hot and damp weather; stool.

Amelioration: Open air, cold weather, firm pressure (during headache), lying down, rest, sleep.

■ **Causation**

Mental overexertion.

■ **Indications**

Backache. *Enlarged prostate.* Headache. Mental exertion. *Priapism.*

■ **Compare**

Argentum nitricum, Gelsemium, Kali phosphoricum, Phosphor, Phosphoricum acidum.

Platinum

Platinum metallicum. Precious metal.

■ Generalities

Physical symptoms alternate with mental symptoms. Complaints only on one side of the body. Pain increasing and decreasing slowly; spasmodic and constricting; along with numbness and cold. Sensation of inner trembling. **Coldness and numbness** in circumscribed areas of the body, in particular around the head and the face. Spasmodic conditions: similar to a *tetanic* stiffening along with chills. Alternating with shortness of breath. Sticky secretions.

■ Mind and Emotions

Conflict between excessive sexual desire and heightened, romantic, idealistic ideas when in a loving relationship. Sensitive; sensual and idealistic at the same time. Intellectual, artistic. **Disappointment** because partner never lives up to requirements. Ailments from grief, disappointed love and disappointing sexuality. Forsaken feeling. Erotomania. Presumptuous, arrogant character; looks down with contempt on other people. **Inflated sense of self, arrogance.** Contempt for the world. Megalomania, fixed ideas of being rich, domineering personality. All objects around him appear to be small, while he himself feels bigger. Great sadness with a pensive nature and a tendency to cry. Taciturnity; involuntary weeping. Mood swings quickly from depression to boisterousness and the other way around. *Apathy*, indifference; brooding and **depression**; despair, suicidal thoughts. Desire to kill other people, especially loved ones and lovers, especially at the sight of a knife. Hypochondriasis. Fear of imminent death; of people; anxiety about relatives. Weakness of memory.

■ Head

Headache with the sensation that head is held in a vise. Pain on vertex along with a feeling of heaviness.

■ **Extremities**

Feeling that one part of the body is excessively big. Weakness and fatigue in limbs, especially when at rest. Trembling, numbness, tingling; pain with coldness. **Bound feeling.** Cramps in calves in the evening when lying down, with the sensation that limbs have gone to sleep.

■ **Digestive Tract**

Cravings: cold drinks. Tobacco. Aversions: meat; especially during *menses. Constipation*; worse when travelling. Passing stool always painful, difficult and scanty, regardless of whether it is hard or liquid; *tenesmus* before and after stool. Great weakness when passing stool. Feces: black, hard balls, as if baked. Stool sticks to the *anus* as if made from soft clay.

■ **Urinary Tract and Reproductive System**

Extreme sexual desire. Nymphomania, worse from staying in bed. **Masturbation** from early childhood. Sexual perversion. Extraordinary sensitivity of genitals, any touch is unbearable; therefore spasms during a gynecological examination; even fainting during *sex*. Sensitivity of *ovaries*; burning pain. *Menses* too early, too copious, dark and clotty. *Menses*; along with cramps or painful heaviness in lower *abdomen*; with *hypersensitivity* of genitals. Violent itching around female genitalia.

■ **Sleep**

Persistent insomnia. Difficulty falling asleep. Sleep is short and restless, interrupted by frequent waking and terrible, obscene dreams.

■ **Modalities**

Aggravation: In the evening, at night; silence; emotions; touch; during *menses*.
Amelioration: Fresh air; motion.

- **Causation**

  Ailments from fright, rage, fits of anger; desertion, losses; sexual excesses, masturbation.

- **Indications**

  Adiposity. Bulimia. Constipation. Depression. *Dysmenorrhea. Epilepsy. Facial nerve paralysis/Bell's palsy.* Headache. Insomnia. Mania. *Metrorrhagia.* Phobias. Sexual disorders.

- **Compare**

  Aurum, Crocus, Gratiola, Hyoscyamus, Ignatia, Kali phosphoricum, Lachesis, Lilium tigrinum, Lycopodium, Medorrhinum, Nux vomica, Palladium, Phosphorus, Pulsatilla, Sepia, Stannum, Sulphur, Valeriana, Veratrum album.

Plumbum

Lead.

▪ Generalities

Lack of vitality. Slowness of all functions; symptoms develop progressively. Affects primarily muscles, tendons, nerves and spinal cord. Great and rapid emaciation; generalized or partial *paralysis* with marked weakness, *anemia* and **chilliness**.

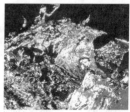

Lead   Photo: DHU

▪ Mind and Emotions

Slow to perceive external impressions, slow mental grasp and reactivity; mental dullness; *apathy.* Loss of memory, especially for words. Quiet melancholy, taciturn; sadness along with anxiety. Desire to destroy self. Great fear of being murdered or poisoned. Suspicion. Feigns sickness. People who have always enjoyed high living; indulged in luxury in an egotistical and self-centered way; they like risky and forbidden adventures.

▪ Head

Sunken and emaciated cheeks. Facial skin is greasy. Eyes and skin yellow during jaundice. Parotid and sublingual glands heavily swollen.

▪ Digestive Tract

Blue lines along margins of gums. Desire for fried and salty foods. Violent *colic*; ameliorated by leaning backwards. Abdominal pain radiating to all parts of body. *Retracted* feeling in *abdomen*; sensation of abdominal wall being drawn toward the spine with a thread. *Constipation* with hard, lumpy, black stools like sheep dung. Anal spasms as if *anus* were being drawn inward.

- **Urinary Tract and Reproductive System**

  Retention of urine due to *paralysis* of the bladder. Chronic inflammation of kidneys. Increased sexual desire. Impotence. *Vaginismus*; *hypersensitivity* of *vagina*. Induration of mammary glands with stitching pain. Miscarriage.

- **Extremities**

  Contracture of tendons. Trembling along with muscular weakness, especially when trying to hold something. Muscular *contractures*. *Atrophy* of affected parts, such as paralyzed muscles. (Painful) progressive *paralysis*; wrist-drop, foot-drop. **Lightning-like pain,** ameliorated by pressure. Pains in limbs are worse at night. *Hypersensitivity* of the skin when touched.

- **Modalities**

  Aggravation: Exertion; cold weather, open air; motion; company; in the evening and at night; touch; fasting; eggs, fish.
  Amelioration: Hard pressure, bending double, rubbing; heat; stretching limbs.

- **Indications**

  Amyotrophic lateral sclerosis. Apoplexy. Arteriosclerosis. Colic. Constipation. Contractures. Dementia. Diabetes. Dupuytren's contracture. Hypertension. Multiple sclerosis. Mumps. *Nephritis. Neuralgia. Neuritis. Parkinson's disease. Proctitis. Sciatica.*

- **Compare**

  Alumina, Cocculus, Dioscera, Lycopodium, Medorrhinum, Mercurius, Opium, Platinum, Podophyllum, Sulphur.

Podophyllum

Podophyllum peltatum, May apple (N.O. Berberidaceae).

■ Generalities

Loosening of tissues; *ptosis*. Extraordinary weakness after passing stool. Perspiration during pain. Alternating complaints.

■ Mind and Emotions

Great loquacity during fever, also delirious. Pretends to be sick; convinced he is going to die soon. Depression during stomach conditions. **Fidgety and restless.**

■ Head

Dull, oppressive headache alternates with diarrhea or liver conditions.

May Apple   Photo: DHU

■ Digestive Tract

Teething problems; grinding teeth during teething. Large, wet tongue showing imprints of teeth; offensive breath. Miserable and empty feeling in *abdomen*, particularly after stool. Diarrhea in the early morning between 2 and 4 am, yellow or green, watery, slimy, copious, offensive-smelling and undigested along with great exhaustion, or diarrhea gushing like a broken pipe. Before onset of diarrhea, spasms and gurgling in the *abdomen* as well as *palpitations*, *nausea* and pale face. Painless diarrhea. Inflammatory states of the duodenum, liver, bile ducts and small intestine, with a sensation of emptiness and *prolapse* in the abdominal organs. Liver area swollen, tender and painful, ameliorated by rubbing. *Rectal prolapse.* Internal and external hemorrhoids.

■ **Urinary Tract and Reproductive System**

Sensation like *uterine prolapse* when passing stool. *Uterine prolapse* from exertion, carrying a heavy load, *constipation* or after delivery. Pain in the ovaries, especially the right side, extending to the thighs, worse from stretching legs. *Amennorrhea* in young girls with a feeling of pressure in the back and *abdomen*.

■ **Modalities**

Aggravation: Early morning, from 3 am on; after eating and drinking; warm weather in summer; teething.

Amelioration: When lying down, in particular on the *abdomen*; rubbing, stroking the liver; applying heat locally, in the evening.

Side most often affected: Right.

■ **Indications**

Amenorrhea. Cholelithiasis. Cholecystitis. Colitis. Dentitio difficilis. Diarrhea. Dysentery. Enteritis. Gastroenteritis. Headache. Hemorrhoids. *Hepatitis. Ovarian cysts. Rectal prolapse. Uterine prolapse.*

■ **Compare**

Aloe, Arsenicum album, Chamomilla, Chelidonium, Croton tiglium, Lycopodium, Mercurius, Natrum sulphuricum, Nux vomica, Sepia, Sulphur.

Psorinum

Psorinum is a nosode made from the contents of a human scabies vesicle.

■ Generalities

Great sensitivity to cold air, **extreme chilliness**; is always cold, can never dress warmly enough; **prone to colds.** All discharges (diarrhea, *leukorrhea*, *menses*, perspiration) have a rotten smell; even with bathing, the body has a **smell of dirt. Generalized weakness**, especially after an acute disease, with excessive perspiration at the slightest exertion. Curiously enough, patient always feels better the day before the onset of an illness.

■ Mind and Emotions

Pessimistic; hopeless and melancholic mood. Enormous despair, making life unbearable for self and others. Suicidal. Very peevish and irritable, discouraged and filled with grief. Misanthropist, nurturing an inferiority complex. **Forsaken feeling.** Melancholy, depression; indifference and *apathy*. Easily frightened. Despairs of recovery. **Great anxiety.** Anxious restlessness at night. Fear of incurable diseases; fear of death. Fear of the future; of disaster; failure in job. Loss of memory; orientation difficult; confusion.

■ Head

Headache dull and numbing; ameliorated by nosebleed, washing with cold water and eating; voracious appetite before or during headache. Crusts and scabs on the scalp or oozing, sticky skin eruptions. Chronic inflammation of eyes, sinuses, ears and tonsils. Offensive pus from ears along with pain in the ears. Even during summer, patient wears a fur hat. Sensitivity to light.

- **Digestive Tract**

  Constant ravenous appetite; gets up at night to eat; loses weight nevertheless. *Flatulence* with a foul smell. Dark brown, watery stools with an unbearable, revolting smell. *Constipation* due to sluggishness of *rectum*.

- **Respiratory System**

  Chronic *recurrent* inflammation of upper respiratory tract and neighboring organs like ears and paranasal sinuses. Marked shortness of breath even in the absense of disease in the thoracic organs, worse when in the open air. Cough and breathing eased when lying on the back with arms spread ("as if crucified"). Hay fever.

- **Skin**

  Itching when body gets warm; **unbearable itching** when in warm bed; scratching skin until it bleeds; itching between fingers and in bends of joints. Dry, scabby eruptions that disappear during summer and reappear in winter. Skin has a black-brownish, dirty look as if the patient never washed, body smells dirty even after taking a bath. Burning and itching soles. Acne worse during *menses*. Washing aggravates all skin symptoms.

- **Modalities**

  Aggravation: Cold, during winter; change of weather, before thunderstorms; touch and pressure; coffee; at night, full moon; mental exertion.

  Amelioration: Heat, during summer, when lying down, rest; when **eating**; nosebleed, sweats; strong pressure.

- **Causation**

  Ailments from suppressed skin eruptions, suppressed diseases, suppressed discharges; emotions; mental exertion; stormy weather; thunderstorms; injuries, sprains and dislocations.

■ **Indications**

Abscess. Acne. Allergy. *Angina tonsillaris.* Asthma bronchial. *Bronchitis.* Common colds. *Conjunctivitis. Constipation.* Depression. *Dermatitis. Diarrhea.* Eczema. Hay fever. Headache. Insomnia. Migraine. *Neuralgia. Otitis media. Pharyngitis. Psoriasis. Rhinitis. Scabies. Sinusitis.*

■ **Compare**

Arsenicum album, Calcarea carbonica, Carbo animalis, Graphites, Hepar sulphuris, Mezereum, Nitricum acidum, Petroleum, Phosphorus, Sulphur.

Pulsatilla

Pulsatilla pratensis, wind flower (N.O. Ranunculaceae).

■ Generalities

Symptoms change and vary: pain and swelling move from one joint to the other; inconsistent stools or chills. Always chilly but still cannot stand a warm room, warm applications or hot water. **Discharges from mucous membranes are thick, like cream, mild, yellow-greenish.**

Wind Flower   Photo: DHU

■ Mind and Emotions

Mild character, weeps easily. Moods change and vary, sad and weepy but not ready to accept consolation. **This is the remedy that weeps most.** Laughing and weeping alternate; changeable mood like April weather. More yielding and ready to give in than provocative and stubborn (but obstinate at times). Strong compassion. Takes care of domestic affairs. Irresolution, insecurity, easily discouraged, very impressionable. Timidity. Anxiousness. **Fear of being left alone.** Anxiety alone in the dark. Fear of robbers, ghosts, enclosed spaces, crowds, insects, dogs, snakes, poverty. Fear of heights. Pathological fear of the opposite sex; aversion to marriage. Religious desperation. Melancholy, depressed mood. Loathing of life, threatens to commit *suicide*, *suicide* by drowning. **Kindness, dependency, conviviality, flexibility, emotionalism.**

■ Head

Headache: *congestive*, pulsating; as if the pain could make the forehead and temples burst; wandering unilateral pain; pain in occiput. Periodical headache; before, during and after *menses*, during suppressed *menses* or *dysmenorrhea*. Ameliorated by external pressure and cold applications. *Vertigo*; fainting.

■ **Eyes**

Conjunctivitis, burning, shooting pain, along with a feeling of dryness; profuse lacrimation. Sties.

■ **Ears**

Otitis media; after perforated eardrum, thick, yellow-greenish mild discharge.

■ **Digestive Tract**

Cravings: sour and fresh food, **hard-to-digest foods like cream cake**, fat, meat. Aversions: meat, butter, fat, bread, milk, smoking. **Thirstless.** Mouth is dry; bad taste especially in the morning. Frequent eructations with a bitter taste. *Nausea* and throwing up of food or bitter mucus. *Gastritis* and *colic* from *flatulence* after a meal. Heaviness, fullness and heartburn after eating, especially fatty, sweet and sour foods, pork, cake and ice cream.

■ **Urinary Tract and Reproductive System**

Frequent urgency; urinary *incontinence* at night, when walking, sneezing, coughing or from a fright or a surprise. Strong sexual desire. *Menses* late and weak, intermittent (especially after wet feet), along with cramps; or *cycle* constantly changes length, intensity and symptoms, often menstruation is too late and scanty; or early and heavy. Relief after *menses*. *Leukorrhea*; in the morning; in young girls.

■ **Sleep**

Insomnia; from thinking after lying down; before midnight. Sleeping position: on the *abdomen* or the back; hands under or above the head. Sweating during sleep, which disappears on waking; often one-sided.

■ Modalities

Aggravation: Heat, warm room, area of low pressure, just before a thunderstorm, fatty food, rest, in the evening and at night.

Amelioration: Motion, **fresh air**, cold external applications.

Side most often affected: Right.

■ Indications

Amenorrhea. Cholecystitis. Conjunctivitis. Cystitis. Depression. *Diarrhea. Dysentery. Dysmenorrhea. Gastritis.* Headache. *Hepatitis. Hordeolum. Hypomenorrhea.* Insomnia. *Leukorrhea. Measles. Menopausal complaints. Nocturnal enuresis. Ophthalmia neonatorum. Orchitis. Orthostatic disorder. Otitis media. Premenstrual syndrome.* Rheumatism. *Sterility. Urinary stress incontinence.* Urinary tract infection.

■ Compare

Argentum nitricum, Baryta carbonica, Capsicum, Kali sulphuricum, Lycopodium, Medorrhinum, Phosphorus, Sepia, Silicea, Staphisagria, Sulphur.

Rhus toxicodendron

Poison ivy, toxicodendron quercifolium (N.O. Anarcardiaceae). Shrub indigenous to North America, found in bushy woods and humid areas in Europe, especially in France.

Poison Ivy   Photo: DHU

- **Generalities**

According to Vithoulkas, the central idea of the remedy is **being stiff**, bound up and unable to relax. Restlessness in bed; has to change position all the time to ease the pain.

- **Mind and Emotions**

Extreme **restlessness**, nervous agitation. Funny, cheerful. Anxious, worried and sad; tendency to weep. Unhappy, discouraged, hopeless. Nice, friendly, timid, cool and mild, but lively. Fears for children. Fear of being injured, of disaster. Great worries at night; feels threatened. Fear of killing someone. Suspicious; fixed ideas. Compulsive, ritualistic behavior. Numbness and mental confusion with typhoidal conditions.

- **Head**

Headache starting with stiffness of the neck, better when moving. Headache along with dullness, head feels empty or heavy. Pain behind the eyes, worse from motion; eye lids are rigid. Swollen parotid gland and lymph nodes. Maxilla is rigid and cracks.

- **Respiratory System**

Hoarseness in the morning, better from talking. Short, dry cough after being in the rain; symptoms worsen after slightest cold or uncovering.

▪ Back and Extremities

Lameness and stiffness as well as pain when beginning to move after rest or when getting up in the morning, better after continuous motion. Stiffness and painful muscles due to exertion, straining or damp cold. Stiffness and cracking in all the joints. *Paralysis* along with numbness. *Hypersensitivity* in the throat area, especially to drafts. Soreness in the back along with stiffness, worse from carrying a heavy weight and from rest, improved by moving, heat, firm pressure. Pain in left shoulder. Restless legs in bed.

▪ Digestive Tract

Dry and dark coated tongue with a triangular red spot at the tip. Craves **cold milk**, cold drinks, sweet foods, cheese, yogurt and oysters. Aversion to meat.

▪ Skin

Vesicular skin eruptions. Very itchy eczema with formation of vesicles. Herpetic eruptions along with swelling, burning, itching and stinging, ameliorated by hot water.

▪ Modalities

Aggravation: Cold, **damp cold weather**, before a thunderstorm, drafts; at night, especially after midnight, in the morning when getting up. **Amelioration:** Continuous **motion**, changing of position; heat; rubbing; stretching of limbs; dry and warm weather.

▪ Causation

Physical exertion, straining, luxation; damp cold, cold, damp, getting wet, common cold when body is very hot and sweaty.

▪ Indications

Arthritis. Asthma bronchial. Backache. *Bronchitis.* Compulsive Behavior. Eczema. *Erysipelas.* Headache. Herpes labialis. *Herpes zoster. Impetigo contagiosa.* Laryngitis. Lumbago. Neuralgia. Pharyngitis. Pneumonia.

Rheumatism. Scarlet fever. *Sciatica*. Strain. *Tenovaginitis. Urticaria. Varicella*. Whiplash.

■ **Compare**

Aconitum, Apis, Arnica, Arsenicum album, Bryonia, Calcarea carbonica, Calcarea phosphorica, Dulcamara, Iodum, Natrum sulphuricum, Phosphorus, Ruta, Sulphuricum acidum, Tarantula, Tuberculinum.

Sepia

Sepia officinalis (N.O. Cephalopodae). Sepia is made from the contents of the ink sac of the cuttlefish, which lives in the Mediterranean, the North Sea and the Atlantic Ocean.

■ Generalities

Stasis **on all levels.** Acts predominantly on the lower *abdomen* and the pelvis, especially in women. **Chilly;** hot flushes along with perspiration and weakness. All discharges have an offensive smell.

Dried Ink of the Cuttlefish   Photo: DHU

■ Mind and Emotions

Aversion/indifference toward everything; to whatever was dear and precious to patient, for example spouse and children, aversion to occupations formerly enjoyed, to domestic duties. Aversion to work; company. Wants to be alone. Needs distance and freedom. Doesn't want people to see through her ("the veil of ink"). Timidity. Fatigue. Weeping for no reason. Sentimental. Overexcited and nervous; laughing and dancing; **loves dancing** and thunderstorms. Hard, hurtful, sarcastic; intelligent, astute; ambitious. Strong sense of justice; perfectionism, enthusiasm for work, conscientious, marked sense of duty. Fault-finder. Nervousness, irritability, anger, aggressivity; despair; melancholy, depression to the point of wanting to commit *suicide*. Weeping; angry irritability. Consolation aggravates symptoms. Anxiety. Desperately worried about health. Fears: that something will happen; ghosts; when driving a car. Easily frightened. Mental dullness; thoughtlessness; confusion, deadening of emotions, *apathy*.

■ Head

Yellow spots, moles; especially prominent on the face, where they tend to take the form of a butterfly or a saddle; on the cheeks, the nose and around the mouth. Tendency to faint; especially in warm rooms; when kneeling down. Lids feel heavy from exhaustion, during headache. Headache; left-sided (above the left eye); preceded by blurred vision; lids droop during headache.

■ Digestive Tract

Cravings: sour foods and chocolate. Aversions: fat and milk, which are not tolerated. Often food tastes oversalted. Painful sensation of emptiness (along with thirst), sunken feeling or faintness in stomach, wretched feeling. Prone to *nausea* and vomiting in the case of emotional but also physical conditions, especially when looking at food or smelling it. Passing stool is difficult even if it is soft. *Constipation*; accompanied by sensation of a lump in *vagina* or in the *rectum*. Fullness in *rectum*. *Constipation* with no urge to defecate.

■ Urinary Tract and Reproductive System

Indifference/aversion to sex. **Heaviness and bearing down** as if contents of the lower *abdomen* were going to fall out through the *vulva*. Patient crosses her legs or pushes *vulva* back. *Menses* mostly too late and scanty. Pregnancy difficult; *abortions*.

■ Extremities

Stiffness and heaviness in extremities, especially after sleep. Weakness of joints. Ankles tend to sprain when walking. Sensation as if a mouse were running up and down the leg.

■ Modalities

Aggravation: In the morning and in the evening, from 2 to 4 pm or from 3 to 5 pm; during full or new moon; at the sea; rest; standing; cold; before, during and after *menses*; *sex* or frequent intercourse; pregnancy; miscarriage, *abortion*; menopause.

Amelioration: In the afternoon; **moving the body vigorously,** dancing, in the open air, especially moving about in fresh air; warmth; occupation.
Side most often affected: Left.

■ Indications

Abortion. Anemia. Bronchitis. Chronic fatigue syndrome. Collagenoses. Condylomata. Connective tissue diseases. *Constipation.* Cough. *Cystitis.* Depression. *Dyspareunia. Endometriosis. Enuresis. Gastric and duodenal ulcers. Gastritis.* Headache. *Herpes. Hirsutism. Hot flushes. Hyperemesis gravidarum. Leukorrhea.* Menopausal conditions. Migraine. Inflammation of the pelvic organs. *Premenstrual syndrome. Prostatitis. Pruritus ani. Psoriasis Raynaud's disease. Rectal fissures. Rhinitis.* Sexual dysfunction. *Sinusitis. Sciatica. Scleroderma.* Stress incontinence. *Uterine prolapse. Vaginitis.* Varicose veins. Warts.

■ Compare

Carbo vegetabilis, Carcinosinum, Gelsemium, Ignatia, Lilium tigrinum, Murex, Natrum muriaticum, Nitricum acidum, Nux vomica, Petroleum, Phosphoricum acidum, Pulsatilla, Thuja.

Silicea

Silica, pure flint, H_2SiO_3. The pure silica found in rock crystal is used to make this remedy.

Generalities

Chilliness, sensitivity to cold; **prone to catching colds.** Weakness of body and mind. Emaciation. Chronic **suppurations,** ulcerations, *tumors, fibroma,* cysts and swelling of lymph nodes with induration. Offensive, aggressive **sweats.** Diseases of bones, spine, teeth and nails. Easily exhausted from mental and physical exertion. **Slowness** in development, growth and recovery. Delicate, weak children with large heads, open fontanelles, head sweat, protruding bellies, late in learning to walk. *Hypersensitivity* of all senses, especially sensitive to touch and noise.

Silicea   Photo: DHU

Mind and Emotions

Yielding, timid, despondent, gentle, reserved. Lack of self-confidence. Fear of *failure;* fear of failing at or undertaking something new. Fear of exams, anticipation; fear of appearing in public. Delusion of failure. Fear of needles or sharp objects. **Fixed ideas about needles. Obstinacy; they give in, but inwardly they stick to their opinions.** Image is important to them. Need a lot of recognition. Irresolution; but sensitive to contradiction. Specialist in one field. Conscientious about details. Lack of mental perseverance. Nervousness, impatience, discontent. Irritable weakness along with absent-mindedness. Weak memory.

■ **Head**

Headache starting at the nape of the neck. moving up to the head, forehead and eyes; often from hard mental work. Pain above one eye, usually worse on the right side. Headache aggravated by all kind of noises, movements or vibrations; better when head is wrapped warmly, from pressure and profuse urination. *Vertigo* rising from the nape of the neck; as if falling forward, from looking up. Sweat all over the head. Inflammations of eyes and ears; sties. Tip of nose is colored vivid red.

■ **Throat**

Recurring *tonsillitis*. Stinging pain in tonsils as though from a needle. Shooting pain when swallowing. Hard swelling of cervical lymph nodes.

■ **Chest**

Cysts in breast. *Mastitis* in breast-feeding women. Sensation of pressure as if from a stone in the breast. Hard lumps in the breast.

■ **Digestive Tract**

Tooth *abscesses*, inflammation of the gums. Sensation of a hair on the tongue. Loss of appetite when trying to eat. **Increased thirst.** Craves cold food, ice cream, eggs, fat and milk. Aversion to fat, meat, salt, warm food, milk and mother's milk. Difficulty in digesting milk. *Constipation* where stool slips back in again; *constipation* is more severe before and during *menses*. Anal *fistulas*.

■ **Respiratory System**

Chronic nasal *congestion*, dryness. Paranasal *sinusitis* with **thick, postnasal catarrh**. Shortness of breath due to drafts. **Violent cough when lying down, with thick, yellow, lumpy** *expectoration*.

■ **Skin**

Skin does not heal easily; every injury suppurates. *Keloid* growths; old scars are suddenly painful. Persistent suppurations, *abscesses*, *furuncles.* Offensive, acrid footsweat. Brittle nails with white spots; *whitlows.* Silicea expels foreign bodies, especially needles and splinters.

■ **Modalities**

Aggravation: Cold, when removing clothes or covers, drafts; pressure; noises; bright light; during *menses*; sex; in the morning, at night; new and full moon; mental exertion; nervous agitation; alcohol, milk.
Amelioration: Warmth, wrapping the head warmly, warm and humid weather.
Side most often affected: Left.

■ **Causation**

Bad effects from vaccination; suppression of (foot) sweat and other discharges; drafts.

■ **Indications**

Abscess. Acne. *Angina tonsillaris.* Asthma bronchial. *Bronchitis. Chronic fatigue syndrome. Conjunctivitis. Constipation.* Eczema. *Fissures.* Furuncles. Headache. *Hordeolum. Keloids. Mammopathia fibrocystica. Mastitis. Migraine. Otitis media. Pharyngitis. Psoriasis. Sinusitis. Scoliosis.* Upper respiratory infections. Vaccinations. *Vertigo. Vitiligo. Whitlows.*

■ **Compare**

Baryta carbonica, Calcarea carbonica, Carbo animalis, Hepar sulphuris, Kali carbonicum, Kali phosphoricum, Mercurius, Natrum carbonicum, Nitricum acidum, Picrinum acidum, Pulsatilla, Sanicula, Staphisagria.

Spongia

Spongia marina tosta or euspongia officinalis. Roasted sponge (N.O. Porifera), which is harvested on the Aegean coast and contains iodine.

■ Generalities

Dryness of mucous membranes, especially of respiratory tract. Enlargement, induration and inflammation of glands. Chilliness. Exhaustion and heaviness of the body. Frightened, anxious look.

Sponge   Photo: DHU

■ Mind and Emotions

Anxious and easily frightened.
Fear of heart disease, the future, death, suffocating. Wakes up with a start at night, with intense anxiety and a feeling of suffocating. Irresistible need to sing, followed by sadness.

■ Throat

Constriction, scratching and dryness in the throat. Frequent clearing of the throat. Goiter; with choking fits at night. *Larynx* very sensitive to touch. Sore throat, worse from eating sweets.

■ Chest

Heart conditions; violent *palpitations* with dyspnea. Rush of blood to throat, head and face.

■ Digestive Tract

Intense thirst and huge appetite.

■ Respiratory System

Coryza with hoarseness. Hoarseness along with pain when swallowing. Hollow, dry, barking, sawing cough. *Expectoration* very scanty and clear. Cough is better from eating and drinking; worse from talking, singing, swallowing and lying down flat. Respiration impeded as if breathing through a sponge. Waking with a start, feeling suffocated, accompanied by a violent, loud, piercing cough with great anxiety and restlessness. Dry asthma without rattling noise of mucus.

■ Modalities

Aggravation: Climbing upward, exertion, motion; dry, cold wind; night, (before) midnight; full moon; sleep, being awakened; lying on the right side; sweats; heat.

Amelioration: Climbing downward; warm food and drinks; humid weather; lying flat, lying on the back.

■ Indications

Angina pectoris. Arrhythmia. Asthma bronchial. *Bronchitis. Goiter. Hyperthyroidism. Laryngitis. Myocarditis.* Pseudocroup.

■ Compare

Aconitum, Bromium, Causticum, Coccus cacti, Hepar sulphuris, Iodium, Kali sulphuricum, Lachesis, Lycopodium, Phosphorus, Rumex.

Stannum

Tin.

■ Generalities

Great weakness, profound exhaustion, which is markedly worse when going down the stairs. Paralytic weakness along with trembling from any exertion. Great **weakness felt in chest. Patient is too weak to talk.** Fatigue. Pains come and go gradually.

■ Mind and Emotions

Miserable and discouraged. **Anxious,** nervous, depressed, **sad; worse before** *menses.* Hopeless and despondent; feels like weeping all the time; weeping makes symptoms worse. Irritability due to tiredness.

■ Head

Neuralgic headache; pressing pain in different spots on the head with *nausea* and choking. Eyes burning when feeling weak.

■ Respiratory System

Sore feeling in *larynx.* Flat, hoarse voice. Cough, provoked by talking, singing and laughing. Chronic conditions of bronchi and lungs, when *expectoration* is profuse, grayish and tastes sweetish but also salty. Chronic loose cough with green *expectoration,* especially in the early morning and in the evening when in bed. Short of breath at slightest exertion. Weakness felt in chest, worse from talking.

■ Digestive Tract

All-gone, empty feeling in stomach, also after eating. Vomiting from the odor of cooking. *Colics* along with cramp-like pain around the navel, better from pressure and bending double.

■ Modalities

Aggravation: Talking; lying on the right side; warm drinks; **during the day;** 5 am, 10 am; cold; motion; when passing stool.

Amelioration: Hard pressure, **bending double; rapid motion.**
Side most often affected: Left.

■ Indications
Asthma bronchial. *Bronchitis*. *Chronic fatigue syndrome*. Headache.
Laryngitis. *Neuralgia*. *Pneumonia*. Upper respiratory infections.

■ Compare
Causticum, Calcarea carbonica, Gelsemium, Kali carbonicum,
Laurocerasus, Muriaticum acidum, Phosphorus.

Staphisagria

The dried seeds of the stavesacre or lousewort, delphinium staphisagria (N.O. Ranunculaceae).

Generalities

Violent, stinging pain. Great sensitivity to pain. Wounds are very delicate, heal slowly; good remedy following abdominal operations. Indurations. Trembling, especially after emotional upheaval. Periodicity of complaints. Chilly.

Stavesacre   Photo: DHU

Mind and Emotions

Suppression of feelings. Bad effects from wounded honor, feeling humiliated. Peevish disposition and exaggerated sensitivity; patient gets angry over nothing. Sadness; irritability. Annoyed, peevish. Easily offended, hurt. Timidity, reserve; kindness. Tactful. Emotionally sensitive. Internal *tremors*. Restlessness. Suppressed anger, anger with silent grief. Capriciousness. Suppressed aggression; throws things from indignation. Cannot defend himself; swallows any insult without bitterness. Resignation. Yielding disposition; cannot say no. Cannot bear any conflict. Conscientious about details. Full of worries; worries about the future, about eternity. Hypochondriasis. Anxiety; fears his own shadow; fear of losing self-control; in high places; out of anger; fear of doctors. Delusion of being followed. Constantly tormented with **sexual thoughts**. Feeling guilty because of masturbation. Tendency toward loneliness. Fear of being close. Feels better when alone. Low self-esteem. Artistic disposition, e.g. painting, music, poetry. Weepy mood. Consolation aggravates symptoms. *Apathy*; indifference toward everything. Melancholy. *Suicide* by shooting. Addictive behavior.

- **Head**

  Headache along with sensation of a leaden lump in the forehead. Sensation as if forehead were about to explode when stooping or moving. Wooden feeling in either the forehead or the occiput. Tooth decay in early childhood; black, decayed on the edges, partially crumbling.

- **Sleep**

  Sleepy during the day, sleepless at night. Insomnia often accompanies sexual thoughts and frequent masturbation so as to get to sleep more easily. **Worse after an afternoon nap.**

- **Eyes**

  Burning eyes, leading to a feeling of dryness despite copious lacrimation. **Sties,** *chalazion* coming on one after the other, sometimes with ulceration; leaving indurations behind.

- **Digestive Tract**

  Cravings: sweets, milk, tobacco/smoking. Aversions: fat, water and milk. Gums soft and spongy, sensitive and tender. Sensitivity of *abdomen*. Extreme appetite, even when stomach is full. All kinds of indigestion after eating meat. Sensation as if stomach were hanging down loose. Gastrointestinal *colic. Constipation*: relatively frequent but dry and insufficient stool. Urge is frequent but inefficent, as if from inactivity of *rectum. Diarrhea*: dysenteric stool with *tenesmus*; after cold drinks. Summer *dysentery* with abdominal pain and *tenesmus* after little food or drink.

- **Cardiovascular System**

  Slightest motion causes *palpitation*.

■ **Respiratory System**

Dry, hollow cough, due to tingling in the *larynx*; tobacco smoke aggravates symptoms. Disgust but also desire for smoking. Coughing only during daytime.

■ **Urinary Tract and Reproductive System**

Burning sensation in *urethra* when not urinating, passing urine ameliorates. *Prostatic* troubles in older men with frequent urge to urinate and dribbling. *Cystitis* after *sex* or catheterization. Strong sexual desire. Easily aroused. **Masturbation.** Impotence, *frigidity*. Backache connected with diseases of the genitals, getting worse at night in bed and in the morning before rising. Highly sensitive genitals; pain in ovaries and testicles. *Menses*: irregular; heavy; bright blood in the beginning and later dark blood with clots. *Uterine* spasms during *menses*.

■ **Skin**

Sensation as of vermin on the skin. Eczema oozing acrid fluid; new vesicles form on spots that have been in contact with this fluid. *Recurrent* itching eruptions with a violent itch that moves to a different spot as soon as it is relieved by scratching; eczema on the head and cradle cap; eczematous eruptions on the ears and eyelids; warts and *condylomata;* mostly pedunculated. Cuts; after operations, especially in the *abdomen*.

■ **Modalities**

Aggravation: Anger, vexation, grief; sexual excesses; smoking; slightest touch on genitals or affected parts; new moon; smallest amounts of solid or liquid food; thinking about complaints.
Amelioration: After breakfast; rest.

■ **Causation**

Diseases due to sexual excesses and masturbation; following sexual abuse. **Conditions resulting from anger or prolonged suppressed**

grief; ailments from lovesickness, disappointed love, humiliation, indignation, outrage, anger.

■ Indications

Apoplexy. Chalazion. Chorea. Chronic fatigue syndrome. Condylomata. Conjunctivitis. Constipation. Cuts. Cystitis. Depression. *Dysentery. Dysmenorrhea.* Eczema. *Enuresis. Gastric and duodenal ulcers.* Headache. Hemorrhoids. *Hordeolum.* Insomnia. *Orchitis.* Postoperative pain. *Prostatitis. Psoriasis. Strabismus. Warts.*

■ Compare

Anacardium, Causticum, Ignatia, Natrum carbonicum, Natrum muriaticum, Nux vomica, Pulsatilla, Silicea.

Stramonium

Datura stramonium or thornapple belongs to the Solanaceae family, like Belladonna, Hyoscyamus, Mandragora, Dulcamara, Tabacum and Capsicum.

■ Generalities

Symptoms are extraordinarily intense; violent course of disease. Almost no pain at all. Rushes of blood. Pulsations felt internally and externally.

■ Mind and Emotions

Vehemence, aggressivity and **violence**. Destructiveness; patient hits, bites, tears things apart, screams or swears. Violent madness; fits of anger, rage. Extreme agitation along with wild delirium and confusion, going wild, great jumpiness and anxiety. Patient is fearful and therefore cannot be alone. Scared to death, **agony. Fears:** of violence; extreme fear of the dark; always wants the lights on because of frightening fantasies, but symptoms worsen in bright light. Unusual fears like fear of cemeteries, tunnels or closed rooms; fear of dogs; of water and aversion to any fluid; marked anxious nervousness when hearing water run. Constantly chattering; laughs, sings, screams or prays constantly without a pause; delirious. Imagining things. Hallucinations when seeing or hearing something. Sensations as if some parts of the body were greatly enlarged. Sadness and melancholy when in the sun. Easily startled; especially by delusions. Suicidal, killing self with a knife or by jumping from a height.

■ Head

Congestion toward the head and brain while face is hot, puffy and bright red. Headache; worse from sun, heat, lying down and motion; mostly in the occiput, but also in the forehead. Eyes wide open, protruding; pupils widely *dilated*. Spasmodic condittions provoked or worsened by looking at shiny objects, being in glaring light, looking at fluids.

■ **Digestive Tract**

Dryness of mouth and throat. Violent hiccups. Spastic constriction in *muscles of pharynx* and *esophagus* which makes swallowing difficult. This is especially true for fluids whose look drives patient into a frenzy. Aversion to water and drinks, cold water. Craving for sweets, sour food. Thirst increased. Vomiting when lifting head from pillow. Offensive *diarrhea*. At times stool is black along with a smell of rotting flesh.

■ **Respiratory system**

Cough, provoked or aggravated by looking at a very bright light. Asthma with dry, warm skin, vivid, hard pulse and a red and puffy face; during the attack head, is superextended backwards.

■ **Extremities**

One side paralyzed, the other seized with *convulsions*. Rhythmic and spasmodic involuntary movement. *Choreic* movements and impaired coordination when moving (staggering when walking, stammering when talking): *tremors,* paralytic conditions. Staggering in the dark or with eyes closed.

■ **Urinary Tract and Reproductive System**

Strong sexual arousal in both sexes; worse before *menses. Menses* heavy, dark, clotty; strong body odor during *menses.*

■ **Sleep**

Nightmares in children. Insomnia in children along with anxiety in the dark and fear of fairy-tale figures after listening to a bedtime story. Awaking with a start, afraid, screams and holds on to people. Jumps out of bed. Panic attacks at night.

■ **Modalities**

Aggravation: Dark; being alone; fear; looking at shining or radiant objects; swallowing; after sleep; cold, **suppressed secretions** (*menses, lochia,* eruptions, perspiration).

Amelioration: Light; company; warmth; cold water.

■ Causation

Sudden shock, vexation with fright, reprimands, head injury, infections with fever involving the central nervous system.

■ Indications

Angina pectoris. Apoplexy. Asthma bronchial. *Chorea.* Craniocerebral trauma. Delirium. *Diarrhea. Enuresis.* Epilepsy. Febrile seizures. Hyperactivity. Headache. Mania. Manic-depressive conditions. *Meningitis. Meningoencephalitis. Metrorrhagia.* Nightmares. *Pavor nocturnus.* Phobias. *Psychosis.* Schizophrenia. Stammering and stuttering. *Strabismus.*

■ Compare

Anacardium, Belladonna, Cuprum, Hyoscyamus, Kali bromatum, Lachesis, Lyssinum, Medorrhinum, Veratrum album.

Sulphur

Brimstone. Volcanic origin. Hahnemann's "anti-psoric". Most symptoms of all the remedies in the materia medica.

- ### Generalities

Corpulent and robust or skinny with drooping shoulders. **Heated. Complaints are of burning nature.** Redness of all orifices. Night sweats, irritant and offensive. Acrid, **repulsive**, revolting, **foul-smelling discharges.** Periodicity: every 7th or 21st day. Lack of reaction. Suppressed skin symptoms. *Vicarious symptoms* of skin and lungs. among others.

Brimstone   Photo: DHU

- ### Mind and Emotions

The "ragged philosopher". Dislike of water and washing; likes to discuss, debate and **theorize.** Explorer, scientist, collector. Absent-minded, overworked, tired, absorbed in thoughts. Full of imagination. Intellectual, materialistic, greedy. Hedonism. Adventurer. Optimist. Egocentric; **egotistical,** haughty, arrogant; boasting, showing off; overestimating self, egoism. Thinks he is better, critical of others, perfectionistic, opinionated. Loner. Insensitive, indifferent toward others. Easily offended, irritable. Anger, vexation, discontent. Restlessness, nervousness, impatience. Lazy, aversion to work, lethargy. Overenthusiastic, hyperactive. Need for admiration and appreciation, ambitious, bad loser. Leader. Independence personified, as well as courage, strength and determination. Untidiness; indifferent to appearance. *Nause*ated by dirt. Fear of contagion, infectious diseases, death. Fear of failing; fear of going insane. Depression, despair, resignation, loathing of life. Worried.

▪ Head

Constant heat on vertex, burning headache on vertex. Headache from relaxation and too much sleep. Flushes of heat to the face frequently followed by gentle perspiration which brings relief.

▪ Digestive Tract

Empty feeling in stomach around 11 am. Craves alcohol, sweets, fat, starchy foods, highly seasoned foods, sour and sweet things. Intense thirst.

Aversion to eggs, meat, sweets, milk and sour foods. Burning or sour eructations after a meal along with heaviness felt in stomach. Painless *diarrhea* very early in the morning, which drives the patient out of bed. Chronic *constipation* with burning and itching around *anus* and hemorrhoids; soreness of *anus*.

▪ Respiratory System

Chronic *coryza*. Asthma bronchiale. Sensation of having swallowed some dust. Oppressed feeling: especially at night when reclining, with *congestion* going to the heart, *palpitations* and shortness of breath as if suffocating. Oppression may also appear during the day in case of physical exertion like climbing stairs.

▪ Extremities

Burning hot soles causing patient to uncover feet; or ice-cold feet. Chronic rheumatism.

▪ Skin

Burning and itching. Dry, flaking, unhealthy, dirty skin. The scalp is dry; tendency to *ulcerations* in skin folds. Diverse eruptions on the skin alternating with other pathological conditions (hemorrhoids, asthma, headache). Itching when in bed.

■ **Sleep**

Insomnia. **Catnaps,** therefore sleep is not very deep. Dreams after midnight.

■ **Modalities**

Aggravation: Heat; water, washing, bathing; upright position, **standing;** warmth of bed; very early in the morning; when getting up; at 11 am and at 5 pm; milk, sugar; change of weather.

Amelioration: Dry and warm weather; fresh air; motion; lying on right side.

Side most often affected: Left.

■ **Causation**

Bad effects of suppressed skin eruptions. Suppression of hemorrhoids or sweat. Prolonged weakness after influenza. Bad effects of vaccination.

■ **Indications**

Abscess. Acne. *Adenopathy.* Alcoholism. Allergy. *Angina pectoris. Angina tonsillaris.* Anxiety. *Arrhythmia. Arthritis.* Asthma bronchial. Backache. *Bronchitis. Chronic fatigue syndrome. Colitis.* Common colds. *Conjunctivitis. Constipation.* Dementia. Depression. *Diabetes. Diarrhea.* Eczema. *Fissures. Fistulas* around rectum. *Gastric and duodenal ulcers.* Gout. Headache. Heat flushes. Hemorrhoids. *Hepatitis.* Herpes. *Hypertension. Impetigo.* Influenza. Menopausal complaints. Migraine. *Otitis media. Pertussis. Pharyngitis. Pneumonia. Prostatitis. Psoriasis.* Rheumatism. *Rhinitis. Sciatica. Sinusitis. Tinea.* Vaccinations.

■ **Compare**

Aloe, Antimonium crudum, Argentum nitricum, Graphites, Lycopodium, Medorrhinum, Mezereum, Nux vomica, Platinum, Psorinum, Pulsatilla.

Sulphuricum acidum
Sulphuric acid

■ Generalities

Great fatigue, exhaustion and weakness with trembling. The whole body trembles and jerks, internal trembling. Sensitive to fumes and smoke. Tendency to bleed. Black blood from all orifices. Weakness after injuries. Pain starts slowly and stops suddenly. All secretions from the body are sour, and so is patient's mood. Chilly. Heat flushes followed by trembling or cold sweats.

■ Mind and Emotions

Extreme hurry. One of the hastiest remedies in the materia medica. Patient does everything in a hurry, is afraid of not being able to finish work, of not getting it done. Nothing is ever fast enough for him. Impatient about trifles. Serious; industrious; restless. Nervous, cannot relax; vexed, irritable. Exhaustion, fatigue. Speech is monosyllabic. Despondent, weepy, discouraged. Lack of self-confidence. Anxiety in the morning, better in the evening.

■ Head

Sensation as if brain is loose and rocking from side to side.

■ Digestive Tract

Canker sores in the mouth; bleeding gums; sour breath. Vomiting, which is worse when lying on the left side. Aversion to alcohol, coffee, fresh fruit, sweet foods, water. Craves alcohol, liquor, fresh fruit, sweets. Patient feels coldness in the stomach after drinking water unless alcohol is mixed into it. Chronic heartburn; sour eructations; hiccups. Stool is orange-yellow or saffron-yellow. *Diarrhea* from eating unripe fruit.

■ **Respiratory System**

Asthma that is worse from smoke and dust. Tiring, irritable cough with copious, loose *expectoration*. Rattling and wheezing respiration during cough.

■ **Skin**

Ailments from mechanical injuries with *hematoma, gangrene* and livid skin. *Ecchymosis.* Scars turn red or blue and are painful. *Petechiae. Purpura* hemorrhagica. Injuries with *hemorrhages.* Itchy fingertips.

■ **Sleep**

Restless sleep, waking up frequently. Sleeps only for two hours and then wakes up. Nightmares before *menses.*

■ **Modalities**

Aggravation: Open air; cold; alcohol; injuries; **fumes, smoke, exhaust fumes, strong odors,** smell of coffee; *menopause.*
Amelioration: Hot drinks; hands on head; pressure; walking fast; at the seaside.
Side most often affected: Right.

■ **Causation**

Ailments from alcohol; injuries.

■ **Indications**

Bronchial asthma. Bronchitis. Ecchymosis. Chemical sensitivities. Diseases due to environmental conditions. Gastritis. Hemorrhagic diathesis. Headache. Purpura. Stomatitis aphthosa.

■ **Compare**

Arnica montana, Arsenicum album, Calendula, Iodium, Lachesis, Ledum, Medorrhinum, Nux vomica, Tarantula.

Syphilinum

Luesinum. Nosode made from a luetic ulceration or syphilitic lesion.

■ Generalities

Extraordinary emaciation of the whole body. **Dwarfish children.**
Tendency to ulcers, abscesses with foul secretions, suppuration and
destructive diseases. Perspiration at slightest exertion or emotions.
Pain gradually growing and receding, changing places; pain, especially
soreness in the bones. Syphilis in family history.

■ Mind and Emotions

Aggressive, peevish, nervous, irritable, malicious, insulting, spiteful,
destructive; desire to kill. Narrow-mindedness; mistrust, suspicion. Fear
of many things: that the worst will happen; vague anxiety and panic.
Fear of catching a cold. Anxiety about health; despair of recovery. Fear
of contagion and diseases. Morbid fear of becoming insane or
paralyzed. Disgusted by dirt. Terrible fear of getting dirty, getting
infected; has to wash body and clothes constantly; obsessional washing.
Anxiety lessens toward evening. Depression, worse when lying down.
Lack of self-confidence/self-esteem; insecurity. **Compulsive behavior**;
has to check everything many times to be sure he didn't get something
wrong. Superstition. **Feeling of being far away.** *Apathy*; indifference
about the future. Mental sluggishness, lack of concentration, mistakes
when doing calculations, forgetfulness, confusion.

■ Head

Hair falling out. Deep, pressing and numbing headache. Pain in bones of
skull. Pain above the right eye. *Neuralgia* in head. Restless during
headache. *Ptosis* of upper lid. Crossed eyes. Vertical double vision.
Contorted features.

- **Digestive Tract**

   Extreme *salivation*; flowing profusely at night. Teeth deformed, decay early. *Canker sores* in the mouth. Craves alcohol. Obstinate, *constipation* lasting years. *Prolapse* of anus. Hemorrhoids.

- **Urinary Tract and Reproductive System**

   Chronic diseases of sexual organs. Profuse, acrid *leukorrhea* running down to the heels. Frequent *abortion*.

- **Back and Extremities**

   Rheumatic stiffness and pain in back and limbs. Inflammation of joints along with stiffness and swelling. Sawing pain in bones, worse in bed warmth, better from cold applications. *Osteomalacia*, decay of bones, *necrosis* of bones, *exostosis*.

- **Skin**

   Coppery-red skin eruptions. Various skin diseases of eczematous and destructive nature, but always without itching. White spot disease/ *vitiligo*.

- **Sleep**

   Insomnia; wakens between 2 and 3 am and cannot go back to sleep.

- **Modalities**

   Aggravation: At night, from sunset to sunrise, humidity, near the sea; **extreme heat and cold;** consolation.

   Amelioration: In the evening, during the day; slow movement; in the mountains; alcohol; cold bath, ice applied locally for pain.

   Side most often affected: Left.

- **Indications**

   Abscess. Alcoholism. *Alopecia*. *Arthritis*. Backache. Compulsive behavior. *Constipation*. Depression. Headache. Insomnia. *Leukorrhea*.

Migraine. *Neuralgia. Psoriasis. Psychosis. Sciatica. Scoliosis. Stomatitis aphthosa. Vitiligo.*

■ Compare

Arsenicum album, Aurum, Kali iodatum, Mercurius, Nitricum acidum, Phytolacca, Platina, Sulphur.

Tarentula hispanica

Tarantula fasciiventris, lycosa hispanica, Spanish tarantula (N.O. Lycosidae).

■ Generalities

Great restlessness, constant motion, never lacking energy. Nervous system is tense, hypersensitive; *hypersensitivity* of all sensory organs. Emaciation. Chilliness but **desires fresh air.** Periodicity of symptoms.

■ Mind and Emotions

Restless and agitated persons with a *hypersensitivity* of all sense organs. Sexually overexcited. Extreme restlessness; hurry, speed; impatience; impulsiveness; anger when others are slow. Industrious, acting quickly, busy, workaholic; also fruitless busyness. Loves **music** (quick, **rhythmic**), **dancing** (wild) and colors, or aversion to strong colors. Irresistible urge to dance, jump and run. Fear of not finishing his work; something will go wrong. Fear of being threatened or injured. Cunning, gloating, mischievous; fits of anger; destructiveness aggressivity, self-mutilation. Disobedient, restless, hyperactive children.

■ Head

Headache as if thousands of needles were sticking into the brain. Spasms; fainting; *vertigo*.

■ Chest

Sudden, violent *palpitations*, *tachycardia*, oppression along with anxiety, difficulty in breathing.

■ Respiratory System

Attacks of suffocation; must have fresh air. Cough, better from smoking, worse from noise.

- **Digestive Tract**

  Craving for highly seasoned and salty foods, raw fruit and vegetables, sand. Aversion to meat. Intense thirst for huge amounts of cold water. *Constipation*, laxatives have no effect.

- **Urinary Tract and Reproductive System**

  Sexual overexcitability in both sexes, but aggravated by sex. *Myoma*; *menses* heavy, too early and too long; nymphomania; extreme itching of *vulva* and *vagina*, worse after *menses*. Pain and *tumors* in testicles.

- **Extremities**

  Motor restlessness; jerking. Wild, crazy and violent movements. Restlessness of extremities, getting better from music. Restless hands. Formication and tingling sensation.

- **Skin**

  Suppuration around the nail beds, on the skin, *furuncles, carbuncles* and *abscesses*. Affected parts are bluish and burning intensely.

- **Modalities**

  Aggravation: Rest, sleep; touching affected parts; noises; change of weather; smoking; after sexual intercourse; cold; motion, exertion.
  Amelioration: Sleep, at night; relaxation; (quick) motion, walking; in the open air; rubbing affected parts of; riding; rhythm and music.

- **Causation**

  Bad effects of unrequited love.

- **Indications**

  Abscess. Angina pectoris. Arrhythmia. Behavioral disorders. *Carbuncle. Chorea minor. Constipation. Furuncles.* Hyperactivity. Headache. Mania. Menorrhagia. Mitral valve disorders. *Neuralgia. Paraesthesia.* Sexual disorders. *Tumors* of testicles. *Uterine myoma. Vaginitis. Whitlows.*

■ **Compare**

Agaricus, Apis, Arsenicum album, Belladonna, Hyoscyamus, Lachesis, Lilium tigrinum, Medorrhinum, Nux vomica, Platinum, Sepia, Stramonium, Sulphuricum acidum, Theridion, Tuberculinum, Veratrum album.

Thuja

Thuja occidentalis, arbor vitae (N.O. Cupressaceae).

■ Generalities

Main remedy for *sycosis*. Rapid exhaustion and emaciation, especially in patients who drink excessive amounts of tea. Lack of reactivity. Skin growths and pathological developments: *condylomata*, *polyps*, warts, sycotic excrescences, etc. **Sweat is cold, oily, has** an **offensive**/sweetish odor and stains clothing yellow. Sweating at slightest exertion; perspiration only on uncovered parts of the skin. Yellowish-green or green discharges. Generalized chilliness, lack of vital heat, intolerant of cold or humidity. Effects of vaccination.

Thuja   Photo: DHU

■ Mind and Emotions

Originally great self-confidence, arrogance, later weak self-esteem, feeling worthless. Materialistic. Closed person, reserved; **deception; feeling of having to hide something ugly.** Deliberately withholding information to put the doctor to the test. Feeling that "others would not like me if they really knew me". Wait-and-see attitude, introverted, cautious, cunning, insidious, deceitful, suspicious. Lying, calculating, manipulative. Alienation, distant from others. Avoids company. Hostility. Hurry, impatience, agitated and excited, fanaticism, workaholic. Creativity. Discontent, irritability, quarrelsome. Peevish, moody. Doubts, anxiety. Pangs of conscience, feeling guilty, blames himself. Anxiety about his soul, religious despair. Fear of strangers. Fear of disease. Fear of wind. Concentration difficult, forgetfulness. Confusion, especially on waking in the morning or when talking. Lets sentences trail off when talking, last words audible only to himself. Oversensitivity, easily hurt.

Fixed ideas: "as if a stranger were at his side; as if body and soul were separated; as if body, especially limbs were made of glass and fragile; as if a live animal were in his *abdomen*; as if under the influence of a higher power." Melancholy, sadness, depression, *apathy*, indifference, hopelessness, loathing of life.

■ Head

Headache starting in the forehead above left eye, extending over the side to the back to the occiput. Pain as if pierced by a nail. Sensation as if head were made of wood. **Facial skin greasy, oily/dry.** Facial hair growth in women. Caries in tooth root, crown looks healthy. Coated tongue, very sensitive at the tip.

■ Respiratory System

Chronic suppurative paranasal *sinusitis* and thick postnasal drip. *Coryza*, hay fever. *Coryza* when passing stool. Asthma bronchiale.

■ Digestive Tract

Lack of appetite and quickly satiated when eating. Craves cold drinks and food, salty and sour foods. Aversion to tobacco/smoking, meat, potatoes, **onions**. Intolerant of onions. Complaints after a meal. Noises and rumbling in *abdomen*.

Obstinate *constipation* with frequent ineffective urge. Watery, yellowish *diarrhea* after breakfast, forcibly expelled; accompanied by a lot of *flatulence* and a gurgling sound, as if water were coming out of a bunghole. *Anal fissures*.

■ Urinary Tract and Reproductive System

Chronic inflammations. *Condylomata* of genitalia. Herpes. Cysts, *tumors*. Urinary stream forked. Feeling that in between *micturations* a drop of urine were passing through *urethra*. Offensive sweat around *scrotum* and *perineum*. Profuse, greenish *leukorrhea*. Proneness to *abortion* during third month of pregnancy. Increased sexual desire.

- **Extremities**

  Rheumatic complaints. Extraordinary weakness in legs. Sudden pain in anterior part of *tibia*. **Brittle, deformed nails.** Warts.

- **Sleep**

  Sleeps on the left side. Insomnia. Wakes around 3 or 4 am. Anxious dreams; dreams of falling, of dead bodies and departed persons. Unpleasant, unrefreshing sleep.

- **Modalities**

  Aggravation: Night, bed warmth, rest (not with joint pain); **cold; humid air,** humidity; change of weather, before and during thunderstorms and other storms; abuse of tea; 3 am and 3 pm, or 3 am to 3 pm, or 4 pm to 4 am; thinking about complaints.

  Amelioration: Perspiration; recurrence of discharges like *coryza*; motion; warmth and warm applications; dry weather; rubbing; pressure; stretching limbs.

  Side most often affected: Left.

- **Causation**

  Bad effects of vaccination.

- **Indications**

  Abscess. Acne. Allergy. *Angina tonsillaris. Arthritis.* Asthma bronchial. *Bulimia. Chronic fatigue syndrome. Condylomata.* Connective tissue diseases. *Constipation.* Depression. *Diarrhea. Dysmenorrhea.* Eczema. *Enlarged prostate.* Epilepsy. *Gonorrhea.* Headache. Herpes. Insomnia. *Leukorrhea.* Malignant diseases. *Neuralgia. Ovarian cysts. Proctitis. Prostatitis. Psoriasis. Rectal fissures.* Rheumatism. *Rhinitis. Sinusitis. Scoliosis. Tinea. Urethral* stricture. *Urethritis. Uterine myoma. Uterine polyps.* Vaccination. Warts. *Whitlows.*

■ **Compare**

Anacardium, Lycopodium, Medorrhinum, Natrum sulphuricum, Nitricum acidum, Phosphorus, Silicea, Staphisagria.

Tuberculinum

Tuberculinum is made from expectoration containing tuberculosis bacilli.

■ Generalities

Great desire **for fresh air though** chilly. Prone to colds, *recurrent* upper respiratory infections. Symptoms change constantly; they appear and disappear suddenly and strike different organs one by one. Perspiration at slightest exertion. **Night sweats.** Urge to move around despite great weakness. Tuberculosis in family history.

■ Mind and Emotions

Discontent. Tuberculinum patients are unhappy because of a romantic dream/longing that remains unfulfilled. They need constant change; lacking roots, **desire to travel.** Desire for freedom. Boldness; looking for risky adventures. Egotism, thoughtlessness. Fickle, non-committal. Changing moods; hopelessness, melancholy, despair. Hurry, speed, hectic rush; anxious not to miss anything. "Burning the candle at both ends". Irritability, anger, rage, aggressivity, maliciousness, violence, destructiveness; children hit their heads against the wall. **Fear of dogs,** especially black dogs, and cats. Compulsive behavior; rituals; superstition. Mental dullness and difficulty concentrating.

■ Head

Terrible headache; as if an iron bandage were wrappted around the head. Headache starting above the right eye, extending to the occiput. Headaches in schoolchildren and college students. Periodic headache. Sties, especially on the red upper lid. Chronic secretion from ears with offensive smell. Lips are bright red.

■ Throat

Enlargement and induration of lymph nodes; enlarged tonsils.

- **Respiratory System**

  Coryza when getting slightly cold, with frequent sneezing. Often very painful *furuncles* in nose with greenish, offensive pus. Hard, dry, hacking cough. Pain penetrating apex of left lung, extending to the back. **Suffocation** even in the open air.

- **Digestive Tract**

  Ravenous hunger; has to get up at night to eat. **Emaciation despite increased appetite.** Craves fat, smoked food, bacon, ice cream, sweets, cold milk. Aversion to meat. Allergic to milk. Chronic diarrhea along with great weakness and profuse night sweats; occurring suddenly and forcibly, especially in the early morning.

- **Urinary Tract and Reproductive System**

  Bed-wetting; bladder weakness and irritability during the day as well. Increased sexual desire; frequent changing of partners; masturbation in early years and in excess. *Menses* early, heavy, prolonged, together with terrible pain.

- **Back and Extremities**

  Wandering pain in joints and limbs, worse in humid weather, before rain or storm; at night and when resting. Stiffness when initiating movement, more relaxed with continued motion.

- **Skin**

  Scaling eczema all over the body with violent itch; worse when undressing and bathing. Oozing eczema behind the ears, on scalp and in folds. Skin eruptions: small, red, itchy spots. Acne; numerous small *furuncles*, appearing one after another.

- **Sleep**

  Head rolls while falling asleep. Sleeps in knee-elbow position. Screaming and tooth-grinding in sleep. Vivid, tormenting and scary dreams. Insomnia. Sleepiness and irritability in the morning.

■ Modalities

Aggravation: Motion, exertion; before a storm, change of weather; in a closed room; when standing upright; wet and cold weather; morning; seaside.

Amelioration: Hot, dry weather; sun, sea, wind, fresh air; mountains, coniferous forests.

■ Indications

Adenopathy. Allergy. *Angina tonsillaris. Arthritis.* Asthma bronchial. Behavioral disorders. *Bronchitis. Cystitis. Diarrhea. Dysmenorrhea.* Eczema. *Enuresis. Furuncles.* Headache. *Hordeolum.* Hyperactivity. *Otitis media. Parodontosis. Pneumonia.* Rheumatism. *Rhinitis.* Sexual disorders. Tooth-grinding/bruxism. Upper respiratory infections.

■ Compare

Calcarea phosphorica, Carcinosinum, Medorrhinum, Platinum, Psorinum, Rhus toxicodendron, Sanicula, Sulphur, Veratrum album.

Veratrum album

Helleborus albus, white hellebore (N.O. Melanthiaceae).

- ### Generalities

Rapid depletion, total exhaustion, **collapse,** along with cold sweat on the forehead, rapid prostration, cold breath. *Cardiac* insufficiency. Coldness of entire body: **cold** from head to feet, icy-cold sweat; sensation of icy needles; coldness as if blood were ice water. All discharges are excessive. Cramps and *convulsions*.

White Hellebore   Photo: DHU

- ### Mind and Emotions

Mental overstimulation. Violence and aggression. Hyperactive, **restless,** industrious; pointless, repeated activity like cutting, tearing things apart. Cheerful, loquacious; singing. Delusions; thinks of self as a great personalitiy. Confusion about identity; religious delusions; imagines self as Jesus or somebody who has saved the world. Delusion of talking to God. Haughtiness, self-righteousness. Melancholy; brooding in silence. Despair about situation; worse in the evening. Despair about social position; anything is justifiable to improve it, even lying and betrayal; **ambition**. Never satisfied with position in society; feels she deserves better. Mania along with desire to tear up everything, especially clothes; lascivious or religious speeches; erotomania. Hyperactive and disobedient children.

- ### Head

Cold sweat on forehead. Fainting, *vertigo*. *Congestive* as well as *neuralgic* headache that drives the patient mad.

- ## Digestive Tract
  Craves sour, unripe fruit, salt, highly seasoned foods, ice, cold drinks, gherkins, herring, sardines, anchovies. Increased thirst for ice water, which is vomited immediately after drinking. Vomiting along with intense *nausea*; aggravated by drinking and on slightest motion. Vomiting and diarrhea simultaneously. **Very profuse, watery diarrhea along with cold sweat.**

- ## Respiratory System
  Cough, especially when entering a warm room or after drinking cold water.

- ## Urinary Tract and Reproductive System
  Cramps during *menses* along with coldness, weakness, vomiting and diarrhea.

- ## Back and Extremities
  Cramps in calves. Rheumatism, aggravated by humidity and lying in bed for a long time. Pain is violent and can bring delirium.

- ## Modalities
  Aggravation: Slightest motion, exertion; by humid and cold weather, spring and fall; when drinking and after; before and during *menses*; during stool; after perspiration; after a fright.
  Amelioration: Rest; horizontal position; warm weather, warmth; walking; eating, meat and milk.

- ## Causation
  Bad effects from fright; from injured pride and honor. Loss of money, excitement, emotions, offense, contempt from others and being looked down on.

- **Indications**
  Behavioral disorders. Cholera. Collapse. *Diarrhea. Dysmenorrhea. Gastroenteritis.* Hyperactivity. Headache. Migraine. *Neuralgia. Psychosis.* Rheumatism.

- **Compare**
  Arsenicum album, Camphora, Carbo vegetabilis, Cuprum, Hyoscyamus, Medorrhinum, Platinum, Tarentula, Tuberculinum, Stramonium.

Zincum metallicum
Zinc.

■ Generalities
Weakness and restlessness (especially in legs). Violent **trembling** of the entire body; jerking movements, contractions and spasms of single muscles and muscle groups. Cerebral irritation and other disorders of the nervous system during *eruptive* diseases or other infectious diseases due to inability or weakness to develop *exanthemata* or as bad effects of suppressed skin eruptions and intermitting discharges.

■ Mind and Emotions
Inner restlessness, always in a hurry; nervousness, irritability, violent temper; irregularity, restlessness, needs to move about. Fiery idealist, full of ideas, loquacity. Pangs of conscience as if he were guilty of a crime. Delusion of being followed. *Hypersensitivity* **to noises.** Moaning and complaining; screaming from pain. Yielding. Mental exhaustion, forgetfulness, **dullness**, confusion. Repeats question before answering. Delirium along with anger, violence and the desire to flee. Depression with suicidal thoughts.

■ Head
Dull, numbing headache, ameliorated by fresh air. Headache with pressure above bridge of nose, confusion, *photophobia* and restlessness; warmth aggravates symptoms, better from firm pressure. *Vertigo*. Impaired vision after eye surgery. Twitching around corners of mouth.

■ Digestive Tract
Aversion to fish, meat, sweets and wine. Wine is not tolerated, even in the smallest quantities. Weakness and trembling from hunger, better from eating. Weakness and sunken feeling in stomach around 11 am, along with the feeling of sudden loss of strength in limbs.

- **Respiratory System**

Shortness of breath due to spasticity, along with constriction as from a bandage around the chest, worse when resting, better from *expectoration*. Asthma caused by suppressed *menses*. Cough, worse from eating sweets.

- **Urinary Tract and Reproductive System**

When bladder is full, patient can only urinate with legs crossed. Retention of urine from *prostate* conditions. Urinary *incontinence*, causesd by spasms, coughing or sneezing.

- **Back and Extremities**

Constant restlessness in legs; involuntary movement of legs, worse when going to sleep; jerking when going to sleep. Restless hands. Burning sensation along the spine. Intense, profound pain at the level of the last thoracic and first lumbar vertebrae, worse sitting than walking.

- **Modalities**

Aggravation: Wine and stimulants, after eating; touch; noise; 11 am and between 5 and 6 pm; mental exertion; **suppressed discharges; hunger,** cold.
Side most often affected: Right.

- **Causation**

Lack of sleep; fear; vexation; stress; exhausting diseases; vaccination; alcoholism.

- **Indications**

Asthma bronchial. Backache. *Chorea. Chronic fatigue syndrome.* Dementia. Depression. *Enlarged prostate. Enuresis. Encephalitis. Epilepsy.* Headache. *Incontinence. Meningitis.* Parkinson's disease. *Neuralgia.* Occupational cramps. *Pertussis.*

■ **Compare**
  Agaricus, Causticum, Cicuta virosa, Cuprum, Ignatia, Kali phosphoricum,
  Lachesis, Nux vomica, Picrinicum acidum, Rhus toxicodendron,
  Stramonium.

Diseases

The following pages explain the diseases listed as indications in the Materia Medica of this book. After a short description, some of the remedies typically given for that disease will be mentioned. These can be employed therapeutically according to their remedy picture.

At this point, it should be re-emphasized that **making a diagnosis and starting a therapeutic treatment are tasks only to be performed by a doctor.**

Abdominal typhus: Bacterial infection with a characteristic 4-week course: First week: fever rises gradually, abdominal pain, headache, relatively slow pulse; Second week: constipation, cough, enlargement of spleen, small red areas on the skin on the upper abdomen; Third week: fatigue, diarrhea of a particular brownish color; Fourth week: amelioration. Possibility of severe complications.

☞ Phosphorus → 250

Abnormal nipple discharge: s. Galactorrhea → 334.

Abscess: Collection of pus within a closed cavity. This cavity did not preexist but was created by a disease. When palpated, a gentle motion can be felt, i.e. the abscess is fluctuant. Often accompanied by high fever.

S. also boil → 320

☞ Calcarea carbonica → 102, Calcarea sulphurica → 108, Crotalus horridus → 148, Graphites → 171, Hepar sulphuris → 177, Ledum → 208, Mercurius solubilis → 225, Psorinum → 264, Silicea → 276, Sulphur → 290, Syphilinum → 295, Tarantula hispanica → 298, Thuja → 301

Acne: Skin disease with nodes and nodules caused by dysfunctional sebaceous glands and hair follicles.

☞ Antimonium sulphuratum aurantiacum → 71, Arnica montana → 80, Bromium → 96, Calcarea carbonica → 102, Calcarea sulphurica → 108, Causticum → 122, Graphites → 171, Hepar sulphuris → 177, Mercurius solubilis → 225, Nitricum acidum → 235, Psorinum → 264, Silicea → 276, Sulphur → 290, Thuja → 301

Acute myelitis: Acute inflammation of the spinal cord. Depending on location and extent of symptoms, this condition can be accompanied by pain, paralysis, or sensory disorders.

☞ Conium maculatum → 144

Adiposity: s. Obesity → 350.

Aging: ☙ Ambra grisea → 65

Agony : Death throes, i.e. progressive restriction of vital functions of the body until death occurs.
☙ Carbo vegetabilis → 119

Alcoholic delirium: Triggered mostly during withdrawal from alcohol. Symptoms like restlessness, trembling, delirious behavior, and possibly delusions.
☙ Cannabis indica → 112, Crotalus horridus → 148, Hyoscyamus niger → 180, Opium → 243

Alcoholism: Alcohol abuse. According to the WHO definition, an alcoholic is a person who has consumed regularly large amounts of alcohol for more than a year and who has lost control over his/her alcohol intake and consequently suffered physical and psychological damage, as well as damage to his/her social status. Clinical symptoms include disturbances of the gastrointestinal tract, pancreas, liver, nerves and muscles, as well as sleep disturbances, trembling and personality changes.
☙ Aurum metallicum → 86, Capsicum → 116, Causticum → 122, Lachesis → 204, Nux vomica → 240 → 240, Sulphur → 290, Syphilinum → 295

Allergic rhinitis: s. Hay fever → 337.

Allergy: Hypersensitivity reaction to certain substances with pathologic symptoms. Acquired through contact with antigens that serve as allergens. The allergy manifests upon a second contact with the particular allergen.
☙ Apis mellifica → 74, Calcarea carbonica → 102, Calcarea sulphurica → 108, Dulcamara → 153, Fluoricum acidum → 163, Iodium → 188, Kali bichromicum → 192, Kali carbonicum → 194, Kali sulphuricum → 199, Lac caninum → 202, Lycopodium → 213, Medorrhinum → 222, Natrum carbonicum → 228, Natrum muriaticum → 230, Natrum sulphuricum → 233, Nux moschata → 238, Psorinum → 264, Sulphur → 290, Thuja → 301, Tuberculinum → 305

Alopecia: s. Baldness → 319.

Alzheimer's disease: Most common type of dementia, caused by a loss of brain cells. The disease mostly manifests in the course of the fifth decade. Symptoms are increasing memory loss, disorientation, diminished energy, and speech disorders.
☙ Ambra grisea → 65, Helleborus niger → 174, Nux moschata → 238

Amebic dysentery: s. Dysentery → 329.

Amenorrhea: Absence of menstruation. Various causes.
✎ Ignatia → 185, Podophyllum → 262, Pulsatilla → 267

Amyotrophic lateral sclerosis: Also known as myatrophical lateral sclerosis. Progressive destruction of the nerves associated with voluntary motor function. Spastic and flaccid paralysis occur simultaneously, in most cases symmetrically on both sides of the body.
✎ Plumbum → 260

Anal fissure: Longish crack in skin and/or mucous membranes in anal area which is very painful.
✎ Nitricum acidum → 235

Anal itch: Pruritus in the anal area, which may be of various origins.
✎ Sepia → 273

Anaphylactic shock: Anaphylaxis is a generalized life-threatening type of allergic reaction is accompanied by redness of the skin, shortness of breath, vomiting, vertigo, and ends in collapse due to shock.
✎ Apis mellifica → 74

Anemia : Number of red blood cells is lower than normal. Various causes. Occurring along with paleness, decreased energy, shortness of breath, during exercise or even at rest. Palpitations, vertigo, ringing in the ears, and headache may occur.
✎ Arsenicum album → 83, Carbo vegetabilis → 119, China officinalis → 130, Ferrum metallicum → 158, Ferrum phosphoricum → 161, Sepia → 273

Angina pectoris: Sudden chest pain, typically (but not necessarily) radiating to the shoulder and the neck. Usually accompanied by shortness of breath and fear of death. Occurs due to insufficient circulation in the heart muscle.
✎ Aconitum napellus → 50, Argentum nitricum → 77, Arnica montana → 80, Arsenicum album → 83, Aurum metallicum → 86, Glonoinum → 169, Lachesis → 204, Nux vomica → 240, Phosphorus → 250, Spongia → 279, Stramonium → 287, Sulphur → 290, Tarantula hispanica → 298

Angina tonsillaris: s. Tonsillitis → 362.

Angioneurotic edema: Acute, allergic reaction, involving redness, edematous swelling, and nettle rash, especially around the mouth; potentially a life-threatening situation if the larynx, pharynx, and gastrointestinal tract are also involved.

 Apis mellifica → 74

Anorexia: s. Anorexia nervosa → 318.

Anorexia nervosa: Eating disorder of psychological origin leading to severe weight loss. In about 10% of cases, patients die.

 Arsenicum album → 83

Anxiety, general: Argentum nitricum → 77, Calcarea carbonica → 102, Gelsemium → 166, Iodium → 188, Kali phosphoricum → 197, Nitricum acidum → 235, Phosphorus → 250, Sulphur → 290

Anxiety, inappropriate to the situation: s. Phobia → 353

Aphthous stomatitis: Inflammation of the oral mucosa, with formation of multiple aphthous ulcers caused by viral herpes simplex infection.

 Nitricum acidum → 235, Sulphuricum acidum → 293, Syphilinum → 295

Apnea during sleep: Episodes of respiratory arrest lasting more than 10 seconds during sleep at night. Occurs mostly in individuals who snore. The oxygen deficiency created can be dangerous.

 Opium → 243

Apoplexy: s. Stroke → 361.

Appendicitis : Inflammation of the appendix. Attacks of strong colic-type right lower quadrant abdominal pain, nausea, and vomiting.

 Aconitum napellus → 50, Bryonia → 99

Arrhythmia : Dysrhythmias. Any disorder of heart rate or rhythm.

 Argentum nitricum → 77, Ferrum metallicum → 158, Glonoinum → 169, Ignatia → 185, Iodium → 188, Lachesis → 204, Lilium tigrinum → 210, Nux vomica → 240, Spongia → 279, Sulphur → 290, Tarantula hispanica → 298

Arteriosclerosis : Sclerosing (hardening) of the arteries. Consequence: insufficient circulation in affected tissue.

 Plumbum → 260

Arthritis: Acute or chronic inflammation of joints involving various causes (often rheumatoid arthritis). Goes along with swelling, pain, redness and hyperthermia of joints, functional inhibition, and contractions.

 Apis mellifica → 74, Arnica montana → 80, Belladonna → 93, Bryonia → 99,

Calcarea carbonica → 102, Calcarea phosphorica → 105, Causticum → 122, Chelidonium → 128, China officinalis → 130, Cimicifuga → 133, Colocynthis → 142, Ferrum metallicum → 158, Graphites → 171, Ignatia → 185, Kali bichromicum → 192, Kali carbonicum → 194, Kali Sulphuricum → 199, Ledum → 208, Lycopodium → 213, Medorrhinum → 222, Natrum muriaticum → 230, Nitricum acidum → 235, Nux vomica → 240, Phosphorus → 250, Phytolacca → 253, Rhus toxicodendron → 270, Sulphur → 290, Syphilinum → 295, Thuja → 301, Tuberculinum → 305

Ataxia: Disturbed coordination of movements, as in the case of the cerebellar diseases.

✎ Argentum nitricum → 77, Causticum → 122, Phosphorus → 250

Atopic dermatitis: s. Eczema → 330.

Atrophy of gums: s. Paradentosis → 352

Atrophy of optic nerve: Atrophy of optic nerve causing blindness after a period of progressive loss of sight.

✎ Phosphorus → 250

Attention–deficit hyperactivity disorder: Hyperactivity in small children and in schoolchildren, accompanied by marked motor restlessness and lack of concentration.

✎ Agaricus muscarius → 55, Fluoricum acidum → 163, Stramonium → 287, Tarantula hispanica → 298, Tuberculinum → 305, Veratrum album → 308

Bacillary dysentery: s. Dysentery → 329

Back pain: ✎Calcarea carbonica → 102, Calcarea phosphorica → 105, Capsicum → 116, Causticum → 122, Cocculus → 137, Dulcamara → 153, Ignatia → 185, Kali bichromicum → 192, Natrum muriaticum → 230, Nitricum acidum → 235, Nux vomica → 240, Picrinicum acidum → 255, Rhus toxicodendron → 270, Sulphur → 290, Syphilinum → 295, Zincum metallicum → 311

Bad effects of vaccination: Damage that has likely occurred due to a prior vaccination.

✎ Silicea → 276, Thuja → 301, Sulphur → 290

Baldness : Increased loss of hair, alopecia.

✎ Baryta carbonica → 90, Fluoricum acidum → 163, Graphites → 171, Kali sulphuricum → 199, Phosphoricum acidum → 247, Syphilinum → 295

Bed wetting: s. Enuresis → 331, Enuresis nocturna → 331.

Bed wetting: s. Enuresis → 331.

Behavioral disorders: ✑Anacardium orientale → 67, Cannabis indica → 112, Cina → 135, Lachesis → 204, Tarantula hispanica → 298, Tuberculinum → 305, Veratrum album → 308

Binge-purging disorder: s. Bulimia. → 321

Bite injury: ✑Ledum → 208

Blackwater fever: s. Malaria → 345.

Blepharitis : Inflammation of eyelids occurring, along with reddened eyelid margins, itching, swelling, occasionally ulceration and abscesses, and loss of eyelashes.
✑ Aconitum napellus → 50, Alumina → 62, Graphites → 171, Hepar sulphuris → 177

Bloody sputum: s. Hemoptysis. → 338

Boil: Painful, acute and purulent inflammation of a single hair follicle. S. also abscess. → 315
✑ Hepar sulphuris → 177, Silicea → 276, Tarantula hispanica → 298, Tuberculinum → 305

Bone fracture: ✑Eupatorium perfoliatum → 156

Bone pain : ✑Aurum metallicum → 86, Eupatorium perfoliatum → 156

Bowel obstruction: s. Paralytic ileus → 352.

Brain contusion: s. Cerebral contusion → 322.

Breast cancer: ✑Conium maculatum → 144

Breath-holding spells: Harmless seizures with no organic cause occurring together with cyanosis (bluish skin), respiratory arrest, and momentary loss of consciousness. Frequent in infants.
✑ Cuprum metallicum → 151

Bronchial asthma: Attacks of constriction of the airways with shortness of breath. Often chronic. Occurs in a hyperreactive bronchial system. Triggered by allergic reactions, infections, emotional factors, exertion or chemical and physical pollutants.
✑ Aconitum napellus → 50, Nitricum acidum → 235, Sulphuricum acidum → 293, Arsenicum album → 83, Baryta carbonica → 90, Belladonna → 93, Bromium →

96, Bryonia → 99, Calcarea carbonica → 102, Carbo vegetabilis → 119, Causticum → 122, Chamomilla → 126, China officinalis → 130, Cuprum metallicum → 151, Dulcamara → 153, Ferrum metallicum → 158, Graphites → 171, Hepar sulphuris → 177, Hypericum → 183, Ignatia → 185, Ipecacuanha → 190, Iodium → 188, Kali bichromicum → 192, Kali carbonicum → 194, Kali Sulphuricum → 199, Lycopodium → 213, Medorrhinum → 222, Natrum muriaticum → 230, Natrum Sulphuricum → 233, Nux vomica → 240, Petroleum → 245, Phosphorus → 250, Psorinum → 264, Rhus toxicodendron → 270, Silicea → 276, Spongia → 279, Stannum → 281, Stramonium → 287, Sulphur → 290, Tartarus stibiatus → 72, Thuja → 301, Tuberculinum → 305, Zincum metallicum → 311

Bronchial pneumonia: Type of pneumonia. The inflammation of the smallest bronchi spreads to the surrounding alveoli.

🖎 Ipecacuanha → 190, Tartarus stibiatus → 72

Bronchitis: Acute or chronic inflammation of the bronchi, which are in the lower respiratory tract. Acute bronchitis may be triggered by the common cold, viral or bacterial infection, chemical irritation, or, in the case of congestive bronchitis, by heart disease. Occurs along with cough, expectoration, chest pain, and light fever. Chronic bronchitis is characterized by a cough that lasts for several months and involves various causes.

🖎 Aconitum napellus → 50, Agaricus muscarius → 55, Allium cepa → 58, Alumina → 62, Ambra grisea → 65, Antimonium crudum → 69, Antimonium sulphuratum aurantiacum → 71, Arsenicum album → 83, Bromium → 96, Bryonia → 99, Calcarea carbonica → 102, Calcarea sulphurica → 108, Camphora → 110, Capsicum → 116, Carbo vegetabilis → 119, Causticum → 122, Chamomilla → 126, China officinalis → 130, Dulcamara → 153, Ferrum metallicum → 158, Hepar sulphuris → 177, Ipecacuanha → 190, Iodium → 188, Kali bichromicum → 192, Kali carbonicum → 194, Kali Sulphuricum → 199, Lycopodium → 213, Mercurius solubilis → 225, Nitricum acidum → 235, Petroleum → 245, Phosphorus → 250, Phosphoricum acidum → 247, Psorinum → 264, Rhus toxicodendron → 270, Sepia → 273, Silicea → 276, Spongia → 279, Stannum → 281, Sulphur → 290, Sulphuricum acidum → 293, Tartarus stibiatus → 72, Tuberculinum → 305

Build-up of pus: s. Abscess → 315, s. Boil → 320, s. Carbuncle → 322.

Bulimia nervosa: Binge-purge behavior. Eating disorder of psychological origin.
🖎 Ignatia → 185, Platina → 257, Thuja → 301

Burn: 🖎 Cantharis → 114

Bursitis : Inflammation of the bursa. Triggered by repeated injuries, constant pressure, or specific inflammation (e.g. tuberculosis).
Ferrum phosphoricum → 161

Canker sores: Skin lesions on mucous membranes of the mouth. Very painful, usually not infectious, white, surrounded by a red area. See also apthous stomatitis → 318.
Calcarea carbonica → 102

Carbuncle: Painful local purulent inflammation that consists of a group of several boils, having multiple sites for the discharge of pus, often found in diabetes mellitus.
Crotalus horridus → 148, Hepar sulphuris → 177, Tarantula hispanica → 298

Cardiac insufficiency: Myocardial insufficiency. The dysfunction of the patient's heart leads to congestion in the pulmonary and the systemic circulation along with shortness of breath, peripheral edema, hypertrophy of the heart muscle, increased heart rate and cyanosis.
Kali carbonicum → 194

Caries: Tooth decay. Progressive destruction of teeth due to external influences, based on genetic predisposition.
Fluoricum acidum → 163

Carpal tunnel syndrome: Mechanical compression of the median nerve in the carpal tunnel in the wrist, causing atrophy of the muscles on the thumb-side of the palm (since these are supplied for by the median nerve) as well as sensory deficits in the palm and the first three fingers.
Calcarea phosphorica → 105

Cataract: Lens opacity. Clouding of the lens of the eye, due to a number of different reasons. Common cause of reduced vision in elderly people.
Aurum metallicum → 86

Catarrh in pharynx and hoarseness after drinking alcohol: Nux vomica → 240

Cerebral concussion: Concussion. Brief reversible damage to the brain caused by an accident. Occurs along with loss of consciousness (for less than an hour), amnesia, nausea, vomiting, instability of cardiovascular system, und headache.
Arnica montana → 80, Opium → 243

Cerebral contusion: Contusion. Closed brain injury after blunt head injury. Symptoms as in case of a concussion but in addition (depending on the size of the

affected brain area) neurologic symptoms and longer period of unconsciousness. In some cases, permanent lesions remain.
- ✎ Helleborus niger → 174

Cerebral trauma: Head injury involving the brain.
- ✎ Natrum sulphuricum → 233, Stramonium → 287

Chalazion: Tarsal cyst. Sterile inflammation of meibomian glands in upper (usually) eyelid by obstructing the gland duct.
- ✎ Staphisagria → 283

Cheyne-Stokes respiration: Periodic long respiration pauses followed by an interval of breaths that increase and then decrease in depth. Occurs after severe brain trauma (respiratory center).
- ✎ Opium → 243

Chickenpox: Viral infection with typical episodes of efflorescent skin eruption, intense itching, and a slight fever caused by varicella virus. Also s. Shingles.
- ✎ Antimonium crudum → 69, Rhus toxicodendron → 270

Cholecystitis: Inflammation of the gallbladder. Mostly in conjunction with gall stones but also from other causes. Goes along with indigestion, intolerance to fatty foods, and occurrence of biliary colic.
- ✎ Bryonia → 99, Calcarea carbonica → 102, Chelidonium → 128, China officinalis → 130, Colocynthis → 142, Lycopodium → 213, Natrum Sulphuricum → 233, Podophyllum → 262, Pulsatilla → 267

Cholelithiasis: Biliary calculi. Gallstones. Only causes symptoms when stones are moving or if the excretion of bile is obstructed. Then results a colic in the gallbladder area, radiating to the right shoulder, accompanied by nausea and vomiting.
- ✎ Chelidonium → 128, Kali carbonicum → 194, Podophyllum → 262

Cholera: Acute, bacterial infectious disease. Occurring along with severe diarrhea, vomiting, and dehydration, which may lead to collapse, convulsions, coma, and finally death.
- ✎ Camphora → 110, Cuprum metallicum → 151, Veratrum album → 308

Chorea: "St. Vitus' dance". Motor disorder with involuntary, arrhythmic, rapid contractions of various groups of muscles almost all over the body.
- ✎ Causticum → 122, Cimicifuga → 133, Cuprum metallicum → 151, Ignatia → 185, Magnesia phosphorica → 220, Staphisagria → 283, Stramonium → 287,

Zincum metallicum → 311

Chorea minor: Form of chorea occurring early in life, especially in young girls; has a favorable prognosis. Associated with rheumatic fever.

🕭 Agaricus muscarius → 55, Tarantula hispanica → 298

Chronic fatigue syndrome: A condition of prolonged and severe weariness or tiredness which is not relieved by rest. Symptoms include exhaustion and depression, sadness, inner restlessness, tension, anxiety, irritability, difficulty in concentrating, and insomnia.

🕭 Ambra grisea → 65, Anacardium orientale → 67, Antimonium crudum → 69, Argentum nitricum → 77, Aurum metallicum → 86, Calcarea carbonica → 102, Calcarea phosphorica → 105, Camphora → 110, Cannabis indica → 112, Carbo vegetabilis → 119, China officinalis → 130, Cocculus → 137, Coffea → 139, Ferrum metallicum → 158, Gelsemium → 166, Ignatia → 185, Kali phosphoricum → 197, Lycopodium → 213, Magnesia carbonica → 216, Magnesia muriatica → 218, Natrum muriaticum → 230, Nux vomica → 240, Phosphoricum acidum → 247, Phosphorus → 250, Sepia → 273, Silicea → 276, Stannum → 281, Staphisagria → 283, Sulphur → 290, Thuja → 301, Zincum metallicum → 311

Cirrhosis of the liver: In cirrhosis of the liver, scar tissue replaces normal, healthy tissue, blocking the flow of blood through the organ. The resulting portal vein congestion can lead to fluid buildup in the abdomen and to enlarged veins in the esophagus. Hepatitis C and chronic alcoholism are the most common causes.

🕭 Lycopodium → 213, Magnesia muriatica → 218

Clap: s. Gonorrhea → 336.

Clavus: s. Corn → 327.

Climacteric symptoms: Menopausal symptoms caused by the changes in hormonal status of a menopausal woman. Symptoms include a disordered menstrual cycle, hot flashes, sudden attacks of sweating, vertigo, palpitations, insomnia, lack of energy, anxiety, mood swings, and depression.

🕭 Lachesis → 204, Pulsatilla → 267, Sepia → 273, Sulphur → 290

Coccygodynia: Circumscribed pain in coccyx, more frequent in women.

🕭 Hypericum → 183

Colic: Spasmodic abdominal pain caused by painful contraction of a hollow organ, usually of the intestine. Often accompanied by autonomous nervous system symptoms.

✎ Magnesia carbonica → 216, Magnesia phosphorica → 220, Nux vomica → 240, Plumbum → 260.

Colitis: Inflammation of the large intestine. Intestinal catarrh with diarrhea.

✎ Abrotanum → 47, Aloe → 60, Argentum nitricum → 77, Arsenicum album → 83, Cantharis → 114, Capsicum → 116, China officinalis → 130, Lachesis → 204, Lilium tigrinum → 210, Lycopodium → 213, Natrum muriaticum → 230, Natrum sulphuricum → 233, Nitricum acidum → 235, Podophyllum → 262, Sulphur → 290

Collagen diseases: Connective tissue disease. General term for a number of diseases that are characterized by inflammatory or degenerative changes in connective tissue due to generalized autoimmune processes such as rheumatoid arthritis, scleroderma, systemic lupus erythematosus, polyarteritis nodosa, polymyositis, and dermatomyositis.

✎ Sepia → 273

Collapse: Circulatory collapse often due to sudden hypotension (e.g. due to excessive bleeding) characterized by a sudden feeling of faintness or by a blackout.

✎ Carbo vegetabilis → 119, Veratrum album → 308

Coma: Deep unconsciousness from which patient cannot be wakened by external stimulation. Many different causes.

✎ Carbo vegetabilis → 119, Helleborus niger → 174, Opium → 243

Common cold: General term for infections of mostly viral origin that present with symptoms of fever and catarrh in the upper respiratory tract, s. also Rhinitis, → 358 Influenza.

✎ Baryta carbonica → 90, Calcarea carbonica → 102, Dulcamara → 153, Ferrum phosphoricum → 161, Kali Sulphuricum → 199, Mercurius solubilis → 225, Nux vomica → 240, Psorinum → 264, Rhus toxicodendron → 270, Sulphur → 290, Eupatorium perfoliatum → 156, Gelsemium → 166

Compulsive behavior: ✎ Argentum nitricum → 77 → 77, Arsenicum album → 83, Iodium → 188, Rhus toxicodendron → 270, Syphilinum → 295

Condylomata: Skin growths in the area of the anus and the genitals, usually transmitted sexually. 1.) Cauliflower-shaped venereal warts (Condylomata acuminata), caused by human papilloma virus; 2.) Broad condylomata, caused by a syphilis infection.

⚕ Sepia → 273, Staphisagria → 283, Thuja → 301

Congenital malformation: Abnormality at birth caused either by genetic defect or acquired during pregnancy due to an infection (e.g. German measles) or other damage or during birth.

⚕ Baryta carbonica → 90

Conjunctivitis: Inflammation of the conjunctiva of the eye with redness, sometimes swelling and discharge.

⚕ Allium cepa → 58, Argentum nitricum → 77, Calcarea sulphurica → 108, Graphites → 171, Hepar sulphuris → 177, Mercurius solubilis → 225, Sulphur → 290, Pulsatilla → 267, Psorinum → 264, Silicea → 276, Staphisagria → 283.

Connective tissue disease: s. Collagen disease → 325.

⚕ Argentum nitricum → 77, Calcarea carbonica → 102, Graphites → 171, Sepia → 273, Thuja → 301

Constipation: Retention of stools. Delayed passing of stools mostly caused by insufficient fluid intake, a diet low in fiber, or an inactive lifestyle.

⚕ Alumina → 62, Ambra grisea → 65, Anacardium orientale → 67, Antimonium sulphuratum aurantiacum → 71, Baryta carbonica → 90, Belladonna → 93, Bryonia → 99, Calcarea carbonica → 102, Causticum → 122, Graphites → 171, Hepar sulphuris → 177, Lycopodium → 213, Magnesia carbonica → 216, Magnesia muriatica → 218, Nux moschata → 238, Nux vomica → 240, Opium → 243, Platina → 257, Plumbum → 260, Psorinum → 264, Sepia → 273, Silicea → 276, Staphisagria → 283, Sulphur → 290, Syphilinum → 295, Tarantula hispanica → 298, Thuja → 301.

Constriction of pupils: s. Miosis → 347.

Continuous fever: Fever at a constantly elevated temperature (>102°F), staying longer than 4 days, with only slight fluctuations in temperature during the day. Many different causes.

⚕ Abrotanum → 47

Contracture: Stiffness in joints. Mostly caused by involuntary, permanent shortening of certain groups of muscles.

⚕ Plumbum → 260

Convulsions: s. Breath-holding spells → 320, s. Epilepsy → 332, s. Febrile seizures → 333.

Coordination disorder: Problems with coordination due to a neurologic problem.
✎ Alumina → 62

Corn : Clavus. Painful callous (local hardening and thickening of epidermis) as a result of chronic pressure on the skin near a bone (e.g. under a toe).
✎ Antimonium crudum → 69

Cough: Cough represents one of the general symptoms of diseases of the respiratory tract, such as bronchitis, diseases of the pulmonary and costal pleura, as well as circulatory disorders. Cough may also be psychogenic.
✎ Antimonium sulphuratum aurantiacum → 71, Hyoscyamus niger → 180, Ignatia → 185, Sepia → 273

Cracks at angles of mouth: s. Rhagade → 358

Cramp in legs: Painful spasm occurring mostly in the muscles of calves or toes.
✎ Calcarea carbonica

Cramps: Involuntary muscular contractions, s. also cramp in legs → 327.
✎ Cuprum metallicum → 151

Crampus-syndrome: s. Cramp in legs → 327.

Cryopathy: s. Frostbite → 334.

Cut-wound: ✎ Staphisagria → 283

Cutaneous hemorrhage: s. Ecchymoses → 330, s. Purpura hemorrhagica → 356.

Cyst in ovaries: s. Ovarian cyst → 351.

Cystitis: Inflammation of the bladder. Symptoms include a burning sensation during urination, frequent micturition, urge to urinate, tenesmus, involuntary passing of urine, and pain in the lower abdomen.
✎ Apis mellifica → 74, Arsenicum album → 83, Camphora → 110, Cannabis indica → 112, Cantharis → 114, Dulcamara → 153, Helleborus niger → 174, Lilium tigrinum → 210, Lycopodium → 213, Medorrhinum → 222, Nux vomica → 240 → 240, Pulsatilla → 267, Sepia → 273, Staphisagria → 283, Tuberculinum → 305

Deafness: s. Hearing loss → 337.

Death throes: s. Agony → 316.

Decubitus ulcer: Skin presenting pressure ulcers, dying of tissue.
✎ Opium → 243

Defects of mucous membrane of the mouth: s. Aphthous ulcers → 334.

Deformation of the spine: s. Scoliosis → 359.

Degeneration of the central and peripheral nervous system:
🐾 Conium maculatum → 144

Delirium: Reversible, severe psychological disorder with decreased consciousness, disorientation, illusions, delusions, and restlessness.
🐾 Belladonna → 93, Stramonium → 287

Dementia: Loss of mental abilities that have been acquired earlier in life.
🐾 Ambra grisea → 65, Graphites → 171, Helleborus niger → 174, Hyoscyamus niger → 180, Plumbum → 260, Sulphur → 290, Zincum metallicum → 311

Depression: Being in a sad mood, gloomy. Other symptoms are a lack of energy, loss of interest, loss of appetite, and diminished sexual desire, as well as sleeping disorders and restlessness.
🐾 Anacardium orientale → 67, Antimonium crudum → 69, Argentum nitricum → 77, Arsenicum album → 83, Aurum metallicum → 86, Calcarea carbonica → 102, Calcarea phosphorica → 105, Cannabis indica → 112, Capsicum → 116, Cimicifuga → 133, Cocculus → 137, Helleborus niger → 174, Hyoscyamus niger → 180, Hypericum → 183, Ignatia → 185, Lilium tigrinum → 210, Lycopodium → 213, Natrum muriaticum → 230, Natrum Sulphuricum → 233, Phosphoricum acidum → 247, Platina → 257, Psorinum → 264, Pulsatilla → 267, Sepia → 273, Staphisagria → 283, Sulphur → 290, Syphilinum → 295, Thuja → 301, Tuberculinum → 305, Zincum metallicum → 311

Dermatitis: Inflammatory skin disease. Various forms, many different causes.
🐾 Psorinum → 264

Diabetes: General term for diseases involving increased excretion of fluid through kidneys.
🐾 Phosphorus → 250, Plumbum → 260, Sulphur → 290

Diabetes mellitus: Increases blood sugar due to insulin deficiency, causing increased urination and excretion of sugar through the urine. Thirst, weight loss, nutrient and water depletion, and multiple complications.
🐾 Phosphoricum acidum → 247

Diaper dermatitis: Diaper rash with redness and swelling.
🐾 Medorrhinum → 222

Diarrhea: Increased quantities of runny stool.
✍ Phosphoricum acidum → 247, Aethusa cynapium → 53, Allium cepa → 58, Aloe → 60, Alumina → 62, Antimonium crudum → 69, Antimonium sulphuratum aurantiacum → 71, Calcarea phosphorica → 105, Chamomilla → 126, China officinalis → 130, Cina → 135, Dulcamara → 153, Ferrum metallicum → 158, Gelsemium → 166, Iodium → 188, Kali phosphoricum → 197, Lachesis → 204, Magnesia muriatica → 218, Natrum Sulphuricum → 233, Nux moschata → 238, Petroleum → 245, Podophyllum → 262, Psorinum → 264, Pulsatilla → 267, Stramonium → 287, Sulphur → 290, Thuja → 301, Tuberculinum → 305, Veratrum album → 308

Diarrhea and vomiting in infants: s. Gastroenteritis → 335.
✍ Aethusa cynapium → 53

Diphtheria: Pharyngeal diphtheria. Infectious disease caused by bacteria. Accompanied by fever, difficulty in swallowing, redness, formation of "pseudomembranes" covering the whole area of the larynx, and swelling of lymph nodes. The toxins of the bacteria may cause severe complications, eventually leading to death.
✍ Bromium → 96, Lac caninum → 202, Lachesis → 204

Diplopia: Double vision. Seeing of double images.
✍ Gelsemium → 166

Disorders of sexual function: Functional disorders of the genitals.
✍ Baryta carbonica → 90, Causticum → 122, Sepia → 273

Disturbance of the cardiac rhythm: s. Arrhythmia → 318.

Double vision: s. Diplopia → 329.

Dropsy of the scrotum: s. Hydrocele → 340.

Drug addiction: ✍ Lachesis → 204

Dupuytren's contracture: Permanent bending of fingers caused by the shrinking of palmar tendons.
✍ Plumbum → 260

Dysentery: Inflammatory bowel disease caused by shigella bacteria (bacillary dysentery) or amebae (amebic dysentery). Bacillary dysentery involves vomiting, colic, and diarrhea containing blood and mucus, leads to dehydration, and possibly to shock. Amebic dysentery may cause complications in bowel and liver later in life.

✍ Aloe → 60, Camphora → 110, Podophyllum → 262, Pulsatilla → 267, Staphisagria → 283.

Dysmenorrhea: Painful menstruation.

✍ Belladonna → 93, Bromium → 96, Cannabis indica → 112, Chamomilla → 126, Cimicifuga → 133, Cocculus → 137, Coffea → 139, Colocynthis → 142, Ferrum phosphoricum → 161, Ignatia → 185, Lac caninum → 202, Lilium tigrinum → 210, Magnesia carbonica → 216, Magnesia muriatica → 218, Magnesia phosphorica → 220, Nux moschata → 238, Nux vomica → 240, Platina → 257, Pulsatilla → 267, Staphisagria → 283, Thuja → 301, Tuberculinum → 305, Veratrum album → 308

Dyspareunia: Pain during sexual intercourse, especially in women. Triggered by physical and/or psychological causes.

✍ Natrum muriaticum → 230, Sepia → 273

Dysphagia: Swallowing disorder involving various causes.

✍ Causticum → 122

Eating disorder: s. Anorexia nervosa, s. Bulimia → 321.

Ecchymoses: Small blotchy areas of skin hemorrhages due to injury or hemorrhagic diathesis.

✍ Sulphuricum acidum → 293, Arnica montana → 80, Ledum → 208

Eczema: Itchy inflammatory skin disease occurring episodically. Most frequent in neurodermatitis (atopic eczema).

✍ Abrotanum → 47, Alumina → 62, Anacardium orientale → 67, Antimonium crudum → 69, Arsenicum album → 83, Calcarea carbonica → 102, Calcarea sulphurica → 108, Cantharis → 114, Carbo vegetabilis → 119, Causticum → 122, Fluoricum acidum → 163 Graphites → 171, Hepar sulphuris → 177, Kali Sulphuricum → 199, Ledum → 208, Lycopodium → 213, Medorrhinum → 222, Mercurius solubilis → 225, Natrum muriaticum → 230, Petroleum → 245, Phosphorus → 250, Psorinum → 264, Rhus toxicodendron → 270, Silicea → 276, Staphisagria → 283, Sulphur → 290, Thuja → 301, Tuberculinum → 305

Emaciation: Severe weight loss, often occurring in severely ill patients (typical for cancer patients), s. Anorexia → 318.

✍ Iodium → 188

Emphysema: Excessive presence of gases in body tissues, as in lung emphysema (overstretching of lung tissue due to hyperdistended lungs).
✎ Lachesis → 204, Phosphorus → 250, Tartarus stibiatus → 72

Encephalitis: Inflammation of the brain caused by bacteria, viruses, fungi, parasites, or as concomitant encephalitis during an infection. Involves reduced states of consciousness, psychological alterations, fever, neurologic symptoms, and seizures.
✎ Cantharis → 114, Cuprum metallicum → 151, Helleborus niger → 174, Ignatia → 185, Opium → 243, Zincum metallicum → 311

Encopresis: Leakage of stool with soiling beyond the age of 4. Caused by emotional conflicts or physical disorders.
✎ Aloe → 60, Hyoscyamus niger → 180

Endometriosis: Tissue growth of normal uterine tissue, involving cyclical alterations, situated in inappropriate sites, e.g. an ovary. Occurs along with pain before and during menstruation (dysmenorrhea).
✎ Lachesis → 204, Sepia → 273

Enlargement of prostate gland: s. Prostatic hypertrophy. → 355

Enlargement of thyroid gland: s. Goiter → 336.

Enteritis: Acute intestinal inflammation of the bowel involving diarrhea, spasmodic abdominal pain, and sometimes fever.
✎ Agaricus muscarius, → 55 Aloe → 60, Ferrum phosphoricum → 161, Ipecacuanha → 190, Nitricum acidum → 235, Petroleum → 245, Podophyllum → 262, Tartarus stibiatus → 72

Enuresis: Bed wetting. Involuntary urination beyondr the age of 4, usually at night. May have a psychological or specific organic cause.
✎ Baryta carbonica → 90, Causticum → 122, Cina → 135, Ferrum metallicum → 158, Hyoscyamus niger → 180, Sepia → 273, Staphisagria → 283, Stramonium → 287, Tuberculinum → 305, Zincum metallicum → 311

Enuresis nocturna: Bed wetting at night, s. also Enuresis → 331
✎ Agaricus muscarius → 55, Magnesia phosphorica → 220, Pulsatilla → 267

Environmental diseases, hypersensitivity to chemicals: Diseases following exposure to pollutants in the environment.
✎ Sulphuricum acidum → 293

Epidemic parotitis: s. Mumps → 348.

Epilepsy: Seizure disorder, convulsions of various origins. Disturbed brain function involving epileptic fits.

🖎 Aethusa cynapium → 53, Agaricus muscarius → 55, Argentum nitricum → 77, Belladonna → 93, Calcarea carbonica → 102, Camphora → 110, Causticum → 122, Cina → 135, Cuprum metallicum → 151, Glonoinum → 169, Helleborus niger → 174, Hyoscyamus niger → 180, Lachesis → 204, Opium → 243, Platina → 257, Stramonium → 287, Thuja → 301, Zincum metallicum → 311

Epistaxis: Nosebleed. Usually locally caused, but may also be due to systemic disorders (e.g. hypertension).

🖎 Antimonium sulphuratum aurantiacum → 71, Ferrum metallicum → 158, Ferrum phosphoricum → 161, Ipecacuanha → 190, Lachesis → 204, Phosphorus → 250

Erysipelas: Bacterial inflammation of the skin caused by streptococci. Clearly circumscribed, tender, red swelling. High temperature and chills.

🖎 Apis mellifica → 74, Arnica montana → 80, Belladonna → 93, Crotalus horridus → 148, Graphites → 171, Ledum → 208, Rhus toxidodendron → 270

Erythema nodosum: Formation of discolored, round, very tender and rough nodules with a blurred demarcation, usually in the lower extremities. Occurs during various general disorders.

🖎 Abrotanum → 47

Esophagitis: Inflammation of esophageal mucosa. Often caused by reflux of gastric juices.

🖎 Argentum nitricum → 77, Carbo vegetabilis → 119,

Excessive vomiting during pregnancy: s. Hyperemesis gravidarum → 340.

Exophthalmic goiter: s. Graves' disease → 336

Eye affections: 🖎 Conium maculatum → 144

Eyelid inflammation: s. Blepharitis → 320.

Facial nerve paresis : Paralysis of VII. cranial nerve (facial nerve) causing paralysis of facial muscles on the affected side, including impaired frowning and eye-closing, drooping of lower eyelid, and dropping of angle of the mouth.

🖎 Causticum → 122, Dulcamara → 153, Platina → 257

Facial neuralgia: Neuralgic pain in the face area.
☙ Conium maculatum → 144

Failure to thrive: In the case of a disorder in the normal development of an infant or small child, many different factors have to be taken into account, such as diet, infections, genetics, insufficient care.
☙ Abrotanum → 47

Faint: Brief episode of unconsciousness.
☙ Carbo vegetabilis → 119

Febrile seizures: Seizures occurring during sudden rise of body temperature, especially in small children.
☙ Belladonna → 93, Stramonium → 287

Fever: Increased body temperature above 100.5°F. Multiple causes.
☙ Belladonna → 93, China officinalis → 130, Eupatorium perfoliatum → 156, Ferrum phosphoricum → 161, Gelsemium → 166

Fever accompanying common colds and other infections: ☙Aconitum napellus → 50, s. Common cold → 325

Fibrocystic breast disease: A benign (non-cancerous) condition characterized by round lumps that move freely within the breast tissue.
☙ Phytolacca → 253, Silicea → 276

Fibroids: Benign tumor of the uterine muscle.
☙ Aurum metallicum → 86, Calcarea carbonica → 102, Kali carbonicum → 194, Tarantula hispanica → 298, Thuja → 301

Fissure: Rhagades. Painful cracks in skin or mucous membranes. S. also Anal fissure → 317, S. Rhagade → 358.
☙ Graphites → 171, Silicea → 276, Sulphur → 290

Fistula in rectal area: ☙Sulphur → 290

Fistulas: Tubular connections between a body cavity and the outer or inner surface of the body.
☙ Calcarea sulphurica → 108

Flatulence: Wind. Distension of the bowel with flatus. May be of psychological, organic, or dietary origin.
☙ Carbo vegetabilis → 119

Flexion deformity of fingers: s. Dupuytren's contracture → 329.

Food allergy and intolerance to certain foods: Symptoms arise in gastrointestinal tract, the airways, or on the skin after intake of certain foods.
 Natrum carbonicum → 228

Food intoxication: s. Food poisoning → 334.

Food poisoning: Ill effects after eating polluted, rotten, or infected food, mostly involving abdominal pain, nausea, vomiting.
 Arsenicum album → 83

Frostbite: Chilblains. Chronic damage due to freezing temperatures. Round, pasty swellings as big as a quarter coin, itching and burning when getting warm. Tendency towards ulceration and blistering.
 Agaricus muscarius → 55, Petroleum → 245

Furunculosis: Recurrent appearance of multiple boils on various parts of the body. Often a complication in metabolic diseases such as diabetes.
 Arnica montana → 80

Galactorrhea: Milky, watery, or bloody secretion from nipple. In cases of secretion from one breast only, or if appearing without prior pregnancy, the cause has to be investigated.
 Lac caninum → 202, Phytolacca → 253

Gallstones: s. Cholelithiasis. → 323

Gangrene: Tissue death. Necrotic tissue of brown and black discoloration.
 Crotalus horridus → 148

Gastric cancer: Malignant tumor of the stomach, causing pain in the upper abdomen, nausea, vomiting, loss of appetite, belching, swallowing difficulties, and general symptoms indicating the presence of a tumor, e.g. weight loss and anemia.
 Conium maculatum → 144

Gastric/duodenal ulcer: Ulcer of stomach/duodenum causing a feeling of pressure and fullness after a meal, lack of appetite, eructation, heartburn, vomiting, pain in upper abdomen (also radiating to the back), and occasionally vomiting of blood or black stools.
 Anacardium orientale → 67, Antimonium crudum → 69, Arsenicum album → 83, Belladonna → 93, Carbo vegetabilis → 119, China officinalis → 130, Graphites → 171, Ignatia → 185, Kali bichromicum → 192, Kali carbonicum → 194, Lachesis →

204, Lycopodium → 213, Medorrhinum → 222, Natrum carbonicum → 228, Nitricum acidum → 235, Nux vomica → 240, Phosphorus → 250, Sepia → 273, Staphisagria → 283, Sulphur → 290

Gastritis: Inflammation of the gastric mucous membranes. Presents symptoms of nausea, gastric pressure, eructation, and general upper abdominal pain.

✍ Aconitum napellus → 50, Anacardium orientale → 67, Antimonium crudum → 69, Argentum nitricum → 77, Arsenicum album → 83, Belladonna → 93, Bryonia → 99, Capsicum → 116, Carbo vegetabilis → 119, Chelidonium → 128, China officinalis → 130, Ferrum metallicum → 158, Ferrum phosphoricum → 161, Graphites → 171, Ignatia → 185, Ipecacuanha → 190, Kali bichromicum → 192, Lac caninum → 202, Magnesia carbonica → 216, Magnesia muriatica → 218, Natrum carbonicum → 228, Natrum muriaticum → 230, Nitricum acidum → 235, Nux vomica → 240, Phosphorus → 250, Sepia → 273, Sulphuricum acidum → 293, Tartarus stibiatus → 72

Gastroenteritis: Acute vomiting and diarrhea, mostly due to contaminated foods. Symptoms begin suddenly and are accompanied by fever and abdominal pain. S. also lymphadenitis with gastroenteritis.

✍ Aethusa cynapium → 53, Antimonium crudum → 69, Arsenicum album → 83, Camphora → 110, Cantharis → 114, Colocynthis → 142, Cuprum metallicum → 151, Helleborus niger → 174, Ipecacuanha → 190, Mercurius solubilis → 225, Nux vomica → 240, Phosphorus → 250, Podophyllum → 262, Pulsatilla → 267, Tartarus stibiatus → 72, Veratrum album → 308

Gastroesophageal reflux disease: Inflammation of the esophagus caused by a movement (reflux) of acidic stomach contents back up into the esophagus. Symptoms (heartburn, sour tasting eructation) occur mostly when lying down, bending, or after having certain foods, alcohol, or tobacco.

✍ Argentum nitricum → 77, Carbo vegetabilis → 119

Glandular fever: s. Mononucleosis → 348.

Glandular induration: ✍ Bromium → 96

Glandular swelling: ✍ Fluoricum acidum → 163

Glandular tumor: Localized proliferation of glandular tissue which can be benign as well as malignant.

✍ Conium maculatum → 144

Glaucoma: Increased intraocular pressure resulting in impaired vision. Acute glaucoma: red, very painful eyes, impaired vision, danger of losing eyesight.
🐾 Aurum metallicum → 86

Globus syndrome: Sensation as if an object has become stuck in the larynx, psychological origin.
🐾 Ignatia → 185, Lachesis → 204

Glomerulonephritis: General term for an inflammatory process within the glomeruli of the kidney due to a number of different reasons. May result in renal insufficiency.
🐾 Apis mellifica → 74

Goiter: Enlargement of thyroid gland.
🐾 Bromium → 96, Calcarea carbonica → 102, Iodium → 188, Spongia → 279

Gonorrhea: Clap. Bacterial infectious disease acquired mostly during sexual intercourse. In men it manifests as painful inflammation of the urethra with purulent discharge. In women there are fewer acute symptoms. May cause severe chronic reactions, such as inflammation of joints, for both genders.
🐾 Thuja → 301

Gout: Acute gout: the attack results from an elevated level of uric acid in the blood, leading to acute inflammation in a particular joint (typically the big toe) associated with severe pain. Chronic gout: joint deformities, tophi, and lesions of inner organs due to deposits of uric acid.
🐾 Bryonia → 99, Calcarea carbonica → 102, Causticum → 122, Ledum → 208, Lycopodium → 213, Sulphur → 290

Graves' diseases: A common type of hyperthyroidism, characterized by general over-activity of the thyroid gland due to an autoimmune defect. The most common symptoms are: goiter (an enlargement of the thyroid gland), a slight protrusion of the eyeballs, weight loss, rapid heart rate, anxiety, and hair loss.
🐾 Fluoricum acidum → 163, Phosphorus → 250

Grinding of teeth: 🐾 Cina → 135, Mercurius solubilis → 225, Tuberculinum → 305

Growth pains: Pain in young people (at night), especially in the legs, without a clear pathology.
🐾 Calcarea phosphorica → 105, Fluoricum acidum → 163,

Hair loss: s. Baldness → 319.

Hardening of arteries: s. Arteriosclerosis → 318.

Hay fever: Also known as pollinosis or allergic rhinitis. Allergic reaction to pollen of weeds, grasses, and trees that results in sneezing fits, itchy nose and eyes, and conjunctivitis.

✎ Agaricus muscarius → 55, Allium cepa → 58, Arsenicum album → 83, Causticum → 122, Dulcamara → 153, Gelsemium → 166, Iodium → 188, Kali Sulphuricum → 199, Natrum muriaticum → 230, Psorinum → 264.

Headache: Pain in the head, may have multiple causes. Different types: tension headache, cluster headache, migraine, as well as headache due to a systemic cause such as hypertension. S. also migraine.

✎ Aconitum napellus → 50, Agaricus muscarius → 55, Allium cepa → 58, Aloe → 60, Anacardium orientale → 67, Antimonium crudum → 69, Argentum nitricum → 77, Arnica montana → 80, Arsenicum album → 83, Aurum metallicum → 86, Belladonna → 93, Bromium → 96, Bryonia → 99, Calcarea carbonica → 102, Calcarea phosphorica → 105, Camphora → 110, Cannabis indica → 112, Capsicum → 116, Carbo vegetabilis → 119, China officinalis → 130, Cocculus → 137, Coffea → 139, Colocynthis → 142, Cuprum metallicum → 151, Dulcamara → 153, Ferrum metallicum → 158, Gelsemium → 166, Glonoinum → 169, Graphites → 171, Hepar sulphuris → 177, Ignatia → 185, Kali bichromicum → 192, Kali carbonicum → 194, Kali phosphoricum → 197, Kali Sulphuricum → 199, Lilium tigrinum → 210, Lycopodium → 213, Magnesia muriatica → 218, Natrum carbonicum → 228, Natrum muriaticum → 230, Natrum sulphuricum → 233, Nitricum acidum → 235, Nux moschata → 238, Nux vomica → 240, Petroleum → 245, Phosphoricum acidum → 247, Phosphorus → 250, Phytolacca → 253, Picrinicum acidum → 255, Platina → 257, Podophyllum → 262, Pulsatilla → 267, Psorinum → 264, Rhus toxicodendron → 270, Sepia → 273, Silicea → 276, Stannum → 281, Staphisagria → 283, Stramonium → 287, Sulphur → 290, Sulphuricum acidum → 293, Syphilinum → 295, Tarantula hispanica → 298, Thuja → 301, Tuberculinum → 305, Veratrum album → 308, Zincum metallicum → 311

Hearing loss: Acquired deafness, may have various causes.

✎ Graphites → 171

Heart attack: s. Myocardial infarction → 348.

Heat stroke: Disorder in heat regulation after overheating. Symptoms are headache, nausea, unconsciousness, rapid pulse, fever (above 104°F), and shock with collapse.
  🠖 Belladonna → 93

Helminthiasis: Infection with worms
  🠖 Abrotanum → 47, Cina → 135

Hemangioma: Benign tumor caused by abnormal growth of blood vessels.
  🠖 Abrotanum → 47, Fluoricum acidum → 163

Hemophilia: Increased tendency to bleeding due to a dysfunctional coagulation factor.
  🠖 Phosphorus → 250

Hemoptysis: Coughing up blood. Bloody sputum has various causes.
  🠖 Lachesis → 204

Hemorrhage: Bleeding.
  🠖 Carbo vegetabilis → 119, China officinalis → 130, Crotalus horridus → 148, Ferrum phosphoricum → 161, Lachesis → 204, Phosphorus → 250

Hemorrhagic diathesis: General term for diseases that have a tendency towards hemorrhaging.
  🠖 Crotalus horridus → 148, Ipecacuanha → 190, Lachesis → 204, Phosphorus → 250, Sulphuricum acidum → 293.

Hemorrhoids: Dilation of veins, taking the form of a lump that protrudes from the rectum into the anal area, leading to circumscribed bleeding, itching, burning, prolapse, pressure, and pain.
  🠖 Abrotanum → 47, Aloe → 60, Anacardium orientale → 67, Antimonium crudum → 69, Arsenicum album → 83, Calcarea phosphorica → 105, Capsicum → 116, Graphites → 171, Kali carbonicum → 194, Lachesis → 204, Lycopodium → 213, Nitricum acidum → 235, Nux vomica → 240, Podophyllum → 262, Staphisagria → 283, Sulphur → 290

Hepatitis: Infection of the liver caused by viruses or other causes. May be acute or chronic. Some clinical signs are lack of appetite, general malaise, enlarged liver, and jaundice.
  🠖 Argentum nitricum → 77, Arsenicum album → 83, Aurum metallicum → 86, Bryonia → 99, Chelidonium → 128, China officinalis → 130, Lachesis → 204, Lycopodium → 213, Magnesia carbonica → 216, Magnesia muriatica → 218,

Natrum sulphuricum → 233, Phosphorus → 250, Podophyllum → 262, Pulsatilla → 267, Sulphur → 290

Hepatopathy: General term for a liver disease.
 ✍ Chelidonium → 128, Lycopodium → 213, Magnesia muriatica → 218

Hereditary bleeding disorder: s. Hemophilia → 338.

Herpes: Skin eruption consisting of painful blisters caused by the herpes virus.
 ✍ Aethusa cynapium → 53, Dulcamara → 153, Graphites → 171, Natrum muriaticum → 230, Nitricum acidum → 235, Petroleum → 245, Rhus toxicodendron → 270, Sepia → 273, Sulphur → 290, Thuja → 301

Herpes labialis: Skin eruption with blisters around the mouth caused by the herpes simplex virus.
 ✍ Natrum muriaticum → 230, Rhus toxicodendron → 270

Herpes zoster: s. Shingles → 359.

Hiccups : Singultus
 ✍ Magnesia phosphorica → 220

High blood pressure: s. Hypertension. → 340

Hirsutism: Male pattern of hair growth in women. May be caused by diseases that result in an increased production of male sex hormones or may have genetic or other causes.
 ✍ Ignatia → 185, Sepia → 273

Hives: Urticaria. Nettle rash. Skin eruption with itchy wheals triggered mostly by a allergic hypersensitivity.
 ✍ Apis mellifica → 74, Hepar sulphuris → 177, Natrum muriaticum → 230, Rhus toxicodendron → 270

Hodgkin's disease: Lymphogranulomatosis. Hodgkin's lymphoma. Disease originating in the lymph nodes, leading to death if remaining untreated. The cause is not known.
 ✍ Baryta carbonica → 90

Hot flashes: Typical menopausal symptom.
 ✍ Graphites → 171, Lachesis → 204, Sepia → 273, Sulphur → 290

Hydrocele: A hydrocele is a fluid-filled sac along the spermatic cord within the scrotum.
Abrotanum → 47, Iodium → 188

Hyperemesis gravidarum: Excessive vomiting during pregnancy.
Ipecacuanha → 190, Nux moschata → 238, Sepia → 273

Hyperesthesia: Hypersensitivity, in particular increased sensitivity to touch stimuli.
Coffea → 139

Hypersensitivity: s. Hyperesthesia → 340.

Hypersensitivity reaction: s. Allergy → 316, s. Anaphylactic shock → 317.

Hypertension: High blood pressure. Can be free of symptoms for many years while nonetheless causing severe blood vessel damage, in particular in the heart, the kidneys, and the brain.
Argentum nitricum → 77, Arnica montana → 80, Aurum metallicum → 86, Belladonna → 93, Calcarea carbonica → 102, Dulcamara → 153, Glonoinum → 169, Kali carbonicum → 194, Lachesis → 204, Lycopodium → 213, Medorrhinum → 222, Nux vomica → 240, Phosphorus → 250, Plumbum → 260, Sulphur → 290

Hypertensive crisis: Critical elevation of blood pressure.
Lachesis → 204

Hyperthyroidism: A hyperactivity of the thyroid gland leading to increased nervousness, insomnia, weight loss despite increased appetite, intolerance to heat, and diarrhea. See also Graves's disease. → 336.
Iodium → 188, Lachesis → 204, Spongia → 279

Hypochondriasis: Excessive preoccupation with one's health, pathological tendency to self-observation, and overrating of one's observations as signs of serious illness.
Conium maculatum → 144

Hypomenorrhea: Weak menstrual flow.
Pulsatilla → 267

Hypothyroidism: Reduced hormonal production in the thyroid gland resulting in lack of energy, poor concentration and memory, insensitivity to cold, muscular weakness, constipation, and a depressed mood.
Calcarea carbonica → 102

Icterus: s. Jaundice → 344.
Chelidonium → 128, Natrum sulphuricum → 233

Ileus: Obstruction of the bowel; can be mechanical (e.g. due to a tumor) or paralytic (e.g. in reaction to an inflammation), s. paralytic Ileus → 352.

Impetigo contagiosa: Contagious, purulent skin eruption with blisters, pustules, and yellow crusts caused by a bacterial infection.
✎ Antimonium crudum → 69, Calcarea sulphurica → 108, Hepar sulphuris → 177, Nitricum acidum → 235, Rhus toxicodendron → 270, Graphites → 171, Sulphur → 290

Impotence: Inability of a man to perform sexual intercourse because of failure to have or maintain an erection - also called erectile dysfunction
✎ Argentum nitricum → 77, Causticum → 122, Lycopodium → 213, Nux vomica → 240, Phosphoricum acidum → 247,

Incontinence: Involuntary passing of urine or stool.
✎ Zincum metallicum → 311

Infantile colic: Intestinal colic in infants during the first three months of life.
✎ Chamomilla → 126, Colocynthis → 142, Magnesia phosphorica → 220

Infection of upper airways: Viral or bacterial infection of the nose or throat.
✎ Antimonium crudum → 69, Tuberculinum → 305

Infection of upper respiratory tract: Catarrh of nose, larynx, and pharynx.
✎ Gelsemium → 166, Mercurius solubilis → 225

Inferiority complex: ✎Anacardium orientale → 67

Infertility : ✎Pulsatilla → 267

Inflammation of appendix: s. Appendicitis → 318.

Inflammation of bladder: s. Cystitis → 327.

Inflammation of bursae: s. Bursitis → 322.

Inflammation of esophageal mucosa: s. Esophagitis → 332.

Inflammation of gallbladder: s. Cholecystitis → 323.

Inflammation of joints: s. Arthritis → 318, s. Synovitis → 362.

Inflammation of larynx: s. Laryngitis → 344.

Inflammation of liver: s. Hepatitis → 338, s. Jaundice → 344.

Inflammation of nerves: s. Neuritis. → 350

Inflammation of paranasal sinuses: s. Sinusitis → 360.

Inflammation of parotid glands: s. Parotitis. → 352

Inflammation of prostate gland: s. Prostatitis → 355.

Inflammation of rectum: s. Proctitis → 355.

Inflammation of spinal cord: s. Acute myelitis → 315.

Inflammation of testicles: s. Orchitis → 351.

Inflammation of the brain: s. Encephalitis → 331, s. Meningoencephalitis → 346.

Inflammation of the breast: s. Mastitis → 346.

Inflammation of the conjunctiva (of the eye): s. Conjunctivitis. → 326.

Inflammation of the cornea (of the eye): s. Keratitis → 344.

Inflammation of the heart muscle: s. Myocarditis → 349.

Inflammation of the iris: s. Iritis → 343.

Inflammation of the middle ear: s. Otitis media → 351.

Inflammation of the pelvis: Inflammation in pelvic area.
⮺ Sepia → 273

Inflammation of the pericardium: s. Pericarditis → 352.

Inflammation of thyroid gland: s. Thyroiditis → 362.

Inflammation of urethra: s. Urethritis → 364.

Inflammation of vagina: s. Vaginitis → 364.

Inflammatory disease of the intestine: Ulcerative colitis and Crohn's disease are the typical chronic inflammatory diseases of the bowel.
⮺ Nux vomica → 240

Influenza: Viral infection with fever, chills, severe malaise, pharyngitis and inflammation of air passages, headache, muscular ache and lower back pain, circulatory weakness, and a long recovery period.
⮺ Arsenicum album → 83, Calcarea carbonica → 102, China officinalis → 130, Eupatorium perfoliatum → 156, Nux vomica → 240, Sulphur → 290

Inguinal hernia: Protrusion of intestine through a weak area in muscles in the abdomen. An inguinal hernia occurs in the area between the abdomen and thigh.

It is called "inguinal" because the intestine pushes through a weak spot in the inguinal canal.
🔊 Aurum metallicum → 86

Injuries and trauma: 🔊 Arnica montana → 80

Insect sting: 🔊 Apis mellifica → 74

Insomnia: 🔊 Arsenicum album → 83, Aurum metallicum → 86, China officinalis → 130, Cimicifuga → 133 Coffea → 139, Gelsemium → 166, Hyoscyamus niger → 180, Kali carbonicum → 194, Lachesis → 204, Magnesia carbonica → 216, Magnesia muriatica → 218, Nux vomica → 240, Opium → 243, Platina → 257, Psorinum → 264, Pulsatilla → 267, Staphisagria → 283, Syphilinum → 295, Thuja → 301, Tuberculinum → 305.

Intermittent claudication: Temporary limping occurring in patients with occlusive arterial disease of the legs. The muscular pain caused by ischemia forces patients to take intermittent rests while walking.
🔊 Lachesis → 204

Intestinal atony: Relaxation, atony of gastrointestinal tract.
🔊 Alumina → 62

Intestinal catarrh: s. Enteritis → 331, s. Colitis → 325.

Iritis: Inflammation of the iris of the eye, frequently also involving the ciliary body.
🔊 Aurum metallicum → 86

Irritable bladder: Frequent urge to urinate and increased frequency of micturition.
🔊 Nux vomica → 240

Irritable bowel syndrome: Irritable colon. Nonorganic bowel condition with alternating pain, diarrhea, constipation, loss of appetite, nausea, bloatedness, and flatulence.
🔊 Agaricus muscarius → 55, Argentum nitricum → 77, Natrum carbonicum → 228, Natrum muriaticum → 230, Nux vomica → 240

Ischialgia: Pain in areas of innervation served by the ischiadic nerve.
🔊 Bryonia → 99, Calcarea carbonica → 102, China officinalis → 130, Cimicifuga → 133, Colocynthis → 142, Kali bichromicum → 192, Kali carbonicum → 194, Lachesis → 204, Magnesia phosphorica → 220, Natrum muriaticum → 230, Nux vomica → 240, Phytolacca → 253, Plumbum → 260, Rhus toxicodendron → 270, Sepia → 273, Sulphur → 290, Syphilinum → 295

Jactatio capitis: Head rolling when falling asleep, especially in small children; occurs in healthy children.
~ Agaricus muscarius → 55

Jaundice: May occur as a symptom in many different diseases. Frequently occurs during inflammation of the liver (s. hepatitis).

Keloid: Hypertrophic scar. Itchy at times. Especially after heat and chemical burns.
~ Graphites → 171, Silicea → 276

Keratitis: Inflammation of the cornea for various reasons.
~ Graphites → 171

Kidney failure: Kidney function is diminished. Kidneys are unable to discharge substances that are usually eliminated with the urine. Depending on the stage of disease, symptoms such as fatigue, increased urination, disturbed sleep, headache, dirty-yellowish skin discoloration, itching, fluid retention, neurologic symptoms, and gastrointestinal disorders may appear.
~ Kali carbonicum → 194

Kidney inflammation: s. Nephritis. → 349

Kidney stones: s. Nephrolithiasis. → 349

Lack of concentration : Increased mental distractibility.
~ Aethusa cynapium → 53

Lactose intolerance: Intolerance to lactose (sugar found in milk) because of a lack or deficiency of the enzyme lactase. In infants it causes diarrhea and a failure to thrive.
~ Aethusa cynapium → 53, Magnesia carbonica → 216, Natrum carbonicum → 228

Laryngeal polyp: Polyp (with the apperance of a swelling) on the vocal cords.
~ Argentum nitricum → 77

Laryngitis: Inflammation of larynx, mostly viral-induced. Characterized by hoarseness and painful cough.
~ Aconitum napellus → 50, Allium cepa → 58, Alumina → 62, Antimonium crudum → 69, Argentum nitricum → 77, Bromium → 96, Carbo vegetabilis → 119, Causticum → 122, Gelsemium → 166, Hepar sulphuris → 177, Kali bichromicum → 192, Phosphorus → 250, Rhus toxicodendron → 270, Spongia → 279, Stannum → 281

Lateral sclerosis: s. Amyotrophic lateral sclerosis → 317
✎ Nux vomica → 240

Leakage of stool: s. Encopresis → 331.

Leukorrhoea: Slight excess of the normal creamy white discharge from the vagina, which can be due to mechanical or inflammatory irritation.
✎ Iodium → 188, Kali phosphoricum → 197, Medorrhinum → 222, Pulsatilla → 267, Sepia → 273, Syphilinum → 295, Thuja → 301.

Locomotor ataxia: s. Tabes dorsalis → 362.

Loss of consciousness: s. faint → 333, s. syncope → 362.

Lower back pain: s. Lumbago → 345, s. Back pain → 319.

Lumbago: Acute lower back pain, often as a result of a slipped disc.
✎ Aloe → 60, Bryonia → 99, Colocynthis → 142, Rhus toxicodendron → 270

Lymphadenitis with gastroenteritis: Gastroenteritis is an inflammation of the digestive tract, often accompanied by swelling of the abdominal lymph nodes. This condition may cause abdominal pain, diarrhea, and vomiting. Severe cases of gastroenteritis can result in dehydration. In such cases, fluid replacement is the primary factor in treatment.
✎ Abrotanum → 47

Lymphadenopathy: Illness involving swelling of lymph nodes.
✎ Baryta carbonica → 90, Bromium → 96, Calcarea carbonica → 102, Hepar sulphuris → 177, Iodium → 188, Kali sulphuricum → 199, Sulphur → 290, Tuberculinum → 305

Lymphogranulomatosis: s. Hodgkin's disease → 339.

Malaria : Malaria is a potentially fatal tropical disease caused by a parasite known as Plasmodium, causing feverish attacks, fatigue, diarrhea, and a range of other symptoms. It is spread through the bite of an infected female mosquito.
✎ China officinalis → 130, Eupatorium perfoliatum → 156

Malformation: s. Congenital malformation → 326.

Malignant goiter: ✎ Fluoricum acidum → 163

Mania: State of elevated mood, hyperactivity, and reduced need for sleep. Often the person will appear euphoric, with an overwhelming sense of well-being and self-importance.

✑ Hyoscyamus niger → 180, Platina → 257, Stramonium → 287, Tarantula hispanica → 298

Manic depression: The sufferer experiences marked mood swings beyond that which most people experience, including the lows of depression as well as the highs of a very elated mood known as mania. S. Mania. → 346

✑ Lachesis → 204, Stramonium → 287

Mastitis: Mostly bacterial breast infection causing fever, pain, redness, enlargement of the breast with the possibility of abscess formation.

✑ Belladonna → 93, Lac caninum → 202, Phytolacca → 253, Silicea → 276.

Mastoiditis: Inflammation of the mastoid bone behind the ear, occurs usually as complication of otitis media.

✑ Aurum metallicum → 86, Calcarea sulphurica → 108, Capsicum → 116

Maturational delay: ✑ Baryta carbonica → 90

Measles: Measles is a very contagious viral droplet infection, causing intense symptoms of catarrh in the upper airways and a typical skin eruption. Typical complications are pneumonia and infection of the middle ear.

✑ Pulsatilla → 267

Meniere's disease: Disease giving rise to sudden attacks of dizziness, vomiting, nausea, impaired hearing, and a buzzing in the ears (tinnitus).

✑ Glonoinum → 169

Meningitis: Meningitis is an inflammation of the lining of the brain and spinal cord and can be a very serious illness. Meningitis may lead to headache, vomiting, high fever, chills, reduced states of consciousness, stiff neck, and photophobia. In young children, it can cause refusal to eat, irritability, and a high-pitched or moaning cry.

✑ Apis mellifica → 74, Arnica montana → 80, Belladonna → 93, Bryonia → 99, Cantharis → 114, Cuprum metallicum → 151, Glonoinum → 169, Helleborus niger → 174, Hyoscyamus niger → 180, Opium → 243, Stramonium → 287, Zincum metallicum → 311

Meningoencephalitis: Combination of meningitis and encephalitis.

✑ Stramonium → 287

Menopausal psychosis: Psychosis during menopause, s. Psychosis. → 356
 ✎ Cimicifuga

Menorrhagia: Excessively heavy or prolonged uterine bleeding, which may be caused by hormone imbalances.
 ✎ Cimicifuga → 133 Ferrum metallicum → 158, Ipecacuanha → 190, Phosphorus → 250, Tarantula hispanica → 298

Mental exhaustion: ✎ Picrinicum acidum → 255

Mental retardation: The overall mental development of a child is retarded due to various reasons. Often genetic.
 ✎ Baryta carbonica → 90

Metrorrhagia: Bleeding between menstrual periods, or bleeding unrelated to the menstrual period.
 ✎ Ambra grisea, Calcarea carbonica → 102, Ipecacuanha → 190, Lachesis → 204, Platina → 257, Stramonium → 287

Migraine: Episodes of intense one-sided headache, often accompanied by nausea, vomiting, and sensitivity to light and sound. Some people also experience visual problems before an attack.
 ✎ Antimonium crudum → 69, Arnica montana → 80, Belladonna → 93, Bryonia → 99, Calcarea carbonica → 102, Chelidonium → 128, China officinalis → 130, Cimicifuga → 133 Cocculus → 137, Coffea → 139, Cuprum metallicum → 151, Ferrum metallicum → 158, Gelsemium → 166, Glonoinum → 169, Helleborus niger → 174, Ignatia → 185, Ipecacuanha → 190, Kali bichromicum → 192, Kali carbonicum → 194, Lac caninum → 202, Lachesis → 204, Lycopodium → 213, Magnesia phosphorica → 220, Medorrhinum → 222, Natrum muriaticum → 230, Nux vomica → 240, Psorinum → 264, Sepia → 273, Silicea → 276, Sulphur → 290, Syphilinum → 295, Veratrum album → 308

Miosis: Constriction of the pupil of the eye as a physiologic, normal response to light.
 ✎ Opium → 243

Miscarriage: s. Abortion → 360.

Mitral valve disease: Disease of the two leaflet heart valve situated between the upper and lower chamber of the left side of the heart. Failure in this valve results in left-sided heart failure. This can lead to an accumulation of fluid in the lungs.
 ✎ Tarantula hispanica → 298

Mononucleosis: Also referred to simply as Mono. Glandular fever, also called Pfeiffer's disease. Infectious mononucleosis, the kissing disease, is an infectious disease caused by the Epstein–Barr virus. Fever, pain in the head and limbs, generalized swelling of lymph nodes, tonsillitis, enlargement of the liver and spleen, and, occasionally, a skin eruption are the most common symptoms.
    ✍ Calcarea carbonica → 102

Multiple sclerosis: Inflammatory disease of the central nervous system of unknown origin, characterized by a slowly progressive disablement. Associated with multiple symptoms, e.g. impaired vision, sensory disturbances, trembling, problems with urination, and spastic paralysis.
    ✍ Agaricus muscarius → 55, Argentum nitricum → 77, Calcarea carbonica → 102, Causticum → 122, Cocculus → 137, Conium maculatum → 144, Gelsemium → 166, Kali phosphoricum → 197, Plumbum → 260

Mumps: Epidemic parotitis. Viral infection with swelling of the parotid glands. Complications in other glands and in the central nervous system are possible.
    ✍ Phytolacca → 253, Plumbum → 260

Muscular dystrophy: Inherited degenerative muscular disease.
    ✍ Calcarea carbonica → 102

Muscular rheumatism: Soft tissue rheumatism affecting the muscles.
    ✍ Nux vomica → 240

Muscular twitching: s. Tics → 362.

Myasthenia gravis: Disorder of neuromuscular transmission of stimuli, causing increased weakness, especially in the muscles in the face, causing drooping of the eyelids and double vision.
    ✍ Gelsemium → 166

Myatrophic lateral sclerosis: s. Amyotrophic lateral sclerosis → 317.

Myocardial infarction: Cardiac infarction. Due to insufficient blood circulation in the heart muscle. Causes severe chest pains behind the sternum (breast bone), often radiating towards the left arm. Symptoms include paleness, rapid pulse and cold sweat, heart failure, shock, and acute cardiac death.
    ✍ Lachesis → 204

Myocardial insufficiency: s. Cardiac insufficiency → 322.

Myocarditis: Inflammation of the heart muscle. Eventually leading to cardiac arrhythmia and progressive heart failure, palpitation, shortness of breath, restlessness, fatigue, and, ultimately, cardiogenic shock.
- Crotalus horridus → 148, Phosphorus → 250, Spongia → 279

Naevus flammeus: Port-wine stain. Due to dilated capillaries, manifested as spots of light blue or red to purple color on the skin, mostly congenital.
- Abrotanum → 47, Fluoricum acidum → 163

Narcolepsy: Attacks of overwhelming drowsiness.
- Nux moschata → 238, Opium → 243

Narcoleptic attacks: s. Narcolepsy. → 349

Neonatal asphyxia: Diminished or deficient breathing mostly accompanied by weak pulse or even pulselessness.
- Tartarus stibiatus → 72

Nephritis: Kidney inflammation.
- Apis mellifica → 74, Camphora → 110, Cannabis indica → 112, Crotalus horridus → 148, Helleborus niger → 174, Lachesis → 204, Nitricum acidum → 235, Phosphorus → 250, Plumbum → 260

Nephrolithiasis: Kidney stone disease. Formation of stones in the kidneys, renal pelvis, and urethra. May cause renal colic and other diseases as consequence.
- Calcarea carbonica → 102, Colocynthis → 142, Kali carbonicum → 194, Lachesis → 204, Lycopodium → 213, Nux vomica → 240

Nephrotic syndrome: General term used for a large number of kidney diseases characterized by the following findings: 1. Profuse proteinuria (proteins in urine); 2. Hypoproteinemia (too little protein in the blood); 3. Hyperlipidemia (too many fats in the blood); 4. Edema (water deposits in body tissue).
- Apis mellifica → 74

Nerve injury: Hypericum → 183

Neuralgia: Pain extending alomg the course of one or more nerves. Neuralgia is thought to be a result of damage to the nerves as a result of physical injury or infection with herpes virus (as in the case of shingles).
- Aconitum napellus → 50, Allium cepa → 58, Belladonna → 93, Chamomilla → 126, Chelidonium → 128, Cimicifuga → 133 Coffea → 139, Colocynthis → 142, Dulcamara → 153, Ferrum metallicum → 158, Gelsemium → 166, Hepar sulphuris → 177, Hypericum → 183, Kali bichromicum → 192, Lycopodium → 213, Magnesia

carbonica → 216, Magnesia muriatica → 218, Magnesia phosphorica → 220, Medorrhinum → 222, Nux vomica → 240, Plumbum → 260, Psorinum → 264, Rhus toxicodendron → 270, Stannum → 281, Syphilinum → 295, Tarantula hispanica → 298, Thuja → 301, Veratrum album → 308, Zincum metallicum → 311

Neurasthenia: "Nervous conditions", including chronic fatigue, fainting, and anxiety.
✎ Kali phosphoricum → 197

Neuritis : Inflammation of nerve → 341
✎ Aconitum napellus → 50, Hypericum → 183, Plumbum → 260

Neurodermatitis: s. Eczema → 330.

Nightmare: ✎ Calcarea carbonica → 102, Stramonium → 287

Nosebleed: s. Epistaxis → 332.

Nymphomania: Increased sexual desire along with intemperate behavior.
✎ Hyoscyamus niger → 180

Obesity: Overweight, or increased Body Mass Index, i.e. >30 kg weight/m² height. May have various different causes. Normally caused by consuming more food than the body can use and by inadequate diet.
✎ Antimonium crudum → 69, Calcarea carbonica → 102, Calcarea phosphorica → 105, Calcarea sulphurica → 108, Capsicum → 116, Carbo vegetabilis → 119, Ferrum metallicum → 158, Graphites → 171, Ignatia → 185, Platina → 257

Obstructive Bronchitis: Spastic bronchitis. Acute bronchitis with obstruction of bronchi, cough, and expectoration. In addition, shortness of breath with prolonged exhalation, stridor (wheezing noise) when exhaling, and an increased respiratory rate.
✎ Ipecacuanha → 190

Occlusive arterial disease: s. Intermittent claudication

Occupational cramp: e.g. writer's cramp. Painful cramps in flexors of hand and fingers after writing.
✎ Zincum metallicum → 311

Ophthalmia neonatorum: Form of conjunctivitis. Mostly contracted during delivery of an infant whose mother is infected with gonorrhea. It can lead to blindness unless promptly treated.
✎ Pulsatilla → 267

Orchitis: Inflammation of testicles, often with swelling, fever, and pain. Often resulting in sterility.

✎ Argentum nitricum → 77, Aurum metallicum → 86, Bromium → 96, Mercurius solubilis → 225, Phytolacca → 253, Pulsatilla → 267, Staphisagria → 283

Orthostatic dysregulation: When changing position from lying down to standing up, blood flows down to the veins of the legs, so that the circulating blood is diminished, and for a short while the blood supply to the brain is insufficient. Symptoms are dizziness, ringing in the ears, vertigo or collapse, profuse sweating, and anxiety.

✎ Phosphorus → 250, Pulsatilla → 267

Osteogenesis imperfecta: Congenital disturbance of ossification.

✎ Calcarea carbonica → 102

Osteomalacia: Softness and tendency to deformation of the bones due to deficient mineralization of the skeletal structure.

✎ Phosphorus → 250

Otitis externa: Otitis of the outer ear is an inflammation of the skin lining the ear canal, along with severe pain in the auricle and ear canal, and swelling.

✎ Graphites → 171

Otitis media: Inflammation of the inner ear. Viral or bacterial otitis media is characterized by violent ear pain, fever, difficulty in hearing, redness, and protrusion of the ear-drum. There is a chance that the suppuration bursts through the ear-drum.

✎ Nitricum acidum → 235, Aconitum napellus → 50, Belladonna → 93, Calcarea carbonica → 102, Calcarea phosphorica → 105, Calcarea sulphurica → 108, Chamomilla → 126, Cina → 135, Dulcamara → 153, Ferrum phosphoricum → 161, Graphites → 171, Hepar sulphuris → 177, Kali Sulphuricum → 199, Lachesis → 204, Mercurius solubilis → 225, Psorinum → 264, Pulsatilla → 267, Silicea → 276, Sulphur → 290, Tuberculinum → 305

Ovarian cyst: Cyst in ovary.

✎ Apis mellifica → 74, Lachesis → 204, Podophyllum → 262, Thuja → 301

Pain extending along the course of one or more nerves: s. Neuralgia → 349.

Painful sexual intercourse: s. Dyspareunia → 330.

Palpitations: Pounding of the heart.

✎ Glonoinum → 169, Lilium tigrinum → 210

Panic attack: ✑ Aconitum napellus → 50, Arsenicum album → 83

Paradentosis: Paradentosis is an inflammation of the gums. It can cause loss of teeth when they become loose.
✑ Tuberculinum → 305

Paralysis: ✑ Gelsemium → 166

Paralytic ileus: Obstruction of the bowel due to intestinal paralysis.
✑ Opium → 243

Paranoia: Mental disorder marked by delusions of grandeur or persecution. In chronic paranoia, patients exhibit a rigid system of false beliefs.
✑ Lachesis → 204

Paresthesia: Abnormal neurologic sensations which include: numbness, tingling, burning, prickling, and increased sensitivity.
✑ Tarantula hispanica → 298

Parkinson's disease: Degenerative disease of the nervous system, associated with trembling of the hands and arms, stiffness and rigidity of the muscles, and slowness of movement.
✑ Argentum nitricum → 77, Mercurius solubilis → 225, Plumbum → 260, Zincum metallicum → 311

Paronychia: Also known as perionychia, felon or whitlow. Purulent inflammation around the nails of fingers and toes, along with swelling, throbbing pain, and redness.
✑ Calcarea carbonica → 102, Hepar sulphuris → 177, Silicea → 276, Tarantula hispanica → 298, Thuja → 301

Parotitis: Inflammation of parotid gland, caused by bacteria or mumps virus (epidemic parotitis).
✑ Bromium → 96, s. Mumps → 348

Pavor nocturnus: Waking with a fright at night in children, anxious confusion, loud screaming.
✑ Agaricus muscarius → 55, Stramonium → 287

Pericarditis: Inflammation of the pericardium (which surrounds the heart). Often occurring with pericardial effusion. Symptoms include pain behind the sternum, fever, rapid breathing, and shortness of breath, and can lead to heart failure.
✑ Bryonia → 99

Periostitis: Inflammation of the outer layer of the bone, where the muscles attach.
✎ Phosphoricum acidum → 247

Peritonsillar abscess: Tonsillitis. Viral or bacterial inflammation of tonsils. Symptoms are a sore throat, fever, and enlarged lymph nodes. Tonsils are red and carry white spots.
s. also Angina tonsillaris → 317.
✎ Baryta carbonica → 90, Belladonna → 93, Bromium → 96, Calcarea carbonica → 102, Crotalus horridus → 148, Ferrum phosphoricum → 161, Hepar sulphuris → 177, Kali Sulphuricum → 199, Lac caninum → 202, Lachesis → 204, Lycopodium → 213, Mercurius solubilis → 225, Phytolacca → 253, Psorinum → 264, Silicea → 276, Sulphur → 290, Thuja → 301, Tuberculinum → 305

Permanent erection: s. Priapism → 355.

Pertussis: s. Whooping cough → 365.

Phantom–limb pain: Paradoxical pain in a non-existing, usually amputated limb which feels to the patient as though it is in its normal position.
✎ Hypericum → 183

Pharyngeal diphtheria: s. Diphtheria. → 329

Pharyngitis: Catarrh of the pharynx; bacterial or viral infection of the pharyngeal mucosa.
✎ Aconitum napellus → 50, Allium cepa → 58, Alumina → 62, Apis mellifica → 74, Argentum nitricum → 77, Arsenicum album → 83, Belladonna → 93, Bromium → 96, Calcarea carbonica → 102, Cantharis → 114, Crotalus horridus → 148, Ferrum phosphoricum → 161, Fluoricum acidum → 163, Hepar sulphuris → 177, Lac caninum → 202, Lachesis → 204, Lycopodium → 213, Mercurius solubilis → 225, Natrum carbonicum → 228, Nitricum acidum → 235, Phosphorus → 250, Phytolacca → 253, Psorinum → 264, Rhus toxicodendron → 270, Silicea → 276, Sulphur → 290

Phlegmon: Extensive progressive purulent inflammation of the connective tissue, with the appearance of red areas with unclear boundaries, swelling, hyperthermia, pain, and, only rarely, fever.
✎ Crotalus horridus → 148

Phobia: Excessive, inadequate anxiety and fear triggered in the context of particular stimuli e.g. spiders.
✎ Agaricus muscarius → 55, Argentum nitricum → 77, Arsenicum album → 83,

Baryta carbonica → 90, Cannabis indica → 112, Cimicifuga → 133 Lac caninum → 202, Phosphorus → 250, Platina → 257, Stramonium → 287

Photophobia: Dread of light. Unpleasant sensitivity of the eyes when light is shone into them.
>≈ Graphites → 171

Pleurisy: Swelling and irritation of the membrane (pleura) that surrounds the lungs. Pleurisy can develop from bacterial or viral infections of the lungs, such as pneumonia.
>≈ Aconitum napellus → 50, Bryonia → 99, Cantharis → 114, Ferrum phosphoricum → 161, Hepar sulphuris → 177, Kali carbonicum → 194

Pleurisy, exsudative: Inflammation of costal pleura with effusion. Depending on the extent of the fluid accumulation, symptoms include shortness of breath, feeling of pressure in the chest, and pain in the shoulder of the affected side.
>≈ Apis mellifica → 74

Pneumonia: Inflammation of the lungs. Mostly caused by infections. Most important symptoms of bacterial pneumonia are fever, cough, expectoration, and chest pain.
>≈ Aconitum napellus → 50, Antimonium sulphuratum aurantiacum → 71, Apis mellifica → 74, Arnica montana → 80, Arsenicum album → 83, Belladonna → 93, Bromium → 96, Bryonia → 99, Camphora → 110, Carbo vegetabilis → 119, Chelidonium → 128, Dulcamara → 153, Ferrum metallicum → 158, Ferrum phosphoricum → 161, Hepar sulphuris → 177, Hyoscyamus niger → 180, Ipecacuanha → 190, Iodium → 188, Kali bichromicum → 192, Kali carbonicum → 194, Lycopodium → 213, Mercurius solubilis → 225, Natrum sulphuricum → 233, Phosphorus → 250, Rhus toxicodendron → 270, Stannum → 281, Sulphur → 290, Tartarus stibiatus → 72, Tuberculinum → 305

Pollinosis: s. Hay fever → 337.

Polyarthritis: s. Rheumatoid arthritis. → 358

Polycythemia: Polycythemia vera is an abnormal increase in red blood cells, resulting from excessive production by the bone marrow. Symptoms include red coloration, especially of the face, itching on the skin, headache, impaired sight, sensory disorders, shortness of breath, and pain in the extremities.
>≈ Lachesis → 204

Port-wine stain: s. Naevus flammeus → 349

Port-wine stain: s. Naevus flammeus → 349.

Post-traumatic headache: Headache following a head injury.
- Arnica montana → 80

Postoperative pain: Pain after surgery.
- Staphisagria → 283

Pounding of the heart: s. Palpitations → 351.

Premenstrual syndrome: Changes in the body and in emotional state appearing 7 to 10 days before the onset of menses and disappearing when menstrual flow starts.
- Calcarea carbonica → 102, Chamomilla → 126, Lac caninum → 202, Lilium tigrinum → 210, Magnesia carbonica → 216, Nux moschata → 238, Pulsatilla → 267, Sepia → 273

Pressure ulcer: s. Decubitus ulcer → 327.

Priapism : Painful persistent erection of the penis without sexual arousal.
- Picrinicum acidum → 255, Cantharis → 114

Proctitis: Inflammation of the rectum with pain in the anal and rectal areas. Resulting discharges are serous or purulent, or even bloody and purulent.
- Plumbum → 260, Thuja → 301

Prolapse of the uterus: s. Uterine prolapse → 364.

Prolapsed rectum: Aloe → 60, Ignatia → 185, Podophyllum → 262

Prostate conditions: Prostate problems.
- Conium maculatum → 144

Prostate hypertrophy: Enlargement of the prostate gland, which can cause frequent urge to urinate, pain when passing urine, urination at night, urination difficulty, and lead ultimately to kidney failure.
- Picrinicum acidum → 255, Baryta carbonica → 90, Iodium → 188, Thuja → 301, Zincum metallicum → 311

Prostatitis: Inflammation of the prostate. Discomfort when passing urine, frequent urination, pain when passing stools, and general symptoms.
- Baryta carbonica → 90, Sepia → 273, Staphisagria → 283, Sulphur → 290, Thuja → 301

Psoriasis: Psoriasis is a common skin inflammation characterized by episodes of redness, itching, and thick, dry, silver-white scabs on the skin.

Arsenicum album → 83, Graphites → 171, Kali Sulphuricum → 199, Lycopodium → 213, Natrum muriaticum → 230, Petroleum → 245, Phosphorus → 250, Psorinum → 264, Sepia → 273, Silicea → 276, Staphisagria → 283, Sulphur → 290, Syphilinum → 295, Thuja → 301

Psoriatic arthritis: Inflammation of joints accompanying psoriasis of the skin. Mostly in the form of polyarthritis, where several joints are affected.

Calcarea carbonica → 102

Psychosis: State of mind characterized by thought disorder and loss of contact with reality, typically including hallucinations and delusions.

Cannabis indica → 112, Helleborus niger → 174, Hyoscyamus niger → 180, Stramonium → 287, Syphilinum → 295, Veratrum album → 308

Psychosis during pregnancy: Psychosis (psychological disturbance with profound changes in perception) occurring during pregnancy.

Cimicifuga → 133

Ptosis: Drooping eyelid which is caused by weakness of the muscle responsible for lifting the eyelid, damage to the nerves which control this muscle, or laxity of the skin of the upper eyelid.

Conium maculatum → 144

Pulmonary emphysema: s. Emphysema → 331.

Purpura hemorrhagica: Spontaneous, multiple, tiny hemorrhages in the skin caused by decreased blood platelet counts or by inflammation of the small blood vessels.

Crotalus horridus → 148, Lachesis → 204, Phosphorus → 250, Sulphuricum acidum → 293.

Pyelonephritis: Bacterial inflammation of the renal pelvis and of renal tissue. Accompanied by fever, chills, pain in the back and flanks, nausea and vomiting, and in some cases discomfort during urination.

Apis mellifica → 74, Belladonna → 93, Cantharis → 114, Crotalus horridus → 148, Lycopodium → 213, Nitricum acidum → 235, Nux vomica → 240

Pyloric stenosis: Narrowing (stenosis) of the outlet from the stomach to the small intestine (called the pylorus) which occurs especially in male infants. Typical

symptoms are projectile vomiting from the 3rd to 4th week onwards, wave-like motions of the abdomen after feeding, diminished stools, and failure to thrive.
🐍 Aethusa cynapium → 53, Nux vomica → 240

Ranula: Retention cyst of the ducts of the sublingual glands present around the floor of the mouth, filled with thickened saliva.
🐍 Abrotanum → 47

Raynaud's disease: Episodes of insufficient circulation in the fingers due to spasms in the blood vessels. During the attack, there is firstly pallor, later cyanosis, and finally reactive hypercirculation in the fingers.
🐍 Sepia → 273

Rectal fissure: Small tear in the rectal mucosa which may cause painful defecation and bleeding.
🐍 Ignatia → 185, Sepia → 273, Thuja → 301

Rectal spasms: Spasms in rectum.
🐍 Ignatia → 185

Reduced range of motion of a joint: s. Contracture. → 326

Relapsing fever: s. Malaria → 345.

Renal colic: Severe, rhythmic pain in the lower back on one side (the loin), which radiates to other areas. It can be caused by kidney stones but by some other diseases as well.
🐍 Colocynthis → 142

Retention of stools: s. Constipation → 325.

Retention of urine: Inability to pass urine in spite of a full bladder.
🐍 Aconitum napellus → 50

Retinal detachment: Due to the detachment of the retina, the patient may experience flashes of light, dark clouding, blurred vision, and complete loss of sight.
🐍 Phosphorus → 250

Retinal hemorrhage: Hemorrhage of the retina of the eye.
🐍 Lachesis → 204, Phosphorus → 250

Rhagades: Cracks or fissures in the skin, occurring especially at the angles of the mouth, due to an infection. Heal with difficulty.
≥ Nitricum acidum → 235

Rheumatoid arthritis: Chronic inflammatory, destructive joint disease which can also affect other organ systems.
≥ Calcarea carbonica → 102

Rheumatoid-collagen disease: Any disorder affecting the connective tissue. Symptoms include muscle stiffness, soreness, and pain in the joints.
≥ Bryonia → 99, Causticum → 122, Cimicifuga → 133 Dulcamara → 153, Ferrum metallicum → 158, Kali Sulphuricum → 199, Ledum → 208, Mercurius solubilis → 225, Phytolacca → 253, Pulsatilla → 267, Rhus toxicodendron → 270, Sulphur → 290, Thuja → 301, Tuberculinum → 305, Veratrum album → 308.

Rhinitis: Coryza, nasal catarrh. Catarrh of the nasal mucosa involving discharge of runny or mucous-purulent secretion. S. also common cold.
≥ Aconitum napellus → 50, Allium cepa → 58, Alumina → 62, Antimonium sulphuratum aurantiacum → 71, Bromium → 96, Calcarea carbonica → 102, Camphora → 110, Fluoricum acidum → 163, Iodium → 188, Kali bichromicum → 192, Mercurius solubilis → 225, Nitricum acidum → 235, Nux vomica → 240, Psorinum → 264, Sepia → 273, Sulphur → 290, Thuja → 301, Tuberculinum → 305

Rickets: Softening and weakening of the bones, primarily caused by vitamin D deficiency. Characterized by skeletal symptoms (skull can be crushed, distention of growth areas in long bones, chest deformations, distentions near the cartilage-bone interface of the ribs, deformations and curvature of entire skeleton) and muscular hypotonia.
≥ Phosphorus → 250

Runny nose: s. Rhinitis → 358

Scabies: Violent itch caused by mites, producing raised sinous burrows (caused by scabies) and skin eruptiosn resembling eczema.
≥ Psorinum → 264

Scarlet fever: Acute bacterial infection associated with tonsillitis, fever, and a characteristic skin eruption. Complications are pneumonia and ear infection.
≥ Belladonna → 93, Lachesis → 204, Phytolacca → 253, Rhus toxicodendron → 270

Schizophrenia: Serious and complex brain disorder. It can include positive "psychotic" symptoms such as delusions and hallucinations, disorganized symptoms such as confused thinking and speech, and negative symptoms such as emotional flatness or lack of expression.
> Anacardium orientale → 67, Hyoscyamus niger → 180, Stramonium → 287

Scleroderma: Autoimmune disease belonging to the collagen diseases, with a tendency to induration of the connective tissue of the skin.
> Calcarea carbonica → 102, Sepia → 273

Scoliosis: Lateral curvature of spine.
> Calcarea carbonica → 102, Calcarea phosphorica → 105, Silicea → 276, Syphilinum → 295, Thuja → 301

Seasickness: Type of travel sickness with nausea.
> Cocculus → 137, Ipecacuanha → 190, Petroleum → 245

Seizure disorder: s. Epilepsy → 332.

Seizure disorder: s. Epilepsy → 332.

Senility: s. Aging → 316.

Sepsis: Blood poisoning. Microbes (bacteria or fungi) in the bloodstream typically cause high fever, a general malaise, and in some cases skin eruptions. Bacterial deposits in organs can be dangerous.
> Camphora → 110, Crotalus horridus → 148

Septicemia: Invasion of the bloodstream by microorganisms from a focus of infection; accompanied by chills and fever. S. Sepsis. → 359
> Lachesis → 204

Sexual disorders: Physical or psychological symptoms during any stage of the sexual act.
> Cantharis → 114, Fluoricum acidum → 163, Graphites → 171, Hyoscyamus niger → 180, Lilium tigrinum → 210, Mercurius solubilis → 225, Platina → 257, Tarantula hispanica → 298, Tuberculinum → 305

Shingles: Herpes zoster. Caused by the re-activation of the varicella-zoster virus, the virus that causes chickenpox. May occur many years after the chickenpox infection, since it usually occurs in old age. Shingles appears strictly confined to the skin area of the infected nerve and presents as a very painful blistery rash on a red background.

🐾 Apis mellifica → 74, Arsenicum album → 83, Cantharis → 114, Causticum → 122, Lachesis → 204, Petroleum → 245, Rhus toxicodendron → 270

Singultus: s. Hiccups → 339.

Sinusitis: Inflammation of paranasal sinuses. Typical symptoms include coryza (mostly purulent), radiating pain, pressing or throbbing pain in certain areas, circumscribed soft tissue edema, headache, and fever.

🐾 Aurum metallicum → 86, Belladonna → 93, Calcarea carbonica → 102, Calcarea sulphurica → 108, Causticum → 122, Dulcamara → 153, Fluoricum acidum → 163, Hepar sulphuris → 177, Kali bichromicum → 192, Kali carbonicum → 194, Kali Sulphuricum → 199, Lycopodium → 213, Medorrhinum → 222, Mercurius solubilis → 225, Natrum carbonicum → 228, Nitricum acidum → 235, Phytolacca → 253, Psorinum → 264, Sepia → 273, Silicea → 276, Sulphur → 290, Thuja → 301

Sjögren's syndrome: Inflammation of lacrimal and salivary glands, with diminished secretions causing dry eyes and mouth.

🐾 Nux moschata → 238

Slipped disk: s. Lumbago → 345.

Soft tissue rheumatism : Rheumatism which is affecting muscle.

🐾 Cimicifuga → 133

Spasmodic abdominal pain: s. Colic → 325, s. Abdominal typhus → 315.

Spasms: Muscular cramps, convulsions, increased muscular tension.

🐾 Ignatia → 185

Speech disorders: 🐾 Agaricus muscarius → 55

Spontaneous abortion: Miscarriage. Spontaneous termination of a pregnancy before the end of the 24th week of pregnancy, with the expulsion of a fetus weighing less than 500 g.

🐾 Apis mellifica → 74, Kali carbonicum → 194, Sepia → 273

Sprain: 🐾 Ledum → 208

Squint: Strabismus

🐾 Hyoscyamus niger → 180, Staphisagria → 283, Stramonium → 287

St. Vitus' dance": s. Chorea → 323.

Stab wound: ✒ Ledum → 208

Stammering: Difficulty in articulating a particular sound, several sounds, or a combination of sounds.
✒ Stramonium → 287

Stiffness of joints: s. Contracture → 326.

Strabismus: s. Squint → 360.

Strain: ✒ Rhus toxicodendron → 270

Stricture of urethra: s. Urethral stricture → 363.

Stroke: Synonyms: Apoplexy, cerebral stroke, cerebrovascular accident or insult. Usually created by an interruption in the blood supply to a specific part of the brain, leading to oxygen deficiency. Occurs along with changes in consciousness and often leads to spastic hemiplegia, various motor and sensory deficiencies, and seizures.
✒ Argentum nitricum → 77, Arnica montana → 80, Causticum → 122, Lachesis → 204, Nux vomica → 240, Opium → 243, Plumbum → 260, Staphisagria → 283, Stramonium → 287

Stuttering: Hesitation with repetition while speaking.

Sty(e): Abscess of one of the glands in the eyelids.
✒ Graphites → 171, Pulsatilla → 267, Silicea → 276, Staphisagria → 283, Tuberculinum → 305

Suicidal behavior: Suicidal behavior indicates that a person intends to, or attempts to, commit suicide.
✒ Aurum metallicum → 86, Natrum sulphuricum → 233

Sun allergy: Inflammatory allergic skin reaction from exposure to light and the presence of a particular allergen.
✒ Fluoricum acidum → 163

Sunburn: Redness and eczema on the skin after exposure to the sun.
✒ Fluoricum acidum → 163, Belladonna → 93

Sunstroke: Violent headache after extensive exposure to the sun; also gives rise to nausea, fever, vertigo, and possibly collapse and death.
✒ Agaricus muscarius → 55, Belladonna → 93, Camphora → 110, Glonoinum → 169

Swallowing difficulty: s. Dysphagia → 330.

Swelling of lymph nodes: s. Adenopathy → 319.

Syncope: Short fainting fit.
Nux moschata → 238

Synovitis: Inflammation of inner lining of the joint capsule; type of joint inflammation leading to joint effusion.
Apis mellifica → 74

Systemic lupus erythematodes: Autoimmune disease belonging to the collagen diseases that can affect joints, skin, kidneys, nervous system, heart, and lungs.
Calcarea carbonica → 102

Tabes dorsalis: Late stage of syphilis, with locomotor ataxia.
Argentum nitricum → 77

Tachyarrhythmia: Heart arrhythmia accompanied by rapid heart rate
Aconitum napellus → 50

Tachycardia: Acceleration of heart rate.
Aconitum napellus → 50

Teething problems: Teething problems almost always accompanied by a disturbed general state of the infant. s. Dentitio difficilis.
Calcarea carbonica → 102, Calcarea phosphorica → 105, Chamomilla → 126, Magnesia muriatica → 218, Magnesia phosphorica → 220, Phytolacca, → 253 Podophyllum → 262

Tenosynovitis: Inflammation of the tendon sheaths.
Fluoricum acidum → 163, Rhus toxicodendron → 270

Testicular tumor: Tumor in testicles, malignant or benign.
Tarantula hispanica → 298

Thyroiditis: Inflammation of thyroid gland.
Lachesis → 204

Tics: Involuntary sudden, quick muscular twitches.
Agaricus muscarius → 55, Cuprum metallicum → 151, Ignatia → 185

Tinnitus: Ringing in the ear, ear noises.
Phosphorus → 250

Tonsillitis: s. Angina tonsillaris → 317, s. Mononucleosis → 348.

Tooth ache: ✍ Chamomilla → 126, Coffea → 139, Magnesia muriatica → 218, Magnesia phosphorica → 220, Phytolacca → 253

Tooth decay: s. Caries → 322.

Travel sickness: Irritation of the equilibrium center in the inner ear caused by a particular motion (seasickness, or sickness when traveling by airplane, train, or car) leading to vertigo, pallor, nausea, vomiting, sudden sweating, and a lowering of blood pressure.
✍ Cocculus → 137, Petroleum → 245

Tremor: Muscular trembling. S. also Parkinson's disease. → 352
✍ Argentum nitricum → 77, Gelsemium → 166

Tuberculosis: Chrinic bacterial infection, mostly confined to the respiratory tract but may also affect any other organ.
✍ Bromium → 96, Conium maculatum → 144, Kali Sulphuricum → 199, Phosphorus → 250

Ulceration of the throat: ✍ Argentum nitricum → 77

Ulcerative colitis: Chronic inflammatory disease of the colon. Characterized by abdominal complaints with violent tenesmus, diarrhea containing mucus and blood, ulceration, shrinking with scar formation, and constriction of intestine.
✍ Helleborus niger → 174

Ulcerative stomatitis: s. Aphthous stomatitis. → 318

Unconsciousness: s. Coma → 325.

Undescended testicles: If the testicles fail to fully drop from their initial abdominal location into the scrotum, these undescended testicles may be the cause of infertility in a man.
✍ Aurum metallicum → 86

Upper respiratory tract diseases: Inflammation of upper airways with symptoms of common cold.
✍ Allium cepa → 58, Silicea → 276, Stannum → 281

Urethral stricture: Abnormal narrowing of the urethra, mostly caused by trauma or infection. Sometimes congenital.
✍ Thuja → 301

Urethritis: Inflammation of urethra. Patient presents with difficulty in urinating, and pain. In chronic cases, constriction of the urethra is possible.
🖎 Cantharis → 114, Capsicum → 116, Lycopodium → 213, Medorrhinum → 222, Nitricum acidum → 235, Thuja → 301

Urinary incontinence: Involuntary loss of urine.
🖎 Causticum → 122

Urinary incontinence: Involuntary urination from straining the bladder sphincter, i.e. through the actions of coughing, laughing etc.
🖎 Natrum muriaticum → 230, Pulsatilla → 267, Sepia → 273

Urinary tract infection: Bacterial infestion of urinary tract. May be confined to the bladder but may also extend to the kidneys.
🖎 Pulsatilla → 267

Urticaria: s. Hives → 339.

Uterine fibroids: s. Fibroids → 333.

Uterine inertia: s. Cimicifuga → 133.

Uterine polyposis: s. Uterine polyp → 364.

Uterine polyps: Pedunculated, benign glandular tumors or growth of mucous membrane within uterus.
🖎 Thuja → 301

Uterine prolapse: Prolapse of uterus.
🖎 Lilium tigrinum → 210, Podophyllum → 262, Sepia → 273

Vaginal discharge: s. Leucorrhoea → 345.

Vaginitis: Inflammation of the vagina. Causes leucorrhoea, often burning pain, itching, feeling of heaviness in pelvis.
🖎 China officinalis → 130, Graphites → 171, Kali phosphoricum → 197, Medorrhinum → 222, Mercurius solubilis → 225, Nitricum acidum → 235, Sepia → 273, Tarantula hispanica → 298

Valvular heart disease: Different symptoms depending on which valve is affected and the disease by which it is affected.
🖎 Aurum metallicum → 86, Lachesis → 204

Varicose veins: Distended, twisted, superficial veins.
🖎 Arnica montana → 80, Calcarea carbonica → 102, Causticum → 122, Fluoricum

acidum → 163, Lachesis → 204, Sepia → 273

Venereal warts: s. Condylomata → 325.

Vertigo: ✍Argentum nitricum → 77, Calcarea carbonica → 102, Cocculus → 137, Conium maculatum → 144, Ferrum metallicum → 158, Gelsemium → 166, Graphites → 171, Lac caninum → 202, Lilium tigrinum → 210, Silicea → 276

Vitiligo: White, benign depigmented spots gradually increasing in size.
✍ Silicea → 276, Syphilinum → 295

Warts: Benign, infectious neoplasm of the skin.
✍ Calcarea carbonica → 102, Causticum → 122, Dulcamara → 153, Lycopodium → 213, Medorrhinum → 222, Nitricum acidum → 235, Staphisagria → 283, Sepia → 273, Thuja → 301

Weak menstrual flow: s. Hypomenorrhea → 340.

Whiplash injury: Straining of muscular fibers in the throat and neck due to the sudden, violent backward and forward snapping motion of the upper body which is typical for head-on collisions. It may cause pain in the nape of the neck, nausea, and vomiting.
✍ Rhus toxicodendron → 270

Whooping cough: Bacterial infection, especially occurring in children, caused by the bacterium Bordetella pertussis. Involves three typical stages. Firstly, 1 to 2 weeks of unspecific upper respiratory tract infections like coryza, conjunctivitis, cough, hoarseness, and temperature slightly above normal. Secondly, 3 to 6 weeks of severe spasmodic cough episodes, mostly at night (staccato cough, shortness of breath, cynosis), and hemorrhaging beneath the conjunctiva. Finally, 2 to 4 weeks in which symptoms slowly fade.
✍ Agaricus muscarius → 55, Antimonium crudum → 69, Arnica montana → 80, Belladonna → 93, Bromium → 96, Bryonia → 99, Capsicum → 116, Carbo vegetabilis → 119, Chelidonium → 128, Cina → 135, Cuprum metallicum → 151, Hyoscyamus niger → 180, Ipecacuanha → 190, Kali carbonicum → 194, Nux vomica → 240, Sulphur → 290,Tartarus stibiatus → 72, Zincum metallicum → 311

Wind: s. Flatulence → 333.

Writer's cramp: Type of professional cramp. Muscular cramp in the hand and fingers after excessive use of muscles during writing.
✍ Magnesia phosphorica → 220

Glossary

Abdomen Belly, tummy

Abortion Miscarriage

Abscess Encapsulated collection of pus

Adenoids Hyperplasia of pharyngeal tonsils

Adenoma Benign glandular tumor

Adenopathy Swelling of the lymph nodes

Adipose Obese, fatty

Adiposity Obesity

Agony Intense pain or anguish of body or mind

Agoraphobia Morbid fear of open places

Albuminuria Presence of albumin in urine

Alcohol embryopathy Lesion in the child caused by alcohol abuse of the mother during pregnancy

Alopecia Loss of hair, baldness

Alzheimer's disease Most common type of dementia

Amenorrhea Failure of menstruation

Amyotrophic lateral sclerosis Disease of the spinal cord with progressive muscular atrophy

Anal fissure Cracks in anal area

Anal prolapse Eversion of anal mucosa

Anaphylactic shock Allergy triggered shock

Anemia Decreased number of red blood cells or decreased amount of hemoglobin

Aneurysm Abnormal dilation of an artery

Angina pectoris Pain in the heart region

Angina tonsillaris Inflammation of tonsils

Angulus infectiosus Migrating cheilitis, inflammation or cracks in angles of the mouth

Anorexia nervosa Mental disorder with extreme fear of becoming obese and with an aversion to food

Anus Lower opening of the digestive tract

Apathy Indifference, absence of interest in the environment

Aphonia Loss of voice

Apnoea Cessation of breathing

Apoplexy Stroke

Appendicitis Inflammation of appendix

Arrhythmia Irregularity of the heart-beat

Arteriosclerosis Hardening of vascular walls

Arthritis Inflammation of joints

Arthritis psoriatica Inflammation of joints caused by psoriasis

Ascites Accumulation of serous fluid in the peritoneal cavity; dropsy of the abdomen

Asphyxia "No pulse"; respiratory arrest

Ataxia Disturbance in locomotive coordination

Atony Lack of tone

Atopy State of hypersensitivity to environmental allergens

Atrophy Wasting of tissues, organs, or the entire body

Blepharitis Inflammation of the eyelids

Borderline syndrome Psychiatric syndrome that is intermediate between neurosis and psychosis

Bronchitis Bronchial catarrh; inflammation of bronchial mucosa

Bulimia Binge eating/overeating with induced vomiting

Bullous Vesiculated

Bursitis Inflammation of synovial bursae

Cachexia General weight loss and wasting

Café-au-lait-spots Spots of café-au lait discoloration

Canker sores Skin lesions on mucous membranes of the mouth.

Carbuncle Deep-seated pyogenic infection of the skin

Cardiac Affecting the heart

Carpal tunnel syndrome Nervus-medianus- compression syndrome

Cataract Loss of transparency of the lens of the eye

Causation Origin of a disease

Celiac disease Indigenous sprue, intolerance to gluten (protein in grain)

Cervix Neck of uterus

Chalazion Tarsal cyst; chronic inflammatory granuloma of a meibomian gland

Cheyne-Stokes respiration Pattern of breathing with gradual increase in depth, followed by a decrease

Cholecystitis Inflammation of gall bladder

Cholelithiasis Presence of gallstones in the gallbladder or bile ducts

Cholera infantum Diarrhea in infants

Chorea Irregular, involuntary, spasmodic movements of the limbs; St. Vitus' dance

Chorea minor St. Vitus' dance in children

Clavus Corn

Clonic characterized by movements with contractions and relaxations of a muscle

Coagulopathy Disturbed coagulation

Coitus Sexual intercourse

Colic Spasmodic abdominal pain

Colitis Inflammation of colon

Collagenoses Disease of connective tissue

Commotio cerebri Concussion of the brain

Condyloma Contagious warty growth on the external genitals or at the anus

Congestion Presence of an abnormal amount of fluid due to increased influx or obstruction to return flow

Congestive Related to congestion

Conjunctivitis Inflammation of conjunctiva in the eye

Constipation Infrequent bowel movements

Continua Constant increase in body temperature above 104°F for more than 4 days

Contracture Involuntary permanent shortening of certain muscles

Contusio cerebri Contusion of the brain

Convulsion Violent spasm or series of jerkings; seizure

Coryza Acute Rhinitis

Cyanosis Dark bluish or purplish coloration of the skin and mucous membranes due to deficient oxygenation of the blood

Cystitis Inflammation of the bladder

Dehydration Deprivation of water

Delirium tremens Alcohol delirium

Dentitio difficilis Difficult teething

Dermatitis Inflammation of the skin

Descensus Descent, prolapse

Diabetes insipidus Hydruria

Diabetes mellitus Glycosuria

Diarrhea Abnormally frequent discharge of semisolid or fluid feces

Diathesis State disposing to a disease

Dilated Expanded

Diplopia Double vision

Dysentery Frequent watery stools with pain, fever, and loss of water

Dysfunction Impairment of functioning of an organ

Dyslexia Developmental reading (and spelling) disorder

Dysmenorrhea Painful menses

Dysphagia Difficulty in swallowing

Dyspnoea Difficulty of breathing

Dystrophy Disturbances and changes in tissues, organs or the whole organism due to a defective nutrition

Dysuria Difficulty or pain in urination

Ecchymosis Extravasation of blood into the skin

Eclampsia Convulsions in pregnancy

Edema Dropsy, morbid accumulation of watery fluid in body tissue

Ejaculation Emission of seminal fluid

Embolism Sudden obstruction of a blood vessel due to a clot

Emphysema Presence of excessivve air in organs e.g. in the lungs

Encephalitis Inflammation of the brain

Encopresis Repeated, generally involuntary passage of feces into inappropriate places

Endometriosis Presence of endometrial tissue outside ot the uterus

Endometritis Inflammation of mucous membrane lining the cavity of the uterus

Enteritis Intestinal inflammation

Enuresis Urinary incontinence; not due to a physical disorder

Epigastrium Region of the stomach

Epistaxis Bleeding from the nose

Erosion Superficial loss of tissue of skin or mucous membrane

Erysipelas Inflammation of the skin

Erythema nodosum Inflammation of subcutaneous adipose tissue with sudden formation of painful nodes on the lower extremities

Esophagitis Inflammation of the esophagus

Esophagus Portion of the digestive canal between the pharynx and the stomach

Exanthema Skin eruption

Exophthalmos Protrusion of one or both eyeballs

Exostosis Hyperostosis, hyperplasia of bone substance

Expectoration Sputum

Exudate Fluid exuded during inflammation

Eyesight Acuity of vision

Facial nerve paresis Paralysis of facial nerve

Failure Weakness; insufficient performance of an organ

Felon Painful purulent infection at the end of a finger or toe in the area surrounding the nail. Also called whitlow, paronychia

Fibroma Benign neoplasm derived from fibrous connective tissue

Fissure Painful crack in the skin

Fistula Abnormal passage from one epithelialized surface to another

Flatulence Excessive amount of gas in the stomach and intestines; wind

Fluor Discharge, leucorrhea

Frigidity Lack of sexual desire

Furuncle Boil

Furunculosis Presence of furuncles

Galactorrhea Secretion from the female breast

Gangrene Necrosis

Gastritis Inflammation of gastric mucous membrane

Gastroenteritis Gastrointestinal catarrh

Gastroesophageal reflux disease Condition in which the liquid content of the stomach backs up into the esophagus

Gingivitis Inflammation of the gums

Glaucoma Increased pressure within the eyeball producing defects in the field of vision

Globus hystericus Sensation of a ball stuck in the pharynx

Glomerulonephritis Kidney disease with inflammation within renal corpuscles

Glottis Part of larynx where sound and speech is formed

Gonorrhea Contagious inflammation of the genital mucous membrane, due to Neisseria gonorrhoeae

Graves' disease Common type of hyperthyroidism

Hemangioma Benign proliferation of blood vessel

Hematoma Bruise

Hemicrania Unilateral headache

Hemiplegia Unilateral paralysis

Hemophilia Inherited disorder of blood coagulation characterized by a permanent tendency to bleed

Hemoptysis Spitting of blood

Hemorrhage Bleeding

Hemorrhagic diathesis Predisposition to bleeding

Hepatitis Inflammation of the liver

Hepatopathy Liver disease

Hernia Protrusion of a structure through the tissues normally containing it

Herpes zoster Shingles

Hirsutism Presence of excessive bodily and facial terminal hair, in a male pattern

Hordeolum Suppurative inflammation of a gland of the eyelid

Hydrocele Collection of serous fluid in a sacculated cavity

Hydrocephalus Abnormal accumulation of fluid in the cerebral ventricles with enlargement of the skull and compression of the brain

Hydrophobia Horror of water

Hyperemesis Excessive vomiting

Hyperemesis gravidarum Exciessive vomiting during pregnancy

Hyperesthesia Hypersensitivity to stimuli

Hyperfunction Hyperactivity, increased function

Hyperhidrosis Excessive or profuse sweating

Hypersensitivity Abnormal sensitivity with an exaggerated response to a stimulus

Hypertension Increased pressure, tension or tonus; high blood pressure

Hyperthyroidism Overactive thyroid gland with an increased secretion of thyroid hormone

Hypertrophy Enlargement

Hypofunction Reduced function

Hypomenorrhea Weak menstrual period

Hypoplasia Underdevelopment of a tissue or organ

Hypotension Diminished pressure, tension or tonus

Hypothyroidism Hypofunction of thyroid gland with a reduced secretion of thyroid hormone

Ileus Intestinal obstruction

Imbecility Intellectual deficit, stupidity

Impetigo contagiosa Contagious pyoderma

Incontinence Involuntary passing of urine or stool

Infantile colic Colic during the first three months

Infectious mononucleosis Acute febrile illness caused by the Epstein-Barr virus

Inspiration Breathing in

Intermittent claudication Intermittent limping caused by ischemia of the muscles

Intoxication Poisoning

Iritis Inflammation of iris

Jactatio capitis Tossing about from side to side, especially of the head

Keloid Nodular, firm, movable mass of hyperplastic scar tissue

Keratitis Inflammation of cornea

Lactose intolerance Disorder with abdominal cramps and diarrhea after consumption of food containing lactose

Laryngitis Inflammation of larynx

Larynx Organ of voice production, part of the respiratory tract

Lateral On the side

Leucorrhea Excessive white vaginal discharge

Leukemia Progressive proliferation of abnormal leukocytes

Lochia Dicharge from the vagina following childbirth

Lumbago Pain in mid and lower back

Lupus erythematodes Autoimmune disease (connective tissue disease) affecting joints, skin, kidneys, nervous system and heart

Lymphadenitis Inflammatory swelling of lymph nodes

Mamma Breast

Marasmus Cachexia, especially in young children, due to prolonged dietary deficiency

Mastitis Inflammation of mammary gland

Mastoiditis Inflammation of the mastoid bone

Mastopathy Disease of the breasts

Menarche First menstrual period

Meningitis Inflammation of the membranes of the brain

Meningoencephalitis Inflammation of the membranes of the brain and of the brain

Menopause Permanent cessation of the menses

Menorrhagia Excessively prolonged menstruation

Menses Periodic physiologic hemorrhage from the uterine mucous membrane

Meteorism Swelling of the abdomen from gas in the intestinal or peritoneal cavity

Metrorrhagia Irregular, acyclic bleeding from the uterus between periods

Miosis Contraction of pupils

Mucopurulent Containing mucus and pus

Multiple Sclerosis Demyelinating disease of the central nervous system, causing plaques in the brain and spinal cord

Muscular dystrophy Progressive degenerative disorders affecting skeletal muscles

Mycosis Disease due to a fungus

Mydriasis Dilation of pupils

Myelitis Inflammation of the spinal cord

Myocardial infarction Sudden necrosis of an area of the heart muscle due to occlusion of a coronary artery

Myocarditis Inflammation of the heart muscle

Myoma Benign muscular tumor

Narcolepsy Recurring episodes of sleep during the day with often disrupted nocturnal sleep

Nausea Feeling of sickness in the stomach with an urge to vomit

Neonatorum Of the new-born

Nephritis Kidney inflammation

Nephrolithiasis Kidney stones

Nephropathy Kidney disease

Nephrotic syndrome Clinical state with edema, albuminuria, and decreased plasma albumin due to kidney disease

Neuralgia Sharp pain extending along a nerve or a group of nerves

Neurasthenia Condition of fatigue accompanying or following depression

Neuritis Inflammation of a nerve

Nevus Circumscribed, usually hyperpigmented malformation of the skin, e.g. a mole or birthmark

Nevus flammeus Large congenital vascular nevus; port-wine stain

Nocturnal enuresis Bed-wetting; urinary incontinence during sleep

Nosode Homeopathic remedy made from secretions of diseased persons or from products of morbid organs

Nystagmus Spasmodic movement of the eyes

Oligophrenia Mental retardation

Ophthalmia Eye disease

Ophthalmia neonatorum Eye inflammation of the new-born

Orchitis Inflammation of the testicles

Osteogenesis imperfecta Hereditary disease with abnormally brittle, easily fractured bones

Osteomalacia Disease with a gradual softening and bending of the bones

Otalgia Earache

Otitis externa Inflammation of the external ear

Otitis media Inflammation of the middle ear/tympanum

Ovarian cyst Cystic tumor of the ovary

Ovary One of the paired female reproductive glands

Palliative Remedy that is alleviating symptoms without curing the underlying disease

Palpitation Irregular, rapid beating or pulsation of the heart

Paracentesis Removal of fluid from a body cavity using a needle, trocar, cannula, or other hollow instrument

Paralysis Loss of voluntary movement (motor function), usually due to damage to the nerve supply

Paresthesia Abnormal sensation of the skin without objective cause, e.g. numbness, tingling, or creeping

Paronychia Infection at the end of a finger or toe in the area surrounding the nail

Parotitis Inflammation of parotid gland

Pathology Science of diseases

Pavor nocturnus Night-terrors; waking with a fright at night in children

Pericarditis Inflammation of the lining around the heart, the pericardium

Perineum Area between the thighs, the genital organs and the anus

Periosteum Dense fibrous membrane covering the surface of bones

Periostitis Inflammation of periosteum

Peritonitis Inflammation of the peritoneum

Pertussis Whooping cough

Petechiae Small red spots on the skin

Pharyngitis Inflammation of the pharynx

Pharynx The upper portion of the digestive tube, between the esophagus below and the mouth and nasal cavities above and in front

Phlegmon Acute suppurative inflammation of the subcutaneous connective tissue

Photophobia Sensitivity to light

Placenta Organ of metabolic interchange between fetus and mother

Placenta accreta Abnormal adherence of the chorionic villi to the myometrium

Plethora Excess of any of the body fluids

Pleurisy Inflammation of the pleura; pleuritis

Pneumonia Inflammation of lungs

Polycythemia Increased number of red blood cells

Polyp Mass of tissue that develops on the inside wall of a hollow organ, e.g. the colon

Polyuria Increased volume of urine

Postencephalitic After encephalitis

Premenstrual syndrome Physical and psychological symptoms, e.g. fatigue, headache, occuring a few days before the onset of menstruation until shortly after menses begins

Priapism Painful persistent erection of penis

Proctitis Inflammation of rectum

Prolapse The falling down or slipping out of place of an organ or part, e.g. the uterus

Prostatitis Prostate inflammation

Proteinuria Proteins in the urine

Pruritus Itching of the skin

Pruritus ani Anal itching

Psoriasis Noncontagious inflammatory skin disease

Psychosis Central disturbance of psychological functions

Ptosis Drooping of upper eyelid

Puerperal fever Fever due to infection of the endometrium following childbirth or abortion

Purpura Multiple hemorrhages

Pustule Small inflamed elevation of the skin filled with pus; pimple

Pyelonephritis Inflammation of the kidney and its pelvis

Pylorospasm Spasmodic contraction of the pylorus

Ranula Cystic tumor on the underside of the tongue due to obstruction of a duct of a salivary gland

Raynaud's disease Episodes of ischemia in fingers

Rectal fissures Painful cracks in mucosa of rectum

Rectum Terminal portion of the digestive tube

Recurrent Returning again

Reflux A flowing back

Retardation (mental) Subnormal intellectual development

Retina Light-sensitive membrane lining the inner eyeball

Retracted Taken back, drawn back

Rhagade Chap, crack, or fissure

Rheumatoid arthritis Chronic joint disease

Rhinitis Runny nose, coryza

Rickets Disease due to vitamin-D deficiency; rachitis

Salivation Secreting saliva

Scabies Contagious skin disease due to a parasitic mite with intensive itching

Sciatica Pain in the lower back and hip due to herniated lumbar disk

Scleroderma Connective tissue disease

Scoliosis Abnormal lateral curvature of the spine

Scrotum External sac of skin enclosing the testes

Sepsis Presence of pathogenic organisms or their toxins in the blood; toxemia, blood poisoning

Septicemia Systemic disease caused by the spread of pathogenic organisms or their toxins via the circulating blood

Singultus Hiccups

Sinusitis Inflammation of paranasal sinuses

Sphincter Muscle that narrows and shuts an orifice

Stasis Arrest of fluid flow

Stenosis Narrowing of a duct or passage

Sterility Incapability of fertilization or reproduction

Stimulus Stimulant that can evoke action

Stomatitis (aphthosa) Inflammation of oral mucosa (ulcerative stomatitis)

Strabismus Lack of parallelism of the visual axes of the eyes

Stridor Noisy respiration, due to respiratory obstruction, especially in the upper respiratory tract

Struma Goiter

Struma maligna Malignant goiter

Stupor State of reduced sensibility or mental numbness

Suicide Act of taking one's own life

Sycosis One of the three miasms in the cure of chronic diseases as defined by Hahnemann

Syncope Partial or complete loss of consciousness, fainting

Synovitis Inflammation of inner lining of joint capsule

Tabes dorsalis Hardening of the dorsal columns of the spinal cord due to syphilis (late form) marked by shooting pains, loss of muscular coordination, and disturbances of sensation

Tachyarrhythmia Fast arrhythmia

Tachycardia Acceleration of heart rate

Tendinitis Inflammation of tendons

Tenesmus Long-continued straining

Testes Testicles

Tetanus Disease with painful tonic muscular contractions due to the neurotropic toxin of Clostridium tetani

Thrombophlebitis Inflammation of veins with formation of blood clots

Thrombosis Formation of blood clots, thrombus

Thyroiditis Inflammation of thyroid gland

Tibia Shin-bone

Tinea Fungus infection of hair, skin, or nails

Tinnitus Ringing in the ears

Tonsillitis Inflammation of tonsils, quinsy

Torticollis Contracted state of the neck muscles that causes the neck to rotate and tilt sideways, forwards, or backwards; wryneck

Trachea Air tube extending from the larynx into the thorax; wind-pipe

Tremor Trembling

Tumor Morbid swelling

Ulcer Lesion of the skin or a mucous surface (e.g. stomach)

Ulcerative colitis Chronic inflammatory disease of the colon

Ulcus duodeni Ulcer in duodenum

Ulcus ventriculi Gastric ulcer

Urethra Canal through which urine is discharged from the bladder

Urethritis Inflammation of urethra

Urticaria Nettle rash, hives

Uterine myoma Bening muscular tumor in the uterus

Uterine prolapse Prolapse of uterus

Uterus Hollow muscular organ located in the pelvic cavity of female

Vagina Genital canal in the female

Vaginism Vaginal spasms

Vaginitis Inflammation of vagina

Varicella Chicken pox

Varices Varicose veins

Varicosis Formation of varicose veins

Vertigo Sensation of dizzyness

Vicarious Occurring in an abnormal situation

Vitiligo White, benign depigmented spots gradually increasing in size

Vulva External female genital organ

Vulvitis Inflammation of vulva

Vulvovaginitis Inflamamtion of vulva and vagina

Xiphoid process Cartilage attached to the lower end of the sternum

About the Author

Almut Brandl studied medicine in Freiburg, Germany, where she was born in 1966. She had become acquainted with homeopathy even before beginning medical school, working in the Lahnhöhe Clinic in Lahnstein under the direction of Dr. Max Bruker. From the beginning of her studies she dedicated herself to learning all about classical homeopathy, starting with lectures by Dr. Ulrich Fischer, and then in working groups with other students, or learning from the teachings of the practitioner Bruno Jakobs. She spent some time studying in Sweden, England, and Switzerland, and upon completion of her Ph.D. she worked as house officer in the Children's Hospital in Karlsruhe. From 1996 to 1998 she practiced classical homeopathy at Hof Bellevue, a special clinic for holistic medicine on Fehmarn Island in the Baltic Sea. During this time she earned professional certification in homeopathy, and attended seminars at the International Academy for Classical Homeopathy in Greece with George Vithoulkas, winner of the 1996 Alternative Nobel Prize. From 1998 to 2000 she worked in a hospital specializing in acute-care internal medicine, concentrating on natural therapies and homeopathy. Since the end of 2000 she worked in homeopathic general practice in Altensteig in the northern Black Forest region.

Important inspiration for her work as homeopathic physician came from Anne Schadde (Munich, Germany) and Massimo Mangialavori (Italy). She continues to be thrilled by her own experiences with homeopathy, both as an attending physician and as a patient. With this book, she hopes to lead the way to homeopathic healing for as many people as possible.

Bibliography

1. Allen, H.C.: Keynotes and Characteristics with Comparisons of some of the Leading Remedies of the Materia Medica with Bowel Nosodes. B. Jain Publishers, Delhi. 1991.

2. Boericke, William: Pocket Manual of Homeopathic Materia Medica. B. JainPublishers, Delhi. 1921.

3. Clarke, John Henry: A Dictionary of Practical Materia Medica in three Volumes. B. Jain Publishers, New Delhi. 1978.

4. Coulter, Catherine R.: Portraits of homoeopathic medicines. 2 v; written under the sponsorship of the National Center for Homoeopathy. North Atlantic Books, Berkeley, Calif. 1986-1988.

5. Currim, Ahmed N.: Guide to Kent's Repertory. Hahnemann International Institute for Homeopathic Documentation. 1996.

6. Hahnemann, Samuel: Organon of Medicine. B. Jain Publishers, Delhi. 2002.

7. Hahnemann, Samuel; Wenda Brewster O'Reilly (Editor), Steven R. Decker: The Organon of the Medical Art. Birdcage Books, Redmond, Washington. 2001.

8. Kent, James Tyler: Lectures on Homoeopathic Materia Medica. B. Jain Publishers, Delhi. 1990.

9. Kent, James Tyler: Repertory of the Homoeopathic Materia Medica and a Word Index. Homoeopathic Book Service, London. 1986.

10. Morrison, Roger: Desktop Guide to Keynotes and Confirmatory Symptoms. Hahnemann Clinic Publishing. 1993.

11. Nash, E.B.: Leaders in Homoeopathic Therapeutics. B. Jain Publishers, Delhi. Reprint 1989.

12. Phatak, S.R.: Materia Medica of Homeopathic Medicines. B.Jain Publishers, Delhi. 1977.

13. Sankaran, Rajan: The Soul of the Remedies. Homoeopathic Medical Publishers, Bombay. 1997.

14. Scholten, Jan: Homoeopathy and Minerals. Stichting Alonissos, Utrecht. 1993.

15. Schroyens, Frederik: Synthesis – Repertorium Homeopathicum Syntheticum.

Homeopathic Book Publishers, London.1993.

16. Tyler, M.L.: Homoeopathic Drug Pictures. B. Jain Publishers, Delhi. 1921.

17. Vermeulen, Frans: Concordant Materia Medica. Merlijn Publ. 1994.

18. Vermeulen, Frans: Synoptic Materia Medica. Merlijn Publishers. 1992.

19. Vithoulkas, George: Essence of Materia Medica. B. Jain Publishers. 1988.

20. Vithoulkas, George: Science of Homeopathy. Grove Press. 1980

21. Wichmann, Joerg; Bolte, Angelika: The Natural Relationship of Remedies. Fagus.1997.

22. Zaren, Ananda: Materia Medica. Core elements of the Materia Medica of the Mind. Ulrich Burgdorf Verlag, Göttingen. 1994.

Index

Diseases italic,
Remedies bold.

A

Abdominal typhus 315
Abortion 76, 196, 275
Abrotanum 47
Abscess 104, 109, 149, 173, 178, 209, 226, 266, 278, 292, 296, 299, 303, 315
Ache, tooth 363
Acidum hydrofluoricum 163
Acne 71, 82, 98, 104, 109, 124, 173, 178, 226, 237, 266, 278, 292, 303, 315
Aconitum napellus 50
Actaea racemosa 133
Addiction
  - *drug* 329
Adenopathy 92, 98, 104, 178, 189, 200, 292, 307
Adiposity 70, 104, 106, 109, 118, 120, 160, 173, 187, 193, 259, 315
Agaricus muscarius 55
Aging 316
Agony 120, 316
Alcoholic delirium 316
Alcoholism 88, 118, 124, 206, 241, 292, 296, 316
Allergic rhinitis 316
Allergies, food 229

Allergy 76, 104, 109, 154, 165, 189, 193, 196, 200, 203, 215, 224, 229, 232, 234, 239, 266, 292, 303, 307, 316
Allium cepa 58
Allopathic 23
Aloe 60
  - **socotrina** 60
Alopecia 92, 165, 173, 200, 248, 296, 316
Alumina 62
Aluminium 62
Alzheimer's disease 66, 239, 316
Amanita muscaria 55
Amara dulcis 153
Ambergris 65
Ambra grisea 65
Amebic dysentery 316
Amenorrhea 187, 263, 269, 317
Amyotrophic
  - *lateral sclerosis* 261, 317
Anacardium orientale 67
Anal
  - *fissure* 237, 317
  - *itch* 317
Anamirta cocculus 137
Anaphylactic shock 76, 317
Anemia 85, 120, 132, 160, 162, 275, 317
Angina
  - *pectoris* 52, 79, 82, 85, 88, 206, 241, 252, 280, 289, 292, 299, 317

  - *tonsillaris* 92, 95, 98, 104, 149, 162, 178, 200, 203, 206, 215, 226, 254, 266, 278, 292, 303, 307, 317
Angina pectoris 170
Angioneurotic
  - *edema* 317
Angulus infectiosus 237
Anorexia 318
  - *nervosa* 85, 318
Antimonium
  - **crudum** 69
  - **sulphuratum aurantiacum** 71
  - **tartarium** 72
Anxiety 79, 104, 168, 189, 198, 237, 252, 292, 318
  - *general* 318
  - *inappropriate to the situation* 318
Aphthous
  - *stomatitis* 318
Apis mellifica 74
Apnea
  - *during sleep* 244, 318
Apoplexy 79, 82, 124, 206, 241, 244, 261, 286, 289, 318
Appendicitis 52, 101, 318
Apple
  - **, bitter** 142
Arbor Vitae 301
Argentum nitricum 77
Argila pura 62
Arnica montana 80

Arrhythmia 79, 160, 170, 187, 189, 206, 211, 241, 280, 292, 299, 318

Arsenic
- trioxide 83
- white 83

Arsenicum
- album 83

Artemisia
- *abrotanum* 47
- *cina* 135

Arteriosclerosis 261, 318

Arthritis 76, 82, 95, 101, 104, 106, 124, 129, 132, 134, 143, 160, 173, 187, 193, 200, 209, 215, 224, 232, 237, 241, 252, 254, 271, 292, 296, 303, 307, 318
- *psoriatic* 104, 356
- *rheumatoid* 104

Asphyxia neonatorum 73

Asthma, bronchial 52, 73, 85, 92, 95, 98, 101, 104, 120, 124, 127, 132, 152, 154, 159, 160, 173, 178, 184, 187, 189, 191, 193, 196, 200, 215, 224, 232, 234, 237, 241, 246, 252, 266, 271, 278, 280, 282, 289, 292, 294, 303, 307, 312, 320

Ataxia 79, 124, 252, 319

Atony of stomach and bowels 64

Atopic dermatitis 319

Atropa belladonna 93

Atrophy of
- *gums* 319
- *optic nerve* 319

Attacks
- *panic* 85

Attention-deficit
- *hyperactivity disorder* 319

Aurum metallicum 86

B

Bacillary
- *dysentery* 319

Bacilli
- of tuberculosis 305

Backache 104, 118, 187, 193, 232, 241, 256, 292, 296, 312

Backpain 106, 124, 154, 271, 319

Bad effects
- of vaccination 292, 319

Baldness 319

Baryta carbonica 90

Bedsores 244

Bed-wetting 319, 320

Behavior
- compulsive 189, 325
- disorder 68, 113, 136, 206, 299, 307, 310, 320

Bell's palsy 154

Belladonna 93

Binge-purging
- *disorder* 320

Biographical
- case-history 19

Bite injury 209, 320

Bites 209

Bitter
- apple 142
- cucumber 142

Bittersweet 153

Black
- cohosh 133
- hellebore 174
- snakeroot 133
- sulphide of antimony 69

Blacklead 171

Blackwater fever 320

Blepharitis 52, 64, 173, 178, 320

Blood
- *high pressure* 339

Bloody
- *sputum* 320

Body weakness 235

Boil 320

Bone
- *fracture* 157, 320
- *pain* 320

Boneset 156

Bönninghausen 21

Bowel obstruction 320

Brain
- *inflammation of* 342

Brain contusion 320

Brazilian
- rattlesnake 148

Breast
- *abnormal nipple discharge* 315
- *cancer* 320

- *inflammation* 342
Breath-holding spells 320
Brimstone 290
Bromine 96
Bromium 96
Bronchial asthma 52, 73,
85, 92, 95, 98, 101, 104,
120, 124, 127, 132, 152,
154, 159, 160, 173, 178,
184, 187, 189, 191, 193,
196, 200, 215, 224, 232,
234, 237, 241, 246, 252,
294, 320
Bronchial pneumonia 73,
321
Bronchitis 52, 57, 59, 64,
66, 70, 71, 73, 85, 98,
101, 104, 109, 111, 118,
120, 124, 127, 132, 154,
160, 178, 189, 191, 193,
196, 200, 215, 226, 237,
246, 252, 266, 271, 275,
278, 280, 282, 292, 294,
307, 321
- *obstructive* 191, 350
Bronchopneumonia 191
Bryonia 99
- *alba* 99
Bryony 99
Build-up of pus 321
Bulimia 187, 259, 303
Burns 115, 321
Bursitis 162, 322
Bushmaster 204

C

Cachexia 189
Calcarea
- **carbonica** 102
- **carbonica**
  Hahnemanni 102
- **phosphorica** 105
- **sulphuratum**
  Hahnemanni 177
- **sulphurica** 108
Camomile
- **common** 126
Camphor 110
Camphora 110
Canker sores 104, 322
Cannabis indica 112
Cantharis 114
- **officinalis** 114
Capsicum 116
- **annuum** 116
Carbo
- **vegetabilis** 119
Carbon containing iron
171
Carbonate
- **of Barium** 90
- **of lime** 102
- **of magnesia** 216
- **of potassium** 194
Carbuncles 149, 178, 299,
322
Cardiac
- *insufficiency* 196, 322
- *valvular diseases* 206
- *weakness* 119

Caries 165, 322
Carpal tunnel
- *syndrome* 106, 322
Case 17
Case-history 17
- *biographical and social*
  19
- *gynecological* 18
- *social* 19
Case-taking 16
Cataract 88, 322
Catarrh in pharynx and
hoarseness
- *after drinking alcohol*
  322
Causticum 122
Cayenne pepper 116
Centesimal potencies 12
Cerebral
- *concussion* 322
- *trauma* 323
Chalazion 286, 323
Chamomilla 126
- **matricaria** 126
Charcoal 119
Chelidonium 128
- **majus** 128
Cheyne-Stokes
- *respiration* 244, 323
Chickenpox 323
Chilblains 246
China officinalis 130
Chloride
- *of magnesia* 218
Cholecystitis 101, 104, 129,
132, 143, 215, 234, 263,
269, 323

Cholelithiasis 129, 196, 263, 323
Cholera 111, 152, 310, 323
- *infantum* 54
Chorea 124, 134, 152, 187, 221, 286, 289, 312, 323
- *minor* 57, 299, 324
Christmas rose 174
Chronic fatigue syndrome 66, 68, 70, 79, 88, 104, 106, 111, 113, 120, 132, 138, 141, 160, 168, 187, 198, 215, 217, 219, 232, 241, 248, 252, 275, 278, 282, 286, 292, 303, 312, 324
Cimicifuga 133
- serpentaria 133
Cina 135
Cinchona
- bark 130
- succirubra 130
Cinnamomum
- camphora 110
Cirrhosis
- *of the liver* 324
Citrullus
- colocynthis 142
Clap 324
Clavus 70, 324
Climacteric
- *symptoms* 324
Club moss 213
Cocculus 137
Coccyalgia 184
Coccygodynia 324

Coffea 139
- arabica 139
- cruda 139
Coffee 139
Cohosh
- black 133
Colds 162
- common 241
Colic 217, 221, 241, 261, 325
- infantile 127, 143, 221, 341
- renal 143
Colitis 49, 61, 79, 85, 115, 118, 132, 206, 211, 215, 232, 234, 263, 292, 325
- ulcerative 175, 363
Collagen
- diseases 325
Collagenoses 275
Collapse 120, 310, 325
Colocynthis 142
Colon irritabile 57, 79, 229, 232, 241
Coma 244, 325
Comatose state 120, 175
Common
- camomile 126
- salt 230
Common
- cold 52, 92, 104, 154, 157, 162, 226, 241, 266, 292
- flu 132
Commotio 184
- cerebri 82, 244

Complementary remedies 27
Compulsive 296
- *behavior* 79, 85, 189, 271, 296, 325
Concentration, weak 54
Concomitant symptoms 20
Conditions
- *manic-depressive* 206, 289
- *menopausal* 275
- *postencephalitic* 57
- *prostate* 146
Condylomata 275, 286, 303, 325
Congenital
- *malformation* 92
Conium maculatum 144
Conjunctivitis 59, 79, 109, 173, 178, 226, 266, 269, 278, 286, 292, 326
Connective tissue
- *diseases* 79, 104, 173, 275, 303, 326
Consciousness
- *Loss* 345
Constipation 64, 66, 68, 92, 95, 101, 104, 124, 173, 178, 215, 217, 219, 232, 239, 241, 244, 259, 261, 266, 275, 278, 286, 292, 296, 299, 303, 326
- *Cough* 71
Constriction of pupils 326
Continua 49
- *fever* 326

Contractures 261, 326
Contusion
- *cerebral* 175, 322
Convulsions 152, 326
- *during fever* 95
Coordination
- *disorder* 327
Copper 151
Corn 327
Cortex peruviana 130
Cough 182, 187, 275, 327
C-potencies 12, 24
Cracks
- *at angles of mouth* 327
Cramp 327
- *in legs* 104, 327
- *occupational* 350
Crampus-syndrome 327
Craniocerebral trauma 234, 289
Crisis
- *hypertensive* 206
Crotalus
- *horridus* 148
Crude rock oil 245
Cryopathy 327
Crystals
- **dark red** 192
Cucumis 142
Cuprum
- **metallicum** 151
Cutaneous hemorrhage 327
Cut-wound 286, 327
Cyst
- *in ovaries* 327
- *Ovarian* 76, 207

- *ovarian* 263, 303
Cystitis 76, 85, 111, 113, 115, 154, 175, 211, 215, 224, 241, 269, 275, 286, 307, 327

D

Dark red crystals 192
Datura
- **stramonium** 287
Deadly nightshade 93
Deafness 327
Death throes 327
Decimal-potencies 12
Decubitus ulcer 327
Defects
- *of mucous membrane of the mouth* 328
Deformation of the spine 328
Degeneration
- *maligant* 104
- *of central and peripheral nervous system* 146, 328
Delirium 95, 289, 328
- *alcoholic* 316
- *tremens* 113, 149, 182, 244
Delphinium
- **staphisagria** 283
Dementia 66, 173, 175, 182, 261, 292, 312, 328
Dentitio difficilis 104, 106, 127, 219, 221, 254, 263
Depleted state 252

Depression 68, 70, 79, 85, 104, 106, 113, 118, 134, 138, 175, 182, 184, 187, 211, 215, 232, 234, 248, 259, 266, 269, 275, 286, 292, 296, 303, 312, 328
Dermatitis 266, 328
- *diaper* 224, 328
Diabetes 252, 261, 292, 328
- *mellitus* 248, 328
Diaper
- *dermatitis* 224, 328
Diarrhea 54, 59, 61, 64, 70, 71, 106, 127, 132, 136, 154, 160, 168, 189, 198, 206, 219, 234, 239, 246, 248, 263, 266, 269, 289, 292, 303, 307, 310, 329
- *and vomiting in infants* 329
Diathesis hemorrhagic 191, 206, 252
Diluting 12
Diphtheria 98, 203, 206, 329
Diplopia 168, 329
Disease
- *manifestation* 26, 27
Disease 25
- *cardiac valvular* 206
- *collagen* 294
- *connective tissue* 173, 275, 303
- *due to environmental conditions* 294
- *gastroesophageal reflux* 335

- *Graves* 252
- *malignant* 173, 206
- *occlusive arterial* 350
- *of liver and pancreas* 241
- *of the connective tissue* 79
- *of the mitral valve* 299
- *Quincke's* 76
- *rheumatoid-collagen* 358
- *upper respiratory tract* 363
- *valvular heart* 88, 364
Disorder
- *attention-deficit hyperactivity* 319
- *behavioral* 299, 307
- *binge-purging* 320
- *hereditary bleeding* 339
- *of sexual function* 329
- *reading (and spelling)-* 369
- *sexual* 115, 165, 173, 182, 211, 226, 259, 299, 307
Disturbance
- *of sexual functions* 92
- *of the cardiac rhythm* 329
Doctrine of Miasms 22
Dog's milk 202
Dosage 22
Dose of a remedy 24
Double vision 329

Dried carbonate of sodium 228
Drinking alcohol 241
Dropsy of the scrotum 329
Drug
- *picture* 22
Drug addiction 206, 329
Dulcamara 153
Dulcis amara 153
Dupuytren's 261
- *contracture* 261
Dysentery 61, 111, 263, 269, 286, 329
- *bacillary* 319
Dysmenorrhea 95, 98, 113, 127, 134, 138, 141, 143, 162, 187, 203, 211, 217, 219, 221, 239, 241, 259, 269, 286, 303, 307, 310, 330
Dyspareunia 232, 275, 330
Dysphagia 124, 330

E

E sophagitis 332
Eating
- *disorder* 330
Ecchymoses 330
Ecchymosis 82, 209, 294
Eczema 49, 64, 68, 70, 85, 104, 109, 115, 120, 124, 165, 173, 178, 200, 209, 215, 224, 226, 232, 246, 252, 266, 271, 278, 286, 292, 303, 307, 330

Edema
- *angiocurotic* 317
Emaciation 330
Emphysema 73, 206, 252, 331
Emptiness 137
Encephalitis 115, 152, 175, 187, 244, 312, 331
Encopresis 61, 182, 331
Endometriosis 206, 275, 331
Enduration of glands 98
Enlargement of
- *prostate gland* 331
- *thyroid gland* 331
Enteritis 57, 61, 73, 162, 191, 237, 246, 263, 331
Enuresis 57, 92, 124, 136, 160, 182, 275, 286, 289, 307, 312, 331
- *nocturna* 57, 221, 269, 331
Environmental conditions
- *diseases due* 294
Environmental diseases
- *hypersensitivity to chemicals* 331
Epidemic parotitis 332
Epilepsy 54, 57, 79, 95, 104, 111, 124, 136, 152, 170, 175, 182, 206, 244, 259, 289, 303, 312, 332
Epistaxis 71, 160, 162, 191, 206, 252, 332
Erection
- *permant* 353

Erysipela 82, 95, 149, 173, 209, 271
Erysipelas 76, 332
Erythema
- *nodosum* 49, 332
Esophageal mucosa
- *inflammation of* 341
Esophagitis 120
Especially pinworms 136
Eupatorium
- **perfoliatum** 156
Euspongia
- **officinalis** 279
Excessive vomiting
- *during pregnancy* 332
Exophthalmic goiter 332
Exudative pleurisy 76
Eye
- *affections* 332
- *diseases* 146
- *eyelid inflammation* 332
- *inflammation of the conjunctiva* 342
- *inflammation of the cornea* 342
Eyesight
- *deficiency* 145

F

Facial
- *nerve paralysis* 124, 154, 259
- *nerve paresis* 332
- *neuralgia* 146, 333

Failure 370
- *to thrive* 49, 217, 333
Faint 333
Fainting 120
Fall Herb 80
Family history 18
Fatigue
- *chronic* 66, 68, 70, 79, 88, 104, 106, 111, 113, 120, 132, 138, 141, 160, 168, 187, 198, 215, 217, 219, 232, 241, 248, 252, 275, 278, 282, 286, 292, 303, 312
Febrile seizures 333
Felon 178, 278, 303
- *gout* 104
Ferrum
- **metallicum** 158
- **phosphoricum** 161
Fever 132, 157, 162, 168, 333
- *accompanying common colds and other infections* 333
- *convulsion during* 95
- *in common colds and inflammatory conditions* 52
Fibrocystic breast disease 333
Fibroids 333
Fissures 173, 278, 292, 333
- *anal* 237, 317
- *rectal* 187
Fistula 109, 333
- *in rectal area* 292, 333

Flammeus 165
Flatulence 120, 333
Flexion deformity
- *of fingers* 334
Fluorescent 250
Fluoricum acidum 163
Fly
- **agaric** 55
- **spanish** 114
Food
- *allergies* 229
- *allergy and intolerance to certain foods* 334
- *intolerance* 229
- *intoxication* 334
- *poisoning* 85, 334
Fool's parsley 53
Fractures
- *bone* 157
Frostbite 57, 334
Functional sexual
- *disorder* 125
Furuncles 82, 178, 278, 299, 307
Furunculosis 334

G

Galactorrhea 203, 254, 334
Gallbladder
- *inflammation of* 341
Gallstones 334
Gangrene 149, 334
Garden poppy 243
Gastric 95, 120, 292
- *cancer* 334
Gastric/duodenal ulcer 334

Gastritis 52, 68, 70, 73, 79, 85, 95, 101, 118, 120, 129, 132, 160, 162, 173, 187, 191, 193, 203, 217, 219, 229, 232, 237, 241, 252, 269, 275, 294, 335

Gastroenteritis 49, 54, 70, 73, 85, 111, 115, 143, 152, 175, 191, 226, 241, 252, 263, 310, 335

Gastroesophageal
- *reflux disease* 79, 335

Gelandine
- **greater** 128

Gelsemium 166
- **sempervirens** 166

General symptoms 20

Gestational psychosis 134

Glandular
- *fever* 335
- *induration* 335
- *swelling* 335
- *tumor* 146, 335

Glauber's
- **salt** 233

Glaucoma 88, 336

Globus
- *hystericus* 187, 206
- *syndrome* 336

Glomerulonephritis 76, 336

Glonoinum 169

Glycerol trinitrate 169

Goiter 336

Gold 86

Golden Sulphuret of Antimony 71

Gonorrhea 303, 336

Gonorrheal pus 222

Gout 101, 124, 209, 215, 292, 336

Grades
- attributed 21

Grading of symptoms 19

Graphites 171

Graves' disease 165, 252

Greater celandine 128

Grinding
- *of teeth* 336
- *of teeth during sleep* 136

Growth pains 106, 165, 336

Guidelines 13

Gums 319

Gynecological
- case-history 18

Gypsum 108

H

Hahnemann 9, 11, 12, 16, 22, 27

Hair loss 336

Hardening
- *of arteries* 337

Hashish 112

Hay fever 57, 59, 85, 124, 154, 168, 189, 200, 232, 266, 337

Headache 52, 57, 59, 61, 68, 70, 79, 85, 95, 98, 101, 104, 106, 111, 113, 118, 120, 138, 141, 143, 152, 154, 160, 168, 173, 178, 187, 193, 196, 198, 200, 211, 215, 219, 229, 232, 234, 239, 241, 246, 248, 252, 254, 256, 259, 263, 266, 269, 271, 275, 278, 282, 286, 289, 292, 294, 296, 299, 303, 307, 310, 312, 337

Healing
- process 25

Health
- concept 9

Heart
- *attack* 337
- *muscle inflammation of the* 342

Heat
- *flushes* 173, 292
- *stroke* 95, 338

Hellebore
- **black** 174

Helleborus
- **albus** 308
- **niger** 174

Helminthiasis 49, 136, 338

Hemangioma 49, 165, 338

Hemlock poison 144

Hemophilia 252, 338

Hemoptysis 206, 338

Hemorrhage 120, 132, 149, 162, 206, 252, 338

Hemorrhagic
- *diathesis* 149
- *diathesis* 191, 206, 252, 294, 338

Hemorrhoids 49, 61, 68, 70, 85, 106, 118, 173, 196, 206, 215, 241, 263, 286,

292, 338
Hemp
- **indian** 112
Henbane 180
Hepar
- **sulphuris** 177
- **sulphuris calcareum** 177
Hepatitis 79, 85, 88, 101, 129, 132, 206, 215, 217, 219, 234, 252, 263, 269, 292, 338
Hepatocirrhosis 215, 219
Hepatopathy 129, 215, 219, 339
Hereditary bleeding disorder 339
Hering 26
Hering's law 26, 27
Herpes 54, 154, 173, 237, 246, 275, 292, 303, 339
- *labialis* 232, 271, 339
- *zoster* 76, 85, 115, 124, 206, 246, 271, 339
Hiccups 339
High
- potencies 23
- potency 23
Higher
- c-potencies 24
- potency 23, 24
Hirsutism 187, 275, 339
History
- family 18
Hives 339
Hoarseness 241

Hodgkin 92
- *disease* 339
Homeopathic
- case-taking 16
- remedies 13, 29
Honey-bee poison 74
Hops
- **wild** 99
Hordeolum 173, 269, 278, 286, 307
Hot
- *flushes* 206, 275, 339
HPUS 13
Hydrargyrum 225
Hydrocele 49, 189, 340
Hyoscyamus 93
- **niger** 180
Hyperactivity 57, 289, 299, 307, 310
Hyperaesthesia 141
Hypercinesia 165
Hyperemesis gravidarum 191, 239, 275, 340
Hyperesthesia 340
Hypericum 183
- **perforatum** 183
Hypersensitivity 340
- *reaction* 340
Hypertension 79, 82, 88, 95, 104, 154, 170, 196, 206, 215, 224, 241, 252, 261, 292, 340
Hypertensive
- *crisis* 206, 340
Hyperthyroidism 189, 206, 280, 340

Hypertrophy
- *of the prostate* 189
- *of the prostrate* 92, 256
Hypochondriasis 146, 340
Hypomenorrhea 269, 340
Hypothyroidism 104, 340

I

Icterus 129, 234, 340
Ignatia 185
- **amara** 185
Ileus 341
- *paralytic* 244
Impaired coordination 64
Impetigo 173, 292
- *contagiosa* 70, 109, 178, 237, 271, 341
Impotence 79, 125, 215, 241, 248, 341
Incontinence 312, 341
- *stress* 275
- *urinary stress* 232
Indian
- **cockle** 137
- **hemp** 112
Indications 226
Indigestion 198
Infantile colic 127, 143, 221, 341
Infection of
- *upper airways* 341
- *upper respiratory tract* 168, 226, 278, 341
- *urinary tract* 269, 364
Inferiority complex 68, 341

Infertility 341
Inflammation of
- appendix 341
- bladder 341
- bursae 341
- esophageal mucosa 341
- gallbladder 341
- joints 341
- larynx 341
- liver 341
- nerves 341
- paranasal sinuses 342
- parotid glands 342
- prostate gland 342
- rectum 342
- spinal cord 342
- testicles 342
- the brain 342
- the heart muscle 342
- the iris 342
- the middle ear 342
- the pelvic organs 275
- the pelvis 342
- the pericardium 342
- thyroid gland 342
- urethra 342
- vagina 342
Inflammatory 241
- conditions of the bowels 241
- disease of the intestine 342
Influenza 85, 104, 157, 241, 292, 342
Inguinal hernia 88, 342

Injury 82
- and trauma 343
- whiplash 272
Insect
- bite 76
- sting 343
Insomnia 259, 266, 269, 286, 296, 303, 343
Intermittent
- claudication 206, 343
Intestinal
- atony 343
- catarrh 343
Intolerance
- of lactose 229
- to lactose 54
Iodine 188
Iodium 188
Ipecacuanha 190
- root 190
Iris
- inflammation of 342
Iritis 88, 343
Iron 158
- phosphate of 161
Irritable
- bladder 241, 343
- bowel syndrome 343
- weakness 137
Ischialgia 134, 221, 232, 261, 271, 292, 296, 343

J

Jactatio capitis 57, 344
Jasmine 166

Jaundice 344
Joints
- inflammation of 341
- stiffness of 361

K

Kali
- bichromicum 192
- carbonicum 194
- phosphoricum 197
- sulphuricum 199
Keloids 173, 278, 344
Kent 21
- Repertory 21
Keratitis 173, 344
Key symptoms 22
Kidney
- failure 344
- inflammation 344
- stones 344
Korsakoff potencies 13

L

Labrador tea 208
Lac caninum 202
Lachesis 204
- muta 204
Lack of
- concentration 344
Lactose intolerance 217, 344
Lapis infernalis 77
Laryngeal
- polyp 344
- polyps 79

Laryngitis 52, 59, 64, 70, 79, 98, 120, 125, 168, 178, 193, 252, 271, 280, 282, 344

Larynx
- *inflammtion of* 341

Lateral sclerosis 345
- *amyotrophic* 261

Laurus camphora 110

Law
- Herings 27
- of Similars 12

Lead 260

Leakage of stool 345

Ledum 208
- *palustre* 208

Leopard's Bane 80

Leukorrhea 189, 224, 269, 275, 296, 303, 345

Lilium tigrinum 210

Limbs feel 248

Lime
- **carbonate of** 102

Liver
- *cirrhosis* 324
- *diseases* 241
- *inflammation* 341

LM-potency 13

Local symptoms 20

Locomotor ataxia 345

Loss
- *of consciousness* 345
- *of hearing* 173

Louse wort 283

Low potencies 23

Lower
- *potencies* 23
- *potency* 13

Lower back pain 345

Luesinum 295

Lumbago 61, 101, 143, 271, 345

Lunar caustic 77

Lupus erythematodes
- *systemic* 362

Lycopodium 213
- **clavatum** 213

Lycosa hispanica 298

Lymphadenitis with gastroenteritis 49, 345

Lymphadenopathy 345

Lymphogranulomatosis 345

Lytta vesicatoria 114

M

Magnesia
- **carbonica** 216
- **muriatica** 218
- **phosphorica** 220

Magnesium
- **chloratum** 218

Main symptoms 22

Malaria 132, 157, 345

Malformation 345

Malignant
- *degenerations* 104
- *diseases* 173, 206, 303
- *goiter* 345

Mammopathia 254
- *fibrozystica* 254, 278

Mania 182, 259, 289, 299, 346

Manic
- *depression* 346
- *depressive conditions* 206, 289

Marking nut 67

Marsh Tea 208

Mastitis 95, 101, 203, 254, 278, 346

Mastoiditis 88, 109, 118, 346

Materia Medica 11, 19, 22, 290

Matricaria
- **chamomilla** 126

Maturationa
- *delay* 346

May apple 262

Measles 269, 346

Medium potencies 23

Medorrhinum 222

Memory
- *weak* 225

Ménière's disease 170, 346

Meningitis 76, 82, 95, 101, 115, 152, 170, 175, 182, 244, 289, 312, 346

Meningoencephalitis 289, 346

Menispermum cocculus 137

Menopausal
- *complaints* 206, 269, 292
- *conditions* 275
- *psychosis* 347

Menorrhagia 134, 160, 191, 252, 299, 347
Mental
- and emotional symptoms 20
- *exertion* 256
- *exhaustion* 347
- *retardation* 92, 347
Mercurius solubilis 225
Mercury 225
Metrorrhagia 66, 104, 191, 206, 259, 289, 347
Migraine 70, 82, 95, 101, 104, 129, 134, 138, 141, 152, 160, 168, 170, 175, 187, 191, 193, 196, 203, 206, 215, 221, 224, 232, 241, 266, 275, 278, 292, 297, 310, 347
Mineral
- oil 245
Miosis 244, 347
Miscarriage 347
Mitral valve
- *disease* 347
- *diseases* 299
Monkshood 50
Mononucleosis 104, 348
Multiple sclerosis 57, 79, 104, 125, 138, 146, 168, 198, 261, 348
Mumps 254, 261, 348
Muscular
- *dystrophy* 104, 348
- *rheumatism* 241, 348
- *twitching* 348
- *weakness* 261

Myasthenia gravis 168, 348
Myatrophic lateral
- *sclerosis* 348
Myelitis acuta 146
Myocardial
- *infarction* 206, 348
- *insufficiency* 348
Myocarditis 149, 252, 280, 349
Myristica
- *fragrans* 238

N

Naevus flammeus 49, 165
Narcolepsy 239, 244, 349
Narcoleptic attacks 349
Natrum
- **carbonicum** 228
- **chloratum** 230
- **muriaticum** 230
- **sulphuricum** 233
Nausea 138
Neonatal
- *asphyxia* 349
Nephritis 76, 111, 113, 149, 175, 206, 237, 252, 261, 349
Nephrolithiasis 104, 143, 196, 206, 215, 241, 349
Nephrotic
- *syndrome* 76, 349
Nerve
- *inflammation of* 341
- *injury* 184, 349

Neuralgia 52, 59, 95, 127, 129, 134, 141, 143, 154, 160, 168, 178, 184, 193, 215, 217, 219, 221, 224, 241, 261, 266, 271, 282, 297, 299, 303, 310, 312, 349
- *facial* 146
Neurasthenia 198, 350
Neuritis 52, 184, 261, 350
Neurodermatitis 350
Nevus flammeus 349
Nightmare 104, 289, 350
Nitric acid 235
Nitroglycerine 169
Noble metal 257
Nose
- *bleed* 350
Nosode 222, 264, 295
Nutmeg 238
Nux
- **moschata** 238
- **vomica** 240
Nymphomania 182, 350

O

Obesity 350
Obstructive bronchitis. 191
Occlusive arterial
- *disease* 350
Occupational
- *cramp* 312, 350
Oil
- **mineral** 245
Oleum petrae album 245

Onion
- red 58
Ophthalmia neonatorum 269, 350
Opium 243
Optic nerve jatrophy 252
Orchitis 79, 88, 98, 226, 254, 269, 286, 351
Organon 16, 27
Orthostatic
- disorder 269
- dysregulation 351
- syndrome 252
Osteogenesis
- imperfecta 104, 351
Osteomalacia 252, 351
Ostrea edulis 102
Otitis
- externa 173, 351
- media 52, 95, 104, 106, 109, 127, 136, 154, 162, 173, 178, 200, 206, 226, 237, 266, 269, 278, 292, 307, 351
Ovarian
- cyst 76, 206, 263, 303
Overall state 22
Oversensitivity to chemicals 294
Oxide of
- Aluminium 62

P

Pain
- extending along the course of one or more nerves 351
- in bones 88, 157
- phantom limb 184
- postoperative 286
Painful sexual intercourse 351
Palpitations 170, 211, 351
Pancreas
- diseases 241
Panic 52
- attack 85, 352
Papaver somniferum 243
Paradentosis 352
Paraesthesia 299
Paralysis 168, 352
Paralytic
- ileus 244, 352
- weakness 137
Paranoia 207, 352
Paresthesia 352
Parkinson's disease 79, 226, 261, 312, 352
Parodontal
- disease 307
Paronychia 352
Parotid glands
- inflammation of 342
Parotitis 98, 342, 352
Pavor nocturnus 57, 289, 352
Pepper
- Spanish 116
Pericarditis 101, 352
Pericardium
- inflammation of the 342
Periostitis 248, 353

Peritonitis 101
Peritonsillar
- abscess 353
Permanent erection 353
Pertussis 57, 70, 73, 82, 95, 98, 101, 118, 120, 129, 136, 152, 182, 191, 196, 241, 292, 312, 353
Phantom limb pain 184, 353
Pharingitis 165
Pharyngeal
- diphtheria 353
Pharyngitis 52, 59, 64, 76, 79, 85, 95, 98, 104, 115, 150, 162, 178, 203, 207, 215, 226, 229, 237, 241, 252, 254, 266, 271, 278, 292, 353
Phlegmon 150, 353
Phobia 57, 79, 85, 92, 113, 134, 203, 252, 259, 289, 353
Phosphate
- of iron 161
- of lime 105
- of magnesia 220
- of potassium 197
Phosphoric
- acid 247
Phosphoricum
- acidum 247
Phosphorus 250
Photophobia 173, 354
Phytolacca 253
- decandra 253
Picric acid 255

Picrinicum
- acidum 255
Plaster of Paris 108
Platinum 257
- metallicum 257
Pleurisy 52, 101, 115, 162, 178, 196, 354
- exsudative 354
Plumbago 171
Plumbum 260
Pneumonia 52, 71, 73, 76, 82, 85, 101, 111, 120, 129, 154, 160, 162, 178, 182, 189, 191, 193, 196, 215, 226, 234, 252, 271, 282, 292, 307, 354
- Bronchial 321
- broncho 191
Podophyllum 262
- peltatum 262
Poison
- hemlock 144
- livy 270
- nut 240
Poke root 253
Pollinosis 354
Polyarthritis 354
Polycythemia 207, 354
Port-wine stain 354, 355
Post
- encephalitic conditions 57
- operative pain 286, 355
- traumatic headache 82, 355
Potash 192, 194
Potassium 192

- sulphate of 199
Potencies 23
Potency 12, 22, 23, 24
- choice 22
- high 23
- higher 23, 24
- Korsakoff 13
- lower 13
- medium 23
Pounding of the heart 355
Premenstrual
- syndrome 104, 127, 203, 211, 217, 239, 269, 275, 355
Pressure ulcer 355
Priapism 115, 256, 355
Process
- disease 25
- of potentization 12
Proctitis 261, 303, 355
Prolapse
- of rectum 187
- of rectum. 61
- of the uterus 355
Prolapsed rectum 355
Prostate
- conditions 146, 355
- gland enlargemant of 331
- gland inflammation of 342
- hypertrophy 312, 355
Prostatic 303
- hypertrophy 303
Prostatitis 92, 275, 286, 292, 303, 355
Prostration 53

Proving symptoms 26, 27
Provings 11
Pruritus ani 275
Pseudo 178
Pseudocroup 52, 109, 178, 189, 193, 280
Psoriasis 85, 173, 200, 215, 232, 246, 252, 266, 275, 278, 286, 292, 297, 303, 356
Psorinum 264
Psychological symptoms 23
Psychomotor or mental 57
Psychosis 113, 175, 182, 289, 297, 310, 356
- during menopause. 134
- during pregnancy 356
Ptosis 146, 356
Pulmonary
- emphysema 356
Pulsatilla 267
- pratensis 267
Pure
- clay 62
- flint 276
Purpura 207, 252, 294
- hemorrhagica 150, 356
Pyelonephritis 76, 95, 115, 150, 215, 237, 241, 356
Pyloric stenosis 356
Pylorospasm 54, 241

Q

Q-potencies 23
Q-potency 13, 23, 25
Quicksilver 225

Quincke's disease 76

R

Ranula 49, 357
Rattlesnake 148
Raynaud's disease 275, 357
Reaction
- to a remedy 25
Reaction
- *hypersensitivity* 340
Rectal 275
- *fissures* 187, 275, 303, 357
- *prolapse* 263
- *spasms* 187, 357
Rectum
- inflammation of 342
Red onion 58
Reduced range of motion of a joint 357
Regulatory therapy 9
Relapsing
- *fever* 357
Remedy 25
- homeopathic 13
- picture 11, 19, 23
- search 19
- searching 19
Renal
- *colic* 143, 357
- *insufficiency* 196
Repertorization 21, 22
- programs 21
- sheet 22

Retardation 57
Retention
- *of stools* 357
- *of urin* 357
- *of urine* 52
Retinal
- *detachment* 252, 357
- *hemorrhage* 252, 357
- *vascular bleeding* 207
Rhagades 358
Rheumatism 101, 125, 134, 160, 200, 226, 254, 269, 272, 292, 303, 307, 310
- *muscular* 241
- *sprain* 209
Rheumatoid
- *arthritis* 104, 358
- *collagen disease* 358
Rhinitis 52, 59, 64, 71, 104, 111, 165, 189, 193, 226, 237, 241, 266, 275, 292, 303, 307, 358
- *allergic* 316
Rhus toxicodendron 270
Rickets 252, 358
Roasted
- **sponge** 279
Runny nose 358

S

Scabies 266, 358
Scarlet fever 95, 207, 254, 272, 358
Schizophrenia 68, 182, 289, 359

Sciatic pain 101, 104, 132
Sciatica 134, 143, 193, 195, 196, 207, 221, 232, 241, 254, 261, 272, 275, 292, 297
Scleroderma 104, 275, 359
Scoliosis 104, 106, 278, 297, 303, 359
Sea salt 230
Seasickness 191, 246, 359
Seizure
- *disorder* 359
Senility 66, 359
Sepia 273
- **officinalis** 273
Sepsis 359
Septicemia 111, 150, 207, 359
Sexual
- *disorders* 115, 165, 173, 182, 211, 226, 259, 299, 307, 359
- *functional disorders* 275, 329
- *weakness* 172
Shingles 359
Shock
- *anaphylactic* 76, 317
Silica 276
Silicea 276
Silver nitrate 77
Similars
- Law 10
Simillimum 22, 27
Singultus 221, 360
Sinusitis 88, 95, 104, 109, 125, 154, 165, 178, 193,

196, 200, 215, 224, 226, 229, 237, 254, 266, 275, 278, 292, 303, 360
Sjögren's syndrome 239, 360
Sleeplessness 88, 132, 134, 141, 168, 182, 196, 207, 217, 219, 241, 244
Slipped disk 360
Slow development. 92
Social case-history 19
Soda 228
Sodium
- chloride 230
- sulfate 233
Soft tissue rheumatism 134, 360
Solanum dulcamara 153
Southernwood 47
Spanish
- fly 114
- pepper 116
Spasmodic
- *abdominal pain* 360
Spasms 187, 360
Speech
- defects 57
- disorders 360
Spinal cord
- Inflammation of 342
Spiritus nitri acidus 235
Sponge
- roasted 279
Spongia 279
- marina tosta 279

Spontaneous abortion 360
Sprain 360
Sputum
- *bloody* 320
Squint 360
St. Ignatius bean 185
St. John's wort 183
St. Vitus' dance 360
Stab
- *wound* 209, 361
Stammering 289, 361
Stannum 281
Staphisagria 283
Stavesacre 283
Sterility 269
Stiffness of
- *joints* 361
Stomach
- *bowels atony* 64
- *cancer* 146
Stomatitis 226
- *aphthosa* 237, 294, 297
- *ulcerative* 363
Strabismus 182, 286, 289
Strachnos ignatii 185
Strain 272, 361
Stramonium 93, 287
Stress
- *incontinence* 275
Stricture of
- *urethra* 361
Stroke 361
Struma 104, 189
- *maligna* 165
Strychnos nux vomica 240
Stuttering 289, 361

Sty(e) 361
Suicidal
- *behavior* 361
- *disposition* 88, 234
Sulphate
- of lime 108
- of potassium 199
Sulphur 290
Sulphuric
- acid 293
Sulphuricum
- acidum 293
Sun
- *allergy* 165, 361
- *burn* 95, 165, 361
- *stroke* 95, 111, 170, 361
Surucucu 204
Swallowing
- *difficulty* 362
Swelling
- *of glands* 165
- *of lymph nodes* 362
Symptom 21
- combination 27
- concomitant 20
- general 20
- graded list 22
- indices 21
- key 22
- local 20
- mental, emotional 20
- picture 11, 26, 27
- proving 11, 26, 27
- psychological 23
Syncope 239, 362

Syndrome
- *chronic fatigue* 66, 68, 70, 79, 88, 104, 106, 111, 113, 120, 132, 138, 141, 160, 168, 187, 198, 215, 217, 219, 232, 241, 248, 252, 275, 278, 282, 286, 292, 303, 312
- *chronic fatigue* 324
- *nephrotic* 349
- *orthostatic* 252
- *premenstrual* 104, 127, 203, 211, 217, 239, 269, 275
- *Sjögren's* 239
Synovitis 76, 362
Syphilinum 295
Systemic
- *lupus erythematodes* 104, 362

T

Tabes dorsalis 79, 362
Tachyarrhythmia 52, 362
Tachycardia 52, 362
Tarantula
- **fasciiventris** 298
- **hispanica** 298
Tartar emetic 72
Tartarus
- **emeticus** 72
- **stibiatus** 72
Teething
- *problems* 362
Tenosynovitis 362
Tenovaginitis 165, 272

Testicles 299
- *inflammation of* 342
- *undescended* 363
Testicular tumor 362
Thornapple 287
Thoroughwort 156
Thuja 301
- *occidentalis* 301
Thyroid gland
- *enlargement of* 331
- *inflammation of* 342
Thyroiditis 207, 362
Tics 57, 152, 187, 362
Tiger lily 210
Tin 281
Tinctura acris sine kalio 122
Tinea 275, 292, 303
Tinnitus 252, 362
Tissue diseases
- *connective* 104
Tonsillitis 362
Tooth
- *ache* 127, 141, 219, 221, 254, 363
- *decay* 363
- *grinding* 226, 307
Torticollis 125
Toxicodendron quercifolium 270
Toxicology 11
Trauma 82
Traumatic headaches
- *post* 82
Travelsickness 246, 363
Tremor 79, 168, 363
Trinitrophenol 255

Trioxide
- **Arsenic** 83
Trituration 12
Tuberculinum 305
Tuberculosis 98, 146, 200, 252, 363
Tumors
- *in female breast* 146
- *of testicles* 299
Typhoid fever 252

U

Ulceration
- *of the throat* 79, 363
Ulcerative
- *colitis* 363
- *stomatitis* 363
Ulcers 120
Ulcus ventriculi et duodeni 68, 85, 95, 120, 132, 173, 193, 206, 215, 224, 229, 241, 252, 275
Unconsciousness 363
Undescended
- *testicles* 88, 363
Upper respiratory tract
- *diseases* 363
- *Infection of* 341
Uragoga Ipecacuanha 190
Urethra
- *inflammation of* 342
- *stricture of* 303, 361, 363
Urethritis 115, 118, 215, 224, 237, 303, 364

Urinary
- *incontinence* 125, 364
- *stress incontinence* 232, 269
- *tract infection* 364

Urticaria 76, 178, 232, 272, 364

Uterine
- *fibroids* 364
- *inertia* 134, 198, 364
- *myoma* 88, 104, 196, 299, 303
- *polyposis* 364
- *polyps* 303, 364
- *prolapse* 211, 263, 275, 364

V

Vaccination 292, 303

Vagina
- *inflammation of* 342

Vaginal discharge 364

Vaginitis 132, 173, 198, 224, 226, 275, 299, 364

Valvular
- *heart disease* 88, 364

Varicella 70, 272

Varicose veins 82, 104, 125, 165, 275, 364

Vegetable charcoal 119

Venereal warts 365

Veratrum
- *album* 308

Vertigo 79, 104, 146, 160, 168, 173, 203, 211, 278, 365

Vithoulkas 10, 25

Vitiligo 278, 297, 365

Vitis
- *alba* 99
- *diaboli* 99

W

Warts 104, 125, 154, 215, 224, 237, 275, 286, 303, 365

Weackness 103

Weak 96, 189, 205
- *concentration* 54, 119, 144, 161, 192
- *memory* 47, 77, 96, 123, 145, 148, 174, 177, 192, 205, 225, 255
- *menstrual flow* 365

Weakness 47, 77, 80, 83, 90, 91, 96, 97, 102, 103, 105, 110, 111, 112, 119, 120, 122, 133, 137, 139, 144, 145, 146, 148, 151, 158, 161, 166, 184, 186, 194, 213, 216, 225, 226, 228, 235, 247, 250, 255, 258, 260, 264, 273
- *after menses* 191
- *after passing stool* 262
- *due to discharges* 130
- *during influenza* 156
- *emotional* 247
- *in back* 195
- *in legs* 138
- *in lumbar region* 138
- *mental* 65, 255

- *of ankles* 229
- *of body* 213
- *of digestion* 161
- *of eyes* 135
- *of joints* 274
- *of memory* 55, 222, 238, 257
- *of mind* 255, 276
- *of muscles* 103, 144, 174
- *of neck muscles* 138
- *of neck of the bladder* 123
- *of senses* 67
- *with trembling* 235

Whiplash
- *injury* 272, 365

White
- *arsenic* 83
- *petroleum* 245

Whitebryony 99

Whitehellbore 308

Whooping cough 365

Wild
- *hops* 99

Wind 365

Wind flower 267

Wolfsbane 50

Wormseed 135

Writer's
- *cramp* 221, 365

X

X-potencies 12, 23, 24

Y

Yellow
- jasmine 166
- phosphorus 250

Z

Zinc 311
Zincum metallicum 311

Medical Spanish pocket family

- For all healthcare professionals • Contains medical terminology specific to Mexico, Puerto Rico, Cuba and other countries

English – Spanish / Spanish – English

Medical Spanish pocket plus

Börm Bruckmeier Publishing

ISBN 1-59103-213-X $22.95

- **2 in 1:** Medical Spanish pocket and Medical Spanish Dictionary pocket
- Vital communication tool for your communication with Spanish-speaking patients
- Bilingual dictionary with accurate translations for almost every health-related term
- Clearly organized by situation: interview, examination, course of visit
- Provides hundreds of essential words and phrases, ready to use

Spanish for Medical Professionals

Medical Spanish pocket

Börm Bruckmeier Publishing

ISBN 1-59103-203-2 $ 12.95

English – Spanish / Spanish – English

Medical Spanish Dictionary pocket

Börm Bruckmeier Publishing

ISBN 1-59103-211-3 $ 14.95

also available for PDA

trial download:
www.media4u.com

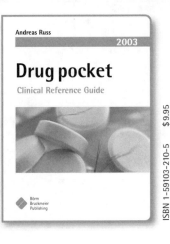

◆ BBP   Order Form

Phone: 888-322-6657 Fax: 419-281-6883	Mail: Börm Bruckmeier Publishing PO Box 388, Ashland, OH 44805	www.media4u.com

Name _____ **E-mail** _____

Address _____

City _____ **State** _____ **Zip** _____

	COPIES		PRICE/COPY		PRICE
Drug pocket 2003		x	$ 9.95	=	
Drug Therapy pocket		x	$14.95	=	
Differential Diagnosis pocket		x	$12.95	=	
ECG pocket		x	$12.95	=	
Homeopathy pocket		x	$14.95	=	
Medical Abbreviations pocket		x	$12.95	=	
Medical Spanish pocket		x	$12.95	=	
Medical Spanish Dictionary pocket		x	$14.95	=	
Medical Spanish pocket plus		x	$22.95	=	
Normal Values pocket		x	$12.95	=	
Antibiotics pocketcard 2003		x	$ 3.95	=	
Antifungals pocketcard		x	$ 3.95	=	
BLS/ALS pocketcard		x	$ 3.95	=	
ECG pocketcard		x	$ 3.95	=	
ECG Evaluation pocketcard		x	$ 3.95	=	
ECG Ruler pocketcard		x	$ 3.95	=	
ECG pocketcards (set of 3 cards)		x	$ 9.95	=	
Emergency Drugs pocketcard		x	$ 3.95	=	
H&P pocketcard		x	$ 3.95	=	
Medical Abbreviations pocketcard (2 cards)		x	$ 6.95	=	
Medical Spanish pocketcard		x	$ 3.95	=	
Neurology pocketcard (2 cards)		x	$ 6.95	=	
Normal Values pocketcard		x	$ 3.95	=	

Sales Tax: CA residents add 8%, OH 6.25%

Shipping & Handling for US addresses:
UPS Standard: 10% of subtotal (minimum $5.00)
UPS 2nd Day Air: 20% of subtotal (minimum $8.00)

Credit Card: ☐ Visa ☐ Mastercard ☐ Amex ☐ Discover

Card Number _____

Exp. Date _____ Signature _____

= **Subtotal**
↳ + Sales Tax
↳ + S&H
= **Total**

For foreign orders, volume discount, shipping and payment questions, please contact us at: service@media4u.com